The Financial Menu

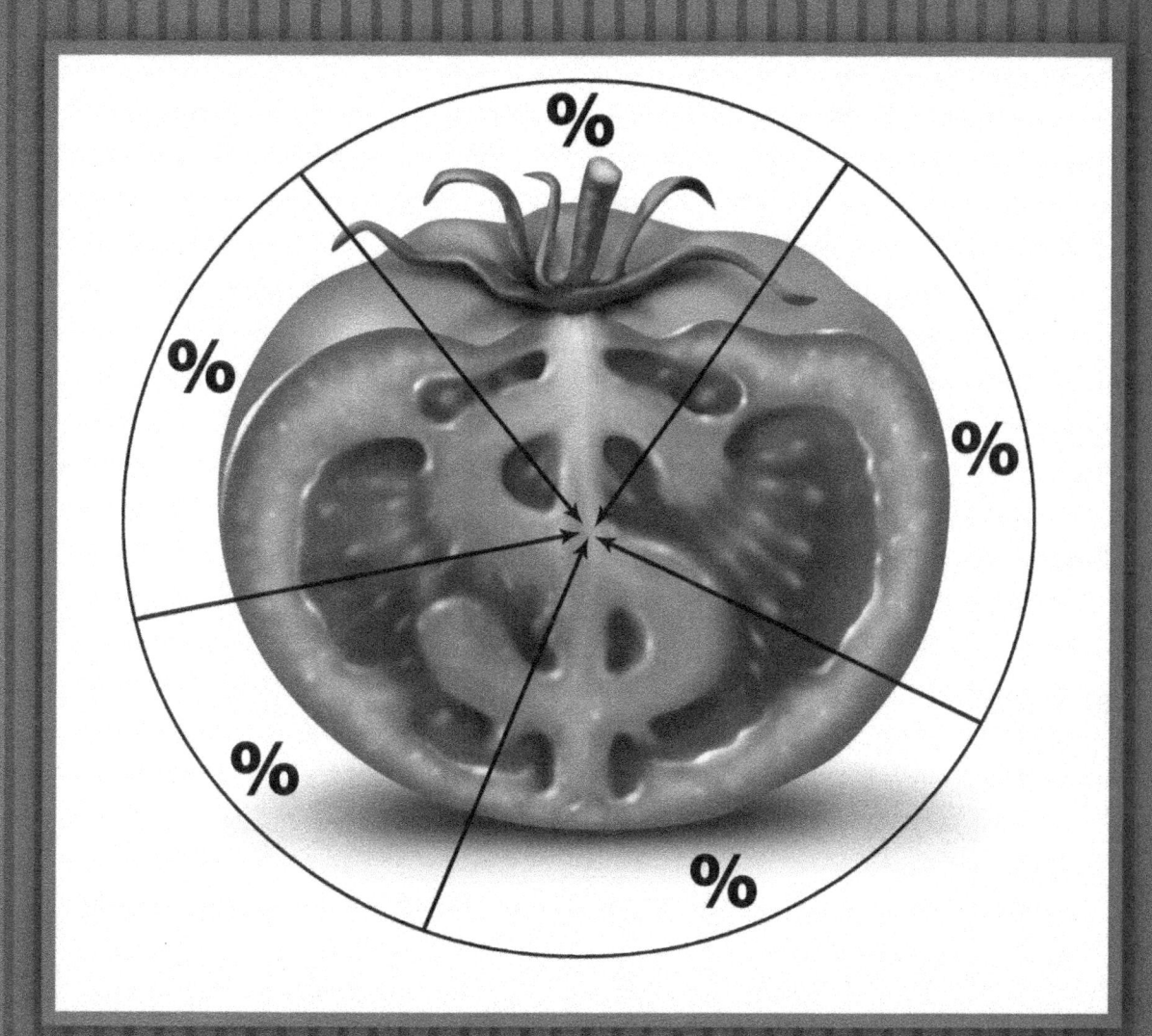

[A Chef's Companion to Cost Control]

FOURTH EDITION

Klaus Theyer, CCC

Kendall Hunt publishing company

Cover image © 2013 Shutterstock, Inc.

Images on pages 162 and 163:
1: © 2013 katalinks. Used under license from Shutterstock, Inc.
2 and 3: © 2013 Petr Salinger. Used under license from Shutterstock, Inc.
4: © 2013 Winnie Chao. Used under license from Shutterstock, Inc.

Kendall Hunt
publishing company

www.kendallhunt.com
Send all inquiries to:
4050 Westmark Drive
Dubuque, IA 52004-1840

Copyright © 2005, 2007, 2011 and 2013 by Klaus Theyer

ISBN 978-1-4652-3186-4

Kendall Hunt Publishing Company has the exclusive rights to reproduce this work,
to prepare derivative works from this work, to publicly distribute this work,
to publicly perform this work and to publicly display this work.

All rights reserved. No part of this publication may be reproduced,
stored in a retrieval system, or transmitted, in any form or by any
means, electronic, mechanical, photocopying, recording, or otherwise,
without the prior written permission of the copyright owner.

Printed in Canada
10 9 8 7 6 5 4 3 2 1

Contents

About the Author   v
Foreword   vii
Letter of Endorsement   ix
Introduction   xi

Chapter 1   **Introduction to Elements of Cost   1**

    The Term Cost Explained   1
    Cost Classification   4
    The Difference Between Cost and Price, and Prime Cost   8

Chapter 2   **Revenue and Cost Areas, Cost of Goods Sold (COGS) and Introduction to Budget and Income Statement   15**

    Introduction to the Term "Business"   15
    C.O.G.S. — Cost of Goods Sold   19
    Introduction to "Budgets" and Budgeting   25
    A Budget Must Be a Realistic Expression of Goals and Objectives in Financial Terms   28
    Depreciation — Capital Cost Allowance and Canada Revenue Agency   31

Chapter 3   **Essential Math and Applied Culinary Conversions   35**

    Basic Math Refresher   35
    From Hours, Minutes to Seconds   55

Chapter 4   **Yield Calculations   65**

Chapter 5   **The Standard Recipe—Unit and Unit Cost   77**

    Unit and Unit Cost   84

Chapter 6   **Additional Important Costs (Hidden, Surrounding, Plate and Line Cost)   85**

    Calculating of Menu Item Cost   85
    Line and Plate Cost   86

Chapter 7	**Demographics, Popular Selling Price Methods and Calculations 88**	
	Popular Selling Price Methods and Calculations	94
	Themes and Concepts	94
	Concept Considerations	96
	Concept Checklist	97
	Menu or Selling Price Strategies	98
	Key Terms	98
	The Factor Method	99
	Cost Behaviour as Business (Sales) Volume Changes	100
	Gross Profit Pricing	100
Chapter 8	**Purchasing, Receiving, Storing, Inventory and Inventory Costing—Simplified 105**	
	Inventory	111
Chapter 9	**Labour Cost, Scheduling Methods and Calculations 121**	
	Scheduling Methods and Costing	125
Chapter 10	**Menu Analysis and Sales Mix 139**	
	Menu Analysis and Menu Engineering	139
	Sales Mix Calculations	146
Chapter 11	**Breakeven Point Calculations for Value and Units 149**	
	The Breakeven Point—Value	149
	The Breakeven Point—Units	150
Chapter 12	**Essential Basic Math Templates, References, Exercises and Workshops 153**	
	Index 173	

About the Author

Klaus, a Canadian Certified Chef de Cuisine, was raised in Vienna, Austria. Klaus' career as a chef started with a cook apprenticeship at 14 years of age after completing eight years of elementary and high school. His culinary experience included working in well-known Viennese, Swiss and Principality Liechtenstein restaurants and hotels and in Montreal, Canada at EXPO67 working in the Austrian Pavilion.

After Expo67 he relocated to Germany to open the "Atrium" the largest restaurant in the Olympic tower in Münich. Klaus returned to Montreal, Canada in 1968 to work again in the Austrian Pavilion at "Man and His World." He moved to Toronto in 1969 and started as Sous chef at "Gasthaus Schrader," which became the leading German restaurant in Toronto. In 1970 he was promoted to Chef, and subsequently became responsible for the financial well-being of the back of the house.

During this time he made his mark on the Toronto culinary scene being the first chef in Toronto to offer wild boar on the menu; his cheesecake was the Toronto-Sun's newspaper favourite in 1971.

In 1972, an opportunity to manage a Commissary supplying 32 food-outlets within Dominion (now Metro) and Bittner's stores with ready-to-eat products and establishing an on-location catering company was an opportunity he could not resist. It was during that time in his career that Klaus was introduced to corporate accounting procedures, management principles and reporting methods.

In 1981, while working at a catering contract at the Toronto Carlsberg Pavilion with Tony Thomas, a teaching master at Humber College and Humber College students, Tony mentioned that Humber College was looking for instructors for the new "Chef de partie" program. Hesitant at first, since he had never done any formal training other than apprentices, Klaus agreed to an interview.

It did not take long for Klaus to discover his love for teaching and he started to successfully use techniques to show the relationship between cooking and financial accountability expected by restaurant management.

He began to incorporate spreadsheet and computer programs into the curriculum, which became the accepted standard both in the culinary programs and the Hospitality programs. Since 1981 Klaus has taught his skills in computer applied cost control to industry colleagues and to thousands of students at Humber College which earned him respect from his colleagues and appreciation from his students.

Klaus became a member with the Canadian Federation of Chefs and the Escoffier Society of Toronto and he held several board of director's positions at the local and national level, including national Secretary, President of the Escoffier Society and National Chairman of The Canadian Culinary Institute. During his chairmanship he was instrumental in the development of the Certified Chef de Cuisine program and implemented the practical examination in Toronto. In 1990 he was elected by his peers as Chef of the year for the Escoffier Society of Toronto. In 2006 he became the first Canadian Chef to receive the Presidential medal from the American Culinary Association president John Kinsella CMC PhD.

This book contains contributions from my Humber College colleagues, Konrad Weinbuch CMC and Leonhard Lechner CMC. This fourth edition is supported by my own website www.menuforprofit.com with ready-made functional worksheets and an industry proven automated Standard Recipe form.

Foreword

This publication was prepared after years of disappointment searching for a quick reference referring to terminology, formulas, and examples of costing applications in the Hospitality Industry.

I have read many publications on this topic without finding one with the right mix of essential information and examples. It appears that the majority of these publications were written for middle management dealing with theoretical cost control on a daily basis, leaving occasional users in need of a quick reference without a resource for their needs.

In this publication I aim to explain cost, identification, principles, usage, formulas, and their intended application, as well as basic control methods in a manner anyone should be able to use.

This publication **does not intend to cover accounting principles or methods**. Readers are encouraged to seek competent professional advice and services.

After reading and using this publication, please let me know if I have achieved my goal. If you have any suggestions for improving this publication or on topics you think should be covered, do not hesitate to contact me and share your thoughts.

For live worksheets, updates, corrections, and communication, please visit my website **www.menuforprofit.com.** Your comments are welcome and appreciated.

Klaus Theyer CCC

Letter of Endorsement

Dear Reader,

I have read many excellent books which explain in great detail theoretical definitions of the numerous costs occurring in the hospitality industry and how to recognize, calculate and control them. Most of these books are between 200 and 500 pages in length and try to encompass all areas of cost in such great detail that the reader who is looking for a quick explanation is not being served.

Working chefs, Educators, and Students have been looking for a condensed reference guide for applied Cost control. The "Financial Menu" formerly "A Chef's Companion to Cost Control" authored by Klaus Theyer, certified Chef de Cuisine, were specifically written for the working Chef, Food and Beverage manager and College students in mind.

The first version of this book, published by Kendall Hunt in Iowa was produced specifically for the Culinary and Hospitality Students at Humber College. After working extensively with this version of the book I asked Klaus to expand the book to encompass the necessary information to satisfy the needs for the Certified Chef de Cuisine program which resulted in the fourth edition of this book.

As the past National Chairman of the Canadian Culinary Institute responsible for all of the association offered and required Certification standards, including the Certified Chef de Cuisine program, and as a teacher of the Cost Control Course for this program I have used Klaus's book, a required textbook for this course successfully in the past.

The feedback from all students and candidates from the basic, the advanced and the certification program has been very positive. The book is a great reference and guide, with easy to follow examples which are used on an ongoing basis by cooks and chefs alike in real life situations.

Klaus also instituted a support website www.MenuForProfit.com, where updates, practical examples and corrections are posted, as well as Excel worksheets for review, practice and for customized expansion for commercial applications. The website also supports the other book Klaus wrote on Menu planning and writing "Today's Menu du jour" which I also recommend to be used in the Certified Chef de Cuisine Menu planning course which is part of the certification curriculum.

I had a sneak preview of the manuscript for this edition of the book, which was expanded with additional chapters, more examples and definitions and I am looking forward to its publication.

Klaus developed many industry related Excel spreadsheets including a versatile two page Standard Recipe form which can be downloaded from www.menuforprofit.com – it is quite comprehensive and easy to use. I recommend it to everyone who needs to cost recipes; but you need to read and follow the built-in help menus.

Respectfully,
Rudi Fischbacher CCC
Past National Chairman, Canadian Culinary Institute,
(www.ccicc.ca), the education arm of the Canadian Culinary
Federation. *www.ccfcc.ca*

Introduction

A cost control system is designed to monitor the performance of planned menus and is usually the responsibility of the Food and Beverage Manager as well as the Chefs or Kitchen Manager and the Bar Manager. This book focuses on Food and Labour cost control.

It is imperative to note that food and beverage and consequently the labour cost associated with food and beverage is primarily dependent on menu planning and subsequent production logistics.

The menu planning process must take into consideration the cost of the raw product, the quantity on hand of each product, the need of production equipment and the subsequent need of real estate, as well as production related labour cost and of course the selling or menu price. Management will also have to look closely at the utility and labour cost when deciding on purchasing raw versus pre-prepared products.

Considering all of the named components of cost control I am sure you can appreciate that it is a financial balancing act comparable to a high wire act performance which needs a full understanding of the risks involved.

The biggest risk is the consumer's acceptance for what you have planned for them. This risk can be greatly reduced by carefully analyzing the findings of demographics and feasibility studies, competitive analysis, and a subsequent profiling of the establishment's concept with a solid marketing plan.

Once all of the above have been considered and the details have been worked out, the planning and control process can begin.

The key to success is to plan costs, analyse occurrences, have control measures in place and reconcile planned costs with actual costs, and if necessary make appropriate adjustments.

This publication will assist you in understanding the term "Cost" and offers examples on how it is applied and used, how it occurs, how the term itself may change depending on who uses it, and to recognise that in different situations it may have different effects as well as that there is a need to monitor in order to have control.

The word Cost, by itself, is often referred to or quoted in many situations and equally often misinterpreted, or not fully understood.

By definition, theoretically, no directly related cost has occurred until a sale is made or the product is no longer available for sale. Practically however, cost does occur in preparation for anticipated sales.

Chapter 1

Introduction to Elements of Cost

Elements of Cost

The composition of costs is classified on a direct and indirect basis including an addition for profit that in summary allows the calculation of a selling price of goods and services to be determined.

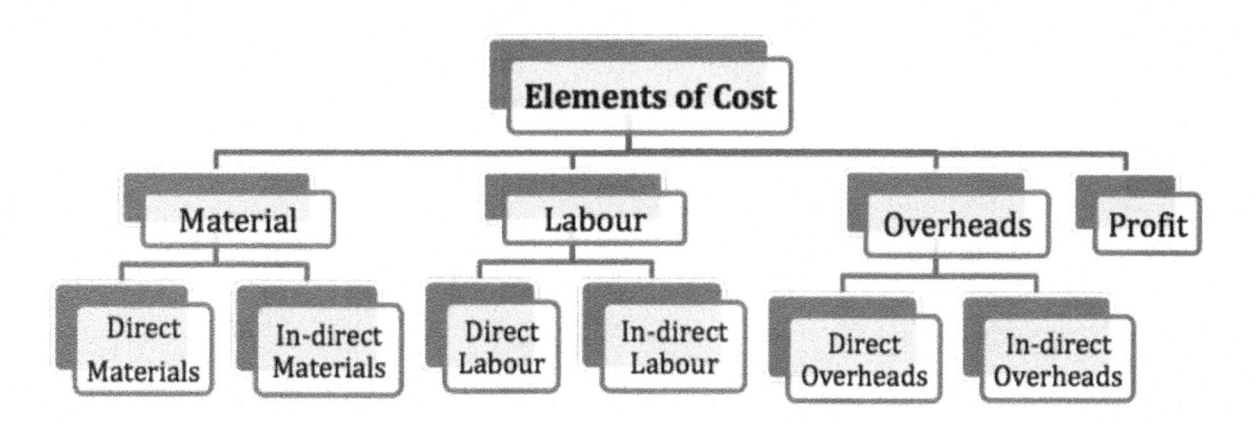

```
                        Elements of Cost
            ┌───────────────┬───────────────┬─────────┐
         Material        Labour         Overheads   Profit
         ┌──┴──┐         ┌──┴──┐         ┌────┴────┐
      Direct In-direct Direct In-direct Direct  In-direct
    Materials Materials Labour Labour  Overheads Overheads
```

The Term Cost Explained

The word cost, by itself, is often referred to or quoted in many situations and equally often misinterpreted or not fully understood. In accounting terms, cost is a REDUCTION IN VALUE OF AN ASSET (an Asset is something the company owns) for the PURPOSE OF SECURING BENEFIT OR GAIN (Sales, Profit).

Cost in *accounting terms* is most often referred to as *expense,* which is true most of the time, unless it refers *directly or indirectly to the Cost of Goods for Sale or Sold,* in which case other factors need to be considered.

Cost

Cost is the amount of money laid-out to produce or offer something for sale, while **price** is the amount of money paid out to make a purchase.

One could argue that the terms are interchangeable. In reality, however, the two words have a very different meaning—one is the amount that the customer pays, and the other is the amount it costs the producer to create or to offer it.

Cost Defined

In summary, cost is money or value equal to money (promissory note) laid out for **consumed** or **depleted** goods or services rendered; while money or value laid out for **consumable** goods is an asset increase (inventory).

What is Money Laid out For?

In business, *money* should only be laid out in anticipation to make a *Sale* and subsequently a *Profit*.

What is Profit?

Profit is the commonly used term for the accounting term Net-income before taxes which refers to the money left over from a sale after all costs are accounted for.

In the hospitality business a *Profit* is usually derived from a *sale* of a product or a service. Commonly products sold in the hospitality business are food, beverage, accommodation and related services.

Therefore, in order to make these before-mentioned sales, the following products or elements of costs are needed:

- Money-Funds
- Establishment (Local-Facility)
- Equipment (Production-Service-Maintenance)
- Furniture & Decor
- Utility services
- Food
- Beverage
- Labour

These elements of cost are divided into three key-categories:

- Investment
- Profit Centres
- Cost Centres

The two categories which this book deals with are *Profit Centres* and *Cost Centres*.

Profit Centre

A *Profit Centre* is an area(s) of a business which is expected to make a profit based on sales. Example: Area(s) of the business which has employees and makes sales.

Cost Centre

A *Cost Centre* is an area(s) of a business which is not expected to make a profit, with or without a sale, but is/are needed to make or support a sale. Example: Area(s) within a business which may or may not make sales but has employees; Maintenance, Custodial, IT, Office, Marketing and Convenience services.

Chapter 1 Introduction to Elements of Cost

The following charts illustrate identified costs.

Restaurant Revenue and Cost Areas—Simplified

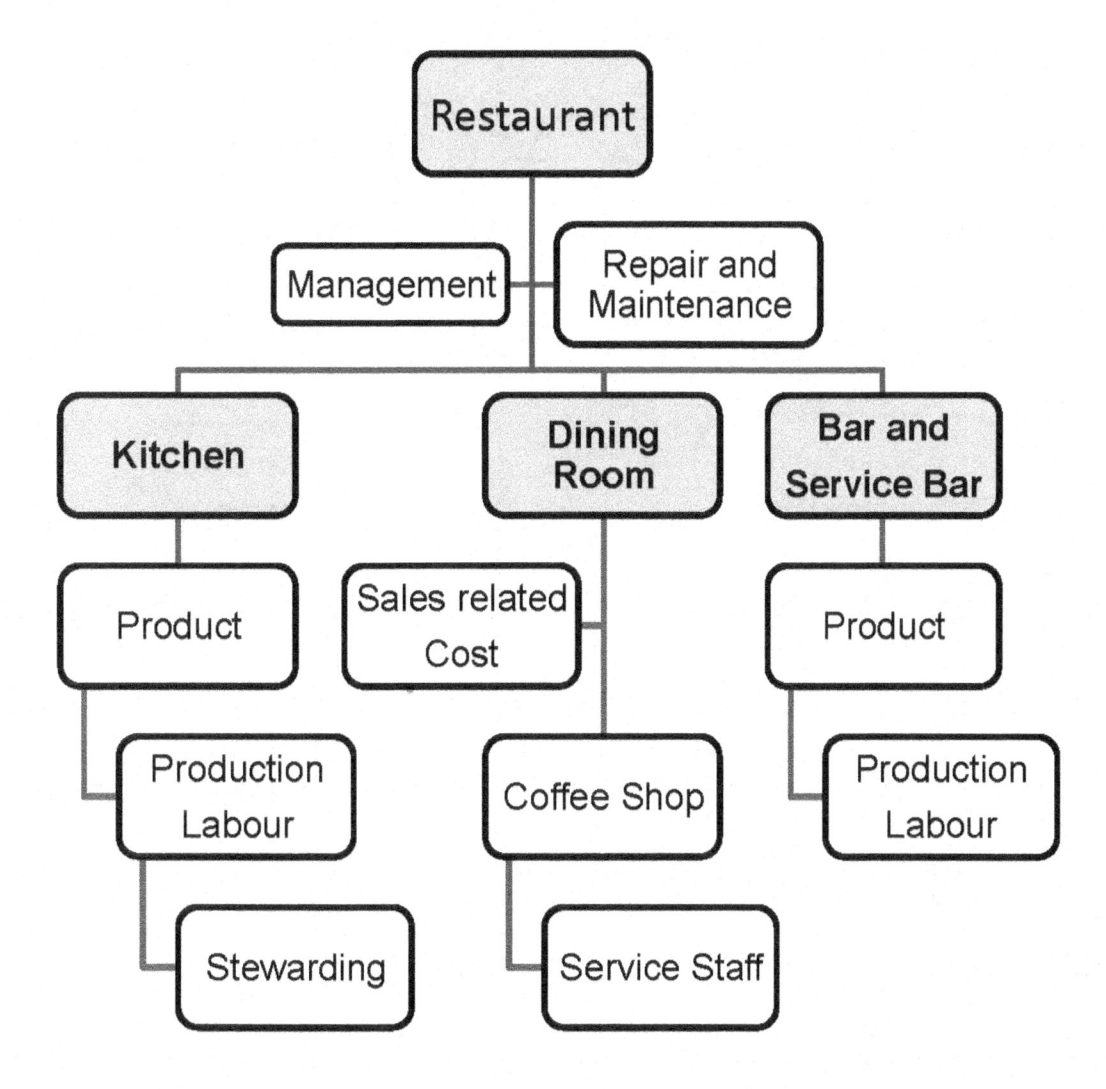

```
                    Restaurant
                        |
          Management ─── Repair and Maintenance
                        |
        ┌───────────────┼───────────────┐
     Kitchen        Dining Room    Bar and Service Bar
        |               |                 |
     Product      Sales related         Product
        |            Cost                 |
   Production          |              Production
    Labour         Coffee Shop          Labour
        |               |
   Stewarding      Service Staff
```

Looking at the simplified Restaurant, Hotel, Revenue, and Cost Area Diagrams, the following should be observed: Sales and cost are calculated either as a budget or income statement for the whole operation and for the departments and their sub-departments separately.

Example

Most restaurants will have a dining room and perhaps a service bar, and/or a sit-down bar/lounge. These areas are being served by the kitchen. Food and bar sales are usually accounted separately from one another. Alcoholic beverage cost is allocated to the bar. Bar labour cost may be allocated to the bar or to the lounge.

The kitchen is accountable for food cost, labour cost, stewarding, and equipment maintenance. Management labour cost (fixed cost) and the dining room service staff labour cost (variable cost) are often allocated against sales from food and beverage. There are no hard-and-fast rules, and cost allocation is usually decided by management.

Hotel Revenue and Cost Areas—Simplified

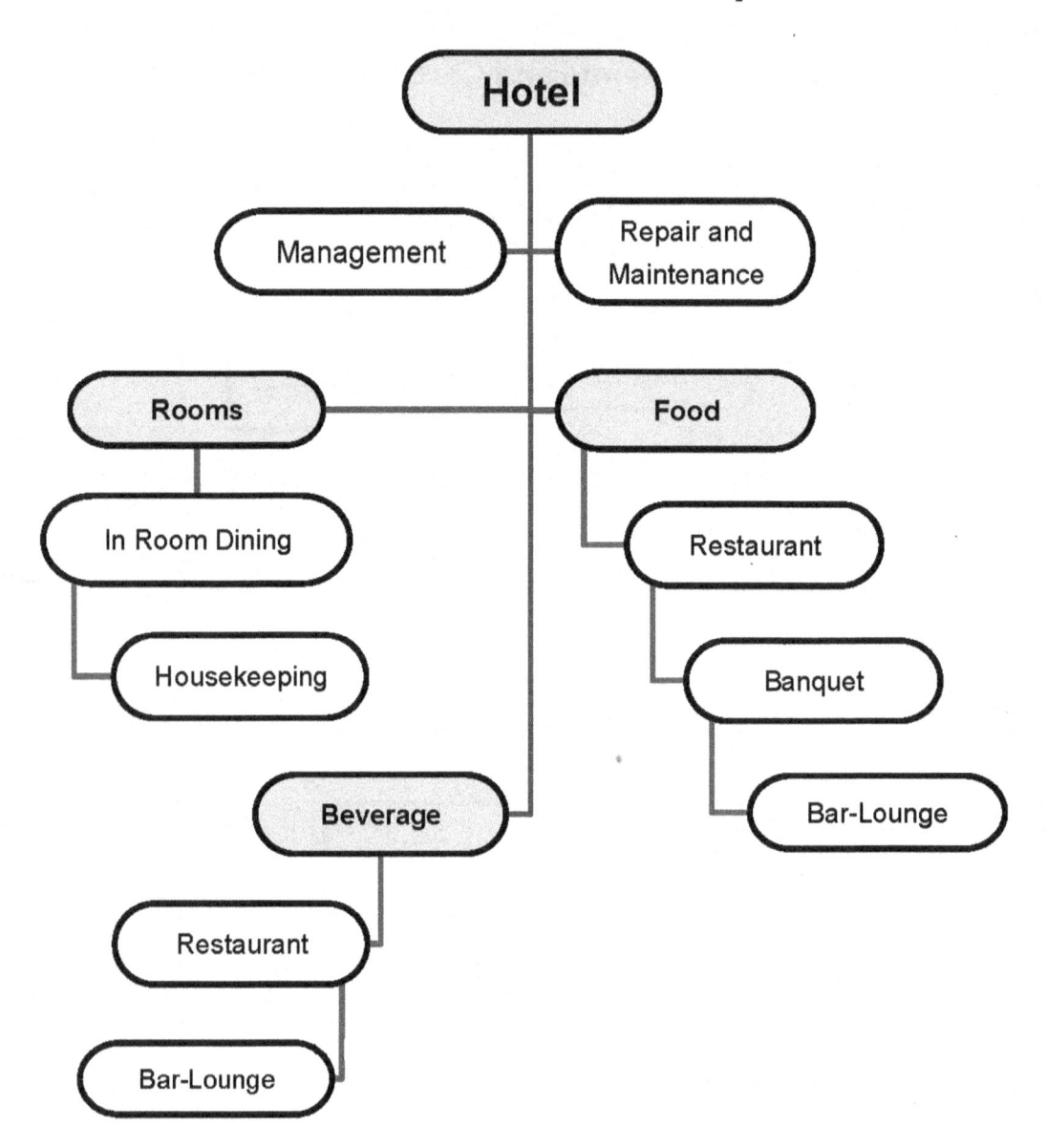

```
                    Hotel
                   /     \
        Management       Repair and
                         Maintenance
         /                  \
      Rooms                 Food
        |                    |
   In Room Dining        Restaurant
        |                    |
   Housekeeping           Banquet
        |                    |
     Beverage            Bar-Lounge
        |
    Restaurant
        |
    Bar-Lounge
```

Cost Classification

In order to keep the various terms in which the word "Cost" is used, uniformly identifiable from one industry person and establishment to another, specific terminology has been developed and used for many years to group all the different costs.

The two key-cost-groups are:

The Group of Variable Costs

A cost that occurs of products being prepared to be sold, and the subsequent sale of it, as well as the cost of having the selling establishment ready for service to receive customers.

Strictly theoretical, because all costs are costs occurring to make a sale, if nothing is sold, no cost should occur. In reality, that does not work; as mentioned before, the establishment must be set-up to be open for business and subsequently product, labour, and other costs like the cost for cleaned/washed tablecloths and napkins, table and silverware, flowers in a vase, and the cost of purchasing the pre-prepared food products.

The term *Variable Cost* implies that cost occurs, increases and/or decreases with **Sales.**

Opposite to the Group of *Variable Costs*, the **group of *Fixed Costs also referred to as Occupancy cost*** is a cost occurring regardless of sales. A simple example is Rent or Mortgage; if the establishment is open for business or closed for vacation, the Rent/Mortgage payments will remain the same. Another example is a part of the total *Labour Cost*; salaried employees are being paid if they are scheduled or not scheduled to work. Subsequently, a cost occurred with or without a sale being made.

The term *Fixed Cost* is applied for cost occurring independent of any **Sales**.

Most books I have read use the acronym **FC** for fixed cost. Throughout this publication I will use the acronym **FXC** for fixed cost and **FC** for food cost to avoid potential confusion and mistakes.

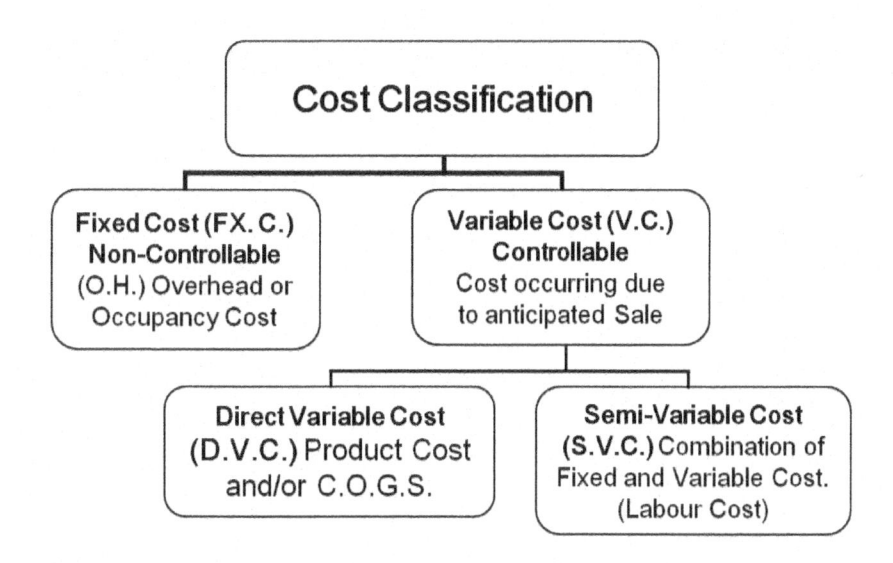

```
                    ┌─────────────────────┐
                    │ Cost Classification │
                    └─────────────────────┘
                       │              │
        ┌──────────────┴──┐     ┌─────┴──────────────┐
        │ Fixed Cost (FX. C.) │   │ Variable Cost (V.C.) │
        │ Non-Controllable   │   │ Controllable        │
        │ (O.H.) Overhead or │   │ Cost occurring due  │
        │ Occupancy Cost     │   │ to anticipated Sale │
        └────────────────────┘   └─────────────────────┘
                                     │           │
                        ┌────────────┴──┐   ┌────┴──────────────────┐
                        │ Direct Variable Cost │ │ Semi-Variable Cost    │
                        │ (D.V.C.) Product Cost │ │ (S.V.C.) Combination of│
                        │ and/or C.O.G.S.       │ │ Fixed and Variable Cost.│
                        │                       │ │ (Labour Cost)          │
                        └───────────────────────┘ └────────────────────────┘
```

Variable Costs are considered controllable, since changes to a cost change can be relatively quickly corrected.

Fixed Costs are considered not controllable, since changes to a cost increase or decrease cannot be quickly implemented.

The term *controllable* implies that it can be controlled within a short period of time. Example: If an unexpected increase in product cost occurs, it may be quickly offset by decreasing portion size or weight or product substitutions.

The term *non-controllable* implies that it cannot be changed within a short period of time. Example: A lease or mortgage can usually only be renegotiated at the end of their term and not at will.

When fixtures and equipment are being purchased, the expense incurred by the business, although it is an expense, is also an investment which establishes, or increases, the value of the business and therefore is recorded as an **Asset** in the financial statements (balance sheet).

Assets fall into two major groups: **fixed assets (long-term and sometimes depreciable),** which are not intended to be sold, and **liquid** assets (short-term), which can easily be converted into cash, such as cash itself, checks, credit card payments, and products for sale (food and beverage).

The saleable **assets** are referred to as **inventory** for sale. At this point, although money may have been laid out to acquire these goods, no cost has occurred, since all these goods are still available for sale.

This situation changes when the product is no longer available for sale due to spoilage, breaks, expiry, or theft. The value of the product that is lost (no longer available for sale) has now changed from an investment (asset inventory) to an expense or cost.

The situation also changes when the product is removed from inventory to be prepared for sale and is subsequently sold (a meal or a drink). It is then referred to as *Cost of Goods Sold*, or abbreviated as *COGS*.

Beverage Costs

Although most establishments are distinctively different from another, industry averages are commonly acceptable as guidelines and can be a starting point for comparing one establishment with another.

The following averages were derived from personal findings while conducting industry research to gather material for the recently published *Today's Menu du jour* menu planning and writing book, and by no means are to be considered to be uniform or complete.

Here in Ontario, Canada, the cost of alcoholic beverages is standardised due to the Liquor Control Board of Ontario "LCBO" www.lcbo.com and the Brewers Retail, "The Beer Store" www.thebeerstore.ca with the exception of private import.

Wine, beer and liquor costs vary among establishments due to a number of reasons. Here is the summary of "Cost percentage ranges are expressed as a Cost of sales," from my personal findings:

- ▶ Liquor—18% to 20% of sale.
- ▶ Bar secondary costs 4% to 5% of liquor sales (includes mixes, olives, cherries, onions and other food products like nuts and nibbles that are used and/or offered at the bar).
- ▶ Bottled beer is 19% to 22% (for mainstream domestic beer. Specialty and imported bottled beer was generally 2% lower).
- ▶ Draught beer from the tap 15% to 20% (assumes mainstream domestic beer, cost percent of specialty and imported draft beer will generally be higher).
- ▶ Wine had the largest range of cost percentage from 25% to 45% from establishment to establishment depending on the types of wines which were offered. In all fairness, in most cases, the higher the cost per bottle was, the higher the cost percentage.

I just read in an industry journal about Non-alcoholic beverage costs: They claim that in the past it has been standard industry practice to record non-alcoholic beverage sales and costs in Food Sales and Food Cost accounts. However, they have found that many operators are now breaking out non-alcoholic beverage sales and costs and report on them separately as "Soft Beverages."

- ▶ Soft drinks (post-mix) 10% to 15% (another rule of thumb for soft drinks is to expect post-mix soda to cost a little more than a penny an ounce for the syrup and CO_2).
- ▶ Regular coffee (remained in Food sales and cost) 15% to 20% (average 8-oz cup, some cream, milk and sugar, no free refill).
- ▶ Specialty coffee, 12% to 18%, no free refills.
- ▶ Iced tea and lemonade, 5% to 10%, iced tea and lemonade are the leaders in low cost of food. The cost of the tea is about a cent per glass, the largest cost is the lemon.

Chef's or Kitchen Managers Common Areas of Cost

The Chef's Budget responsibilities towards contributing to Profit

- **Revenue Sales**
  - ▶ Menu planning, writing and design
  - ▶ Promotions
  - ▶ Participation in public events, Associations

- **COGS DVC**
  - ▶ Accurate Recipes
  - ▶ Production
  - ▶ Portion Control
  - ▶ Purchasing
  - ▶ Storing
  - ▶ Inventory

- **Labour Cost**
  - ▶ Hiring
  - ▶ Scheduling
  - ▶ Productivity
  - ▶ Motivation
  - ▶ Menu Item selection

- **Variable Cost**
  - ▶ Uniforms
  - ▶ Knife Service
  - ▶ Condiments
  - ▶ Presentations

- **FXC may be shared proportionally**

The Difference Between Cost and Price, and Prime Cost

Cost is the *amount* of money laid-out to make something, while price is the amount of money paid out to make a purchase. One could argue that the terms are interchangeable. In reality, however, the two words have a very different meaning—one is the amount that the customer pays, and the other is the amount it cost the manufacturer to produce it.

Costs: Cost of Sale and Cost of Goods Sold

Now let's have a look at the same terminology for the structure of a basic Income Statement, with Revenue being converted to the shape of a Dollar Coin (Circle) and where all Costs are part (Slice) of that Coin (Circle) adding up the Value of the Sale ($) to 100%.

Think dimensional: Look at Sales as a Circle or Coin representing 100%

- Any Costs allocated against Sales become a fraction of Sales—or, if you like, a slice of a coin.
- Profit becomes a Budgeted Cost or Alternative Cost.
- Knowing that any or all Costs are fractions of Sales, the value of a fraction is easily calculated if the size of the fraction is known.
- Management determines the size of the fractions based on the Business Plan and subsequent Budget.

The following are examples only. There are no standards implied. Each establishment, based on the type of business they are, will set their own standard, which is not comparable from one establishment to another. Within a chain of establishments one is tempted to compare; however, cost of product and cost of labour as well as fixed costs will most likely be different based on location. Formula used in this calculation:

Sales × Cost % equals Cost in $ (S × C% = $)

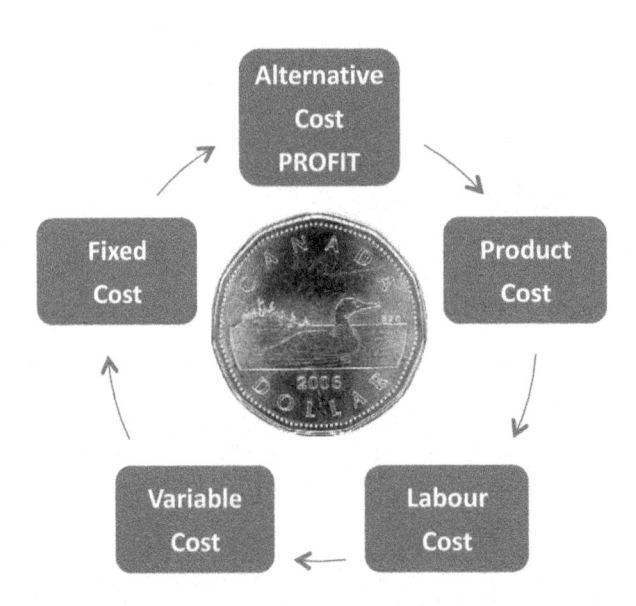

Chapter 1 Introduction to Elements of Cost 9

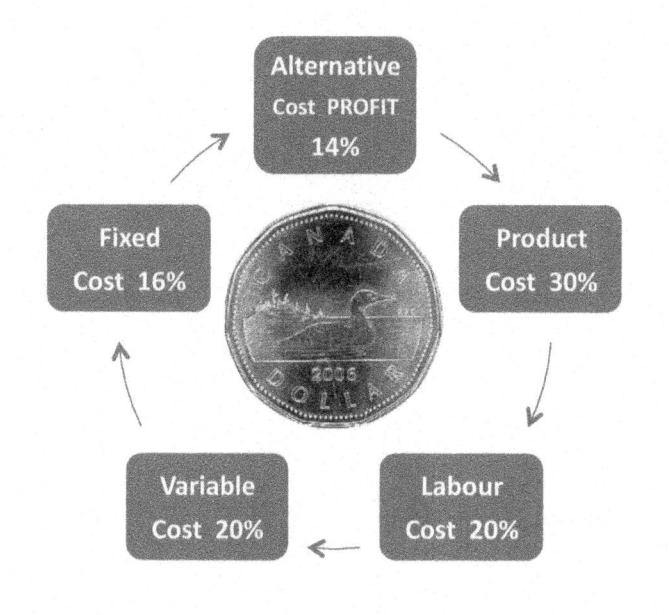

In this scenario (Clockwise)

Product Cost = 30%

Labour Cost = 20%

Sales related Cost = 20%

Overhead Cost = 16%

Alternative Cost = 14%

Total Costs = 100%

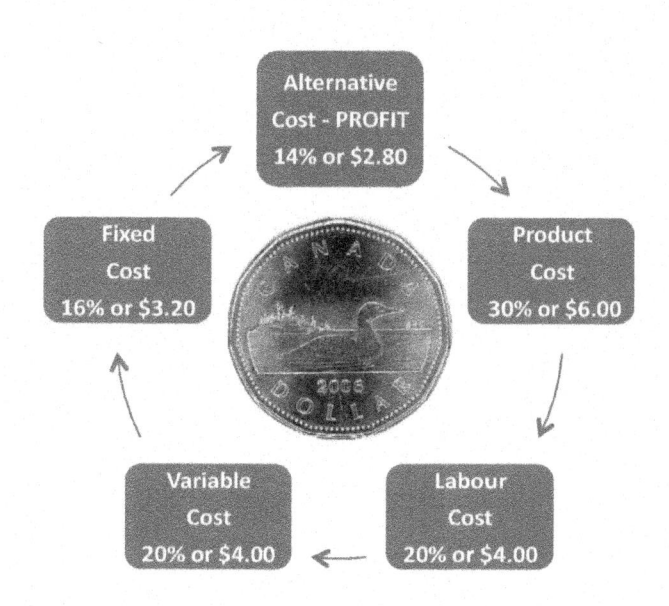

Assuming the Sale was $20.00 equalling 100%

Product Cost being 30% of Sales = $6.00

Labour Cost being 20% of Sales = $4.00

Sales related Costs being 20% = $4.00

Overhead being 16% of Sales = $3.20

Alternative Cost being 14% of Sales = $2.80

Total Costs = $20.00

Once all identified Costs have a percentage allocation assigned, they become Projected Costs that must be closely and frequently monitored and compared to Actual Costs. If there is a difference between the forecast and the actual, it is referred to as a Variance, which could be either positive or negative.

Any **increase** in the Projected Cost(s) percentages or dollars, however caused, will result in a **reduction** of the Alternative Cost % and, subsequently, in Profit.

Any **decrease** in the Projected Cost(s) percentages or dollars, however caused, will result in an **increase** of the Alternative Cost % and, subsequently, in Profit.

$ 20.00 Selling Price break-down

Selling Price (without taxes)	S or REV	100.00%	$20.00
Product Cost (COGS)	DVC	30.00%	$6.00
Labour Cost/Payroll	SVC	20.00%	$4.00
Sales Related Costs	VC	20.00%	$4.00
Overhead/Operating Costs	FXC	16.00%	$3.20
Net Income, Profit before taxes	ALTC	**14.00%**	**$2.80**

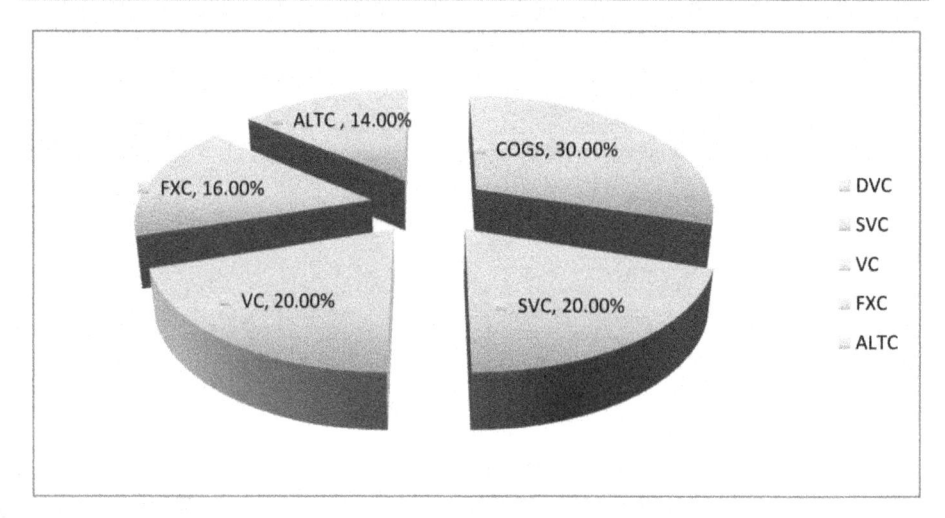

For Cost Control purposes, all Costs are calculated as a fraction of Sales (Revenue), the result being the ACTUAL COSTS, whereas, for Budgeting purposes, Costs are established and subsequently SELLING PRICES are most often calculated based on DESIRED Cost percentage (%).

The two most common methods of calculating a Selling Price are GROSS PROFIT or PRIME COST pricing and DESIRED or IDEAL COST PERCENTAGE (%) pricing.

Let's calculate how **DESIRED or IDEAL COST PERCENTAGE (%) pricing** works:

DESIRED COST pricing	
Product Cost	$1.50
Desired Cost	30%
Product Cost	1.50
divided by DC% of	30%
	= S.P. of 5.00

PRIME COST pricing	
Product $1.50	Labour Cost $00.75
Prime Cost of	45%
P + L Cost	2.25
div. by PC%	45%
	= S.P. of 5.00

In this example there is no difference in the Calculated Selling Price. Increase or decrease the Labour and Product Cost and recalculate. Keep track of the Results for comparison purposes.

Prime Cost may be calculated by department or for the whole operation, although most commonly prime cost is allocated as "Direct labour cost" to produce an item or items.

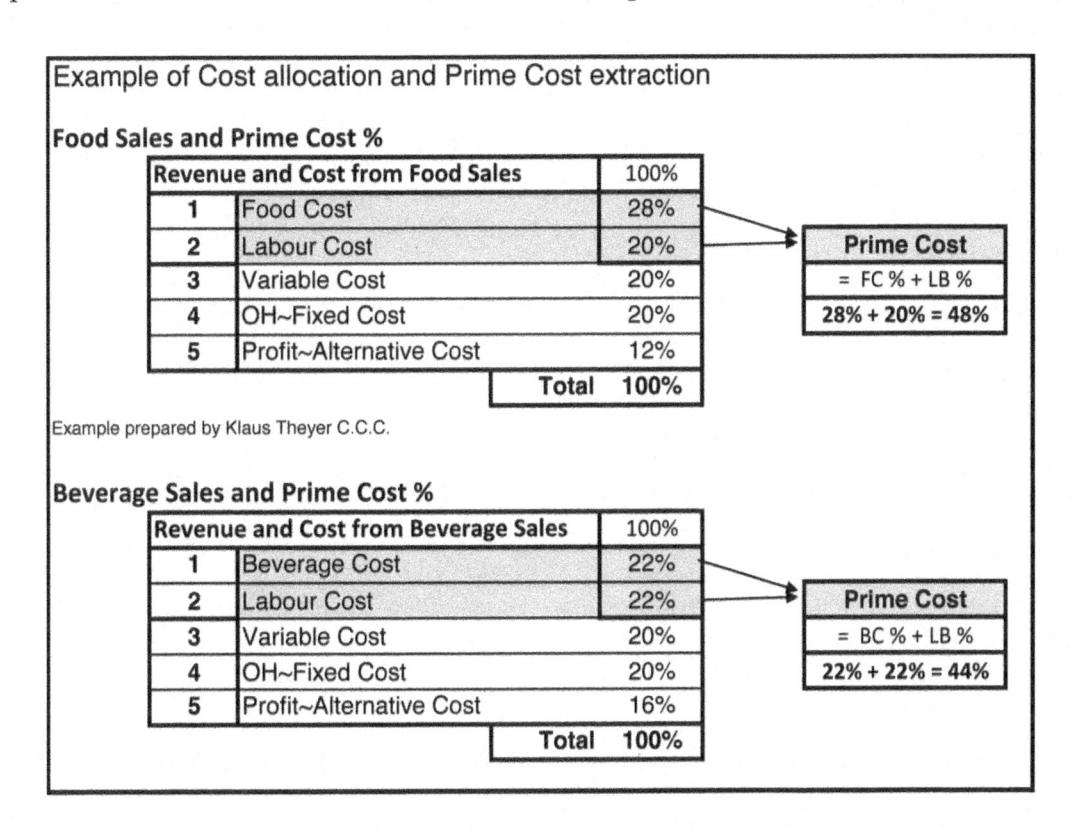

Example of Cost allocation and Prime Cost extraction

Food Sales and Prime Cost %

Revenue and Cost from Food Sales		100%
1	Food Cost	28%
2	Labour Cost	20%
3	Variable Cost	20%
4	OH~Fixed Cost	20%
5	Profit~Alternative Cost	12%
	Total	100%

Prime Cost = FC % + LB %
28% + 20% = 48%

Example prepared by Klaus Theyer C.C.C.

Beverage Sales and Prime Cost %

Revenue and Cost from Beverage Sales		100%
1	Beverage Cost	22%
2	Labour Cost	22%
3	Variable Cost	20%
4	OH~Fixed Cost	20%
5	Profit~Alternative Cost	16%
	Total	100%

Prime Cost = BC % + LB %
22% + 22% = 44%

Food and Beverage Sales and Prime Cost %

Revenue and Cost from Combined Sales		100%
1	Food & Beverage Cost	25%
2	Combined Labour Cost	21%
3	Variable Cost	20%
4	OH~Fixed Cost	20%
5	Profit~Alternative Cost	14%
	Total	100%

Prime Cost 25% + 21% = 46%

Example prepared by Klaus Theyer C.C.C.

Prime Cost % based on Food & Beverage Sales in this example it is 46%

- Alternative Cost 14%
- Food & Beverage Cost 25%
- Combined Labour Cost 21%
- Variable Cost 20%
- OH~Fixed Cost 20%

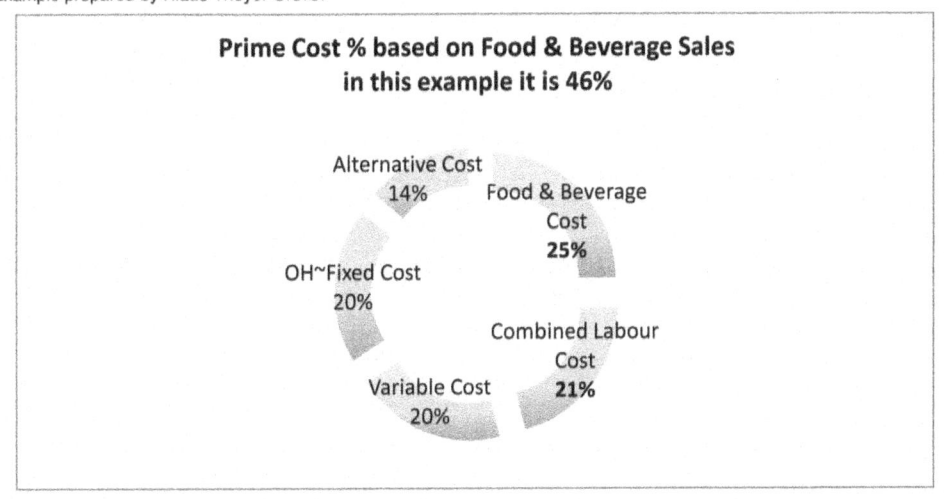

Example Scenarios

Scenario 1

To prepare a chicken stock, the ingredients cost $10.00, and the labour cost for the half hour it takes to set-up, skim, and strain the stock is $7.50; therefore, the prime cost is $17.50.

Scenario 2

The food production area has a 30% Food cost and a 20% Labour cost; therefore, the prime cost would be 50%. If the Bar has a 22% Beverage cost and a 23% Labour cost, then the prime cost would be 45%. For each example, prime cost is calculated based on their separate sales (100%).

If you were to combine the sales from the two (or more) different departments then the various product and labour costs would also have to be combined and the prime cost percentage (%) re-calculated.

Since Cost is a part of the Selling Price and directly influences Profit or Loss, it is expected that everyone working in the hospitality field is knowledgeable of what Cost is, how it occurs (planned and otherwise), and how to check on/for it.

In order to communicate effectively, terminology was developed over the years to identify the different Cost applications. Some terms are more commonly used in the USA than in Canada and some terms are more popular in Canada. Since employees in our industry are often working abroad, it is beneficial to know as many terms as possible.

Think of Cost in relation to Sales and expected Profit. See for yourself how a small increase in Product Cost can affect Profit expectation.

Selling Price of Item:	= 100%	$10.00	= 100%	$10.00	= 100%	$10.00
- COGS	- 25%	2.50	- 27.5%	2.75	- 30%	3.00
= Gross Profit	= 75%	7.50	= 72.5%	7.25	= 70%	7.00
- Variable Cost (to Sales)	- 12%	1.20		1.20		1.20
- Semi-Variable Cost	- 28%	2.80		2.80		2.80
- Fixed Cost	- 15%	1.50		1.50		1.50
= Profit (Net income (Loss))	= 20%	2.00	= 17.5%	1.75	= 15%	1.50

Management must monitor Product Cost; however, since some menu items will have a higher Labour Cost than Product Cost and some Products will have a much higher Product Cost than Labour Cost, it is important to calculate the Prime Cost for each item sold. The Prime Cost is the combination of Product and Labour Cost.

Selling Price of Item:	= 100%	$10.00	= 100%	$10.00	= 100%	$10.00
- COGS	- 25%	2.50	- 15%	1.50	- 45%	4.50
- Semi-Variable Cost	- 28%	2.80	- 40%	4.00	- 15%	1.50
Prime Cost	= 53%	5.30	= 55%	5.50	= 60%	6.00
= Gross Profit	= 47%	4.70	= 45%	4.50	= 40%	4.00
- Variable Cost (to Sales)	- 12%	1.20		1.20		1.20
- Semi-Variable Cost	- 28%	2.80		2.80		2.80
- Fixed Cost	- 15%	1.50		1.50		1.50
= Profit (Net income (Loss))	= 20%	2.00	= 18%	1.80	= 13%	1.30

Common Hospitality Terms and Their Acronyms

Definitions, Terminology	Abbreviation	Explanation, if Necessary
Actual Cost %	A. C. %	Calculated based on COGS and Revenue
Adjusted	ADJ	Projected +/− Variance
Alternative Cost	ALT. C.	Term used for Profit in Cost Control
As Purchased	A. P.	Considered to be 100%
Average and/or mean	AVG	For a data set, the mean is the sum of the observations divided by the number of observations
Average Contribution Margin	A. C. M.	ACM = (AVS − AVC)
Average Sales	AV.S.	Sales divided by # of customers
Average Variable Cost	A. V. C.	AVC = (VA div. # Customers)
Average Variable Rate	A. V. R.	Ratio of AVC to AVS (decimal)
Break Even Point	B. E. P.	When Revenue covers all Costs
Budget (Long-term or Short-term, Static or Flexible)	Budget	Financial Forecast, usually based on Historical information, most often for Sales and Costs
Capital Cost	C. C.	Cost of Capital investment
Capital Cost Allowance	C. C. A.	Reduction of Income by claiming the Value of Loss over Time from grouped Assets. The Loss is determined by Class # and percentage.
Closing Inventory	C. I.	The Value of Inventory at end of (Time/Date)
Contribution Margin	C. M.	CM = (S − COGS)
Contribution Rate	C. R.	CR = (1 − VR) Break-even point calculations
Cost of Goods Sold (COGS)	D. V. C.	Directly Variable Cost − Product used for Sales
Depreciation	DEP	Loss of Value over time − offset by CCA
Desired or Planned or Target or Budgeted or Forecasted or Standard or Ideal Cost %	D.C. %	Percentage used to calculate potential Selling Prices
Edible Consumable Portion	E. P.	Final Consumable Product (See Yield)
Fixed Cost or Overhead Cost	FX. C. or O. H.	Occupancy Cost − Does not change with sales
Gross Profit; also CM	G. P.	Contribution toward Profit (S − COGS)
Historical Cost	All Costs	Budgetary Term for Cost in the past
Indirect Costs	V. C.	Variable Cost − Anticipated Sales surrounding cost
Loss	L	Difference between AP and EP
Menu Mix or Sales Mix or Popularity Index (%)	M. M. or S. M. or P. I.	Item sold divided by total items sold, usually expressed as %
Net Income	Net Inc.	Accounting expression for Profit

Chapter 1 Introduction to Elements of Cost

Definitions, Terminology	Abbreviation	Explanation, if Necessary
Opening Inventory	O. I.	The Value of Inventory at the beginning of (Time/Date) usually closing inventory from previous period
Overhead Cost — Occupancy Cost	FX. C. or O. H.	Fixed Cost occurring with or without a Sale
Popularity Index, Sales, and/or Menu Mix	P. I. or S. M. or M. M.	Item sold divided by total items sold, expressed in a %
Planned Cost	See D. C. %	Historical or other Cost information applied
Point of Sales (System)	P. O. S. (S)	Cash register, Computer terminal recording orders and sales
Prime Cost	PR. C.	Combined Cost of Product and Labour
Profit Margin	P. M.	Difference between Revenue and Costs
Profit or Alternative Cost	P	Another word for Net Income
Projected Cost Percentage	P. C. %	Based on anticipated Sales mix
Proportional Share of Total Sales (Revenue)	P. S. T. S.	Ratio of one (type) Unit Sale to total Units Sold
Purchase	P	Abbreviation used in COGS calculation
Purchase Order	P. O.	External requisition for selected Vendor
Purchase Order Number	P. O. #	A unique number for each P.O. issued
Ratio	RATIO	A method of evaluating comparables
Return On Investment	R. O. I.	Usually expressed as a percentage
Revenue	REV	Accrued Sales (Income)
Sale(s)	S	Earnings in exchange for Goods sold or Services rendered
Semi-Variable Cost (FXC and VC)	S. V. C.	Labour Cost (however, most often calculated as part of FXC)
Un-depreciated Capital Cost	U. C. C.	B/Y or E/Y Beginning or End of Year
Unit or Recipe Unit	Unit - R. U.	Smallest dividable amount of quantity, or predetermined quantity
Unit Sales Required to Break Even	U. S. R. B.	See Break Even Point USRB = (FXC per Unit div. CM per Unit)
Usable Portion	U. P.	Trimmed/Boned, prior to cooking
Variable Cost	V. C.	Cost that changes with Sales volume
Variable Rate (breakeven point)	V. R.	VR = (VC div. by S) usually expressed as fraction
Variance	VAR	Difference between Desired/Projected and Actual
Zero-Based Budget	Z. B. B.	In simple terms, ZBB does not consider Historical costs. Budget items must be defended.

Chapter 2

Revenue and Cost Areas, Cost of Goods Sold (COGS) and Introduction to Budget and Income Statement

Introduction to the Term "Business"

A business is a registered entity (it can be created by one or more persons). A business, like an individual, must keep books and records for income tax purposes as well as for knowing the financial state of the business. Any profit or loss is reported on the owner's tax return.

A business, if owned by one individual, is referred to as a sole ownership or proprietorship. If there is more than one person registered as an owner, then it is referred to as a partnership. Each partner may own a proportional share of the business. In either case, the responsibility for the business lies with the owner(s) in direct proportion to ownership.

At some point, if not from the day of registration, the business may be registered as a corporation. (That is, a company with limited liability—also referred to as a limited "Ltd" company or incorporated entity.) There are situations where an individual may incorporate him/her/themselves.

Corporations do not have owners; they have shareholders. A corporation files its own tax return and shareholders report their share of income or loss on their own tax returns.

The key purpose for going into or being in business is to make a "profit." Profit is another term for net income, usually referring to income before taxes.

Profitability = Ability to Make a Profit

Keeping records (Excerpts from the Canada Revenue Agency Website)

http://www.cra-arc.gc.ca/tx/bsnss/tpcs/kprc/menu-eng.html
http://www.cra-arc.gc.ca/E/pub/tg/rc4409/rc4409-e.html

If you are carrying on a business or engaged in a commercial activity in Canada, you are required by law to keep adequate records.

Your records have to provide enough details to determine your tax obligations and entitlements. Also, your records have to be supported by original documents.

Many people do not realize the rules of being in business—for example, having a defendable (realistic) business plan on record or the reporting of business activities. I strongly recommend informing yourself of the requirements prior to contemplating going into business. Even if you have no intention of going into business yourself, it is good knowledge to have. It will help you understand your employer's responsibility in managing the business. Any employer will have a preference for employees who have an understanding of business rules and regulations.

A little history about taxation from Canada Revenue Agency's Website:

http://www.cra-arc.gc.ca/tx/ndvdls/tchtx/pdf/2007TS18/nglsh/pp1-2-eng.pdf

Record-keeping requirements and filing business reports and tax returns are not unique to Canada—as a matter of fact, there are only a few countries (at the time of writing) on this planet that do not require filing a tax return.

The Basic Internal Income Statement Structure with Cost Control Terms

as of: yyyy/mm/dd

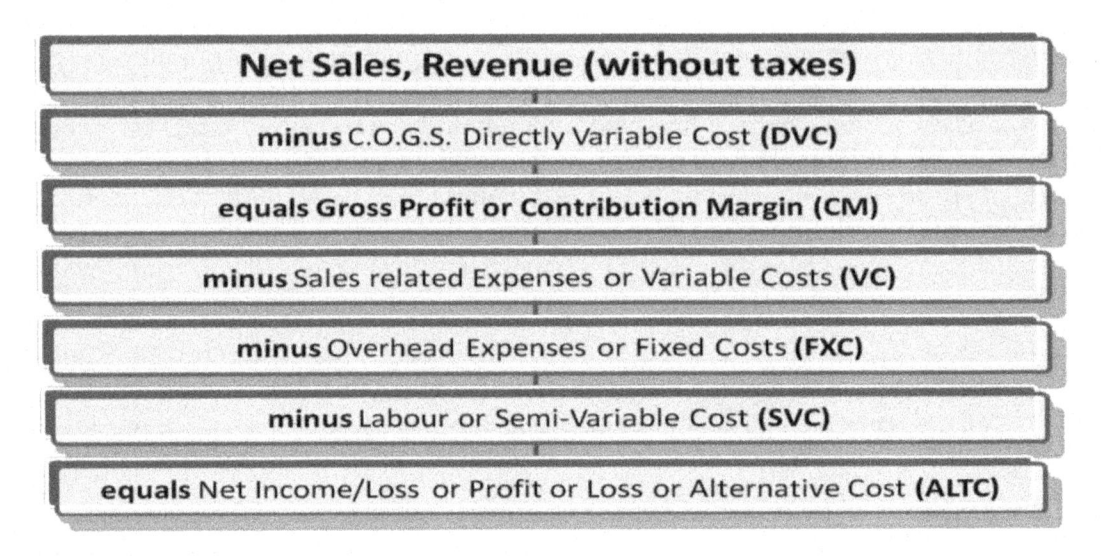

Net Sales, Revenue (without taxes)

minus C.O.G.S. Directly Variable Cost **(DVC)**

equals Gross Profit or Contribution Margin **(CM)**

minus Sales related Expenses or Variable Costs **(VC)**

minus Overhead Expenses or Fixed Costs **(FXC)**

minus Labour or Semi-Variable Cost **(SVC)**

equals Net Income/Loss or Profit or Loss or Alternative Cost **(ALTC)**

Cost Control Terminology vs. Accounting Terminology

Using the Income Statement format, the official name for it is: "Statement of Income and Expenses." The same format is also commonly used as a template for a "Budget" to demonstrate the difference between the terms used in accounting and cost control.

NOTE: **Fixed cost** can be defined as any cost or expense occurring independent of a sale.

Accounting Terms	Cost Control Terms
INCOME:	INCOME:
Sales, Revenue (Accrued Sales, may include taxes)	**Sales, Revenue** (Accrued Sales before taxes–Net Sales)
Cost of Sale Material Cost (Cost of goods or COGS)	**Cost of Goods Sold (COGS)** The actual cost of sold products (**DVC** Directly Variable Cost)
Gross Profit or Profit Margin	Gross Profit or Contribution Margin
EXPENSES:	COSTS:
Operational Expenses: Sales-related expenses, Advertising, and Promotions	**Variable Cost** (in relation to Sales) This cost is an indirect cost, occurring because of a sale being anticipated or made (e.g., condiments)
Fixed Expenses: Overhead (like rent, insurance, and sometimes labour)	FIXED Cost (FXC): (Occupancy Cost) Overhead (like rent, insurance, and sometimes labour)
Labour Expense including Benefits—Sometimes included in Operating Expenses	**Labour Cost (SVC)** Semi-Variable Cost Note: Most establishments handle Labour Cost as a Fixed Cost
Net Income (Loss)	Profit (Loss) Alternative Cost (ALTC)

Accrued Means Accumulated

Sales become revenue when measured for a period of time (i.e., accrued sales from the lunch period become lunch revenue).

A *Cost of Goods Sold* (COGS), which could be Food or Beverage, requires purchased products to be converted to consumables, either through handling or cooking of food, or mixing a drink.

In either case, the purchased product is taken from the inventory which is listed as an *Asset* on the *Balance sheet*. The Balance sheet is one of the two reporting documents a company needs to file with their tax returns. The other is a Statement of Income and Expenses, often referred to as a P & L (Profit and Loss statement).

Chapter 2 — Revenue and Cost Areas, Cost of Goods Sold (COGS) and Introduction to Budget and Income Statement

The chart below explains the transfer from an *Asset* to *COGS*.

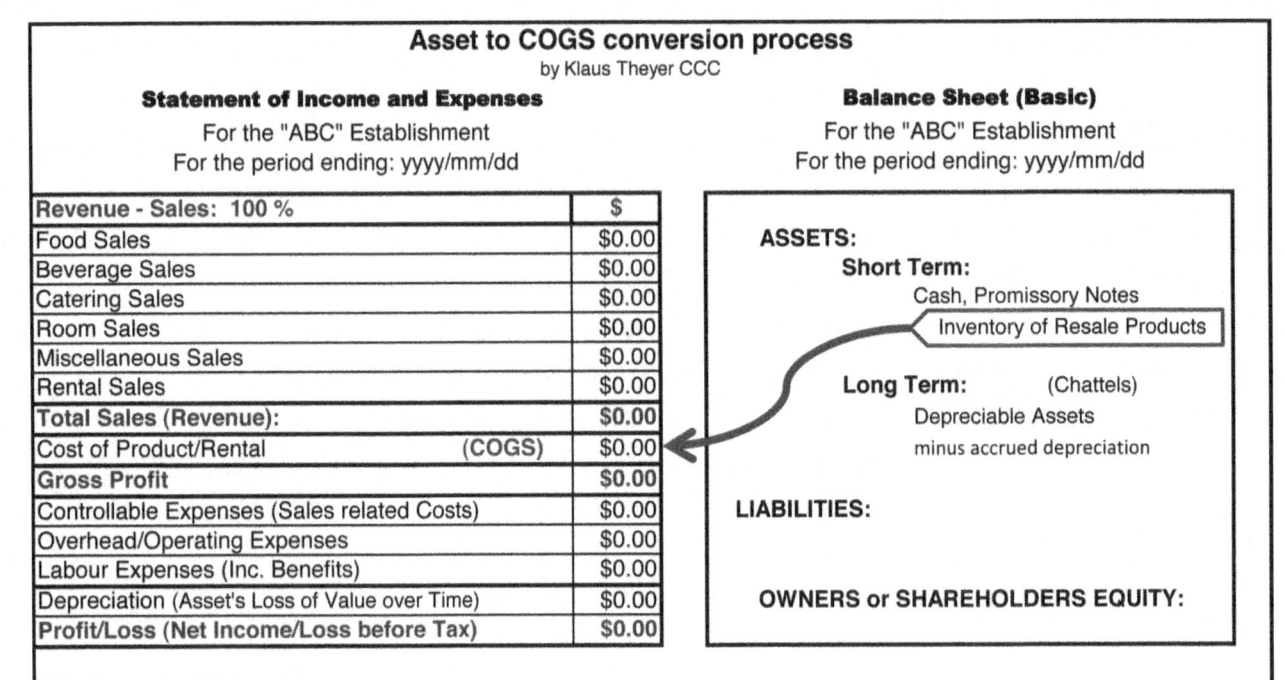

Asset to COGS conversion process
by Klaus Theyer CCC

Statement of Income and Expenses
For the "ABC" Establishment
For the period ending: yyyy/mm/dd

Revenue - Sales: 100 %	$
Food Sales	$0.00
Beverage Sales	$0.00
Catering Sales	$0.00
Room Sales	$0.00
Miscellaneous Sales	$0.00
Rental Sales	$0.00
Total Sales (Revenue):	$0.00
Cost of Product/Rental (COGS)	$0.00
Gross Profit	$0.00
Controllable Expenses (Sales related Costs)	$0.00
Overhead/Operating Expenses	$0.00
Labour Expenses (Inc. Benefits)	$0.00
Depreciation (Asset's Loss of Value over Time)	$0.00
Profit/Loss (Net Income/Loss before Tax)	$0.00

Balance Sheet (Basic)
For the "ABC" Establishment
For the period ending: yyyy/mm/dd

ASSETS:
    Short Term:
        Cash, Promissory Notes
        Inventory of Resale Products

    Long Term: (Chattels)
        Depreciable Assets
        minus accrued depreciation

LIABILITIES:

OWNERS or SHAREHOLDERS EQUITY:

What you should know!

The **Asset** to **COGS** (Cost of Goods Sold) **Conversion** occurs when **Product** is removed from the **Inventory** to be **Sold** (to generate Revenue).   At this point the **Inventory** is reduced by the **Value** ($) of the removed **Asset** and a Cost Of Sale **(COS)** or a Cost Of Goods Sold **(COGS)** has been established.

If there is product left which is not sold, it maybe returned to Inventory for credit against COGS. (This transaction may not occur physically, but should be so recorded in the company's bookkeeping)

FORMULAE: Sales Price (SP) - (minus) Recipe Product Cost = (equals) **Anticipated Gross Profit.**

Revenue - COGS = **Actual Gross Profit**

COGS = OI (Opening Inventory) + P (Purchases) - CI (Closing Inventory)

C.O.G.S.—Cost of Goods Sold

When Menu Prices are being established, the Cost of the Product is used to calculate the Selling Price. Depending on the Pricing method, sometimes Labour Cost is included to establish the Gross Profit (CM).

Although these methods are being commonly used, they will not provide sufficient information to evaluate and calculate Actual Cost and allow for comparison with Projected Costs and, subsequently, any Variance.

Business is required by law to take Inventory once a year but should at least take it once a month, although more often is even better for control purposes.

When a Perpetual or Physical Inventory is taken, the Value of the Stock on hand is calculated based on purchase costs. This Value is recorded and used for the Actual Cost percent (%) calculation.

The most basic equation is:

Opening Inventory + Purchases − Closing Inventory = C.O.G.S.

C.O.G.S. divided (÷) by Revenue for this measured period calculates the Actual Cost percentage (%). The Actual Cost percentage is compared to the Projected or Ideal Cost percentage to calculate any Variances (Positive or Negative).

The Projected Cost % is established by adding the Cost of each menu item and dividing the total by the total from all menu Selling Prices.

Total Recipe Cost divided by Total Selling Price	= Projected Cost %
C.O.G.S. divided by Revenue	= Actual Cost %
Projected C % minus Actual Cost %	= Variance % (Positive or Negative)
That is, if the Projected C %	= 29.00%
and the Actual C % is	28.50%
then the Variance is	+ 0.50% (Positive = subsequently good)
if the Projected C %	= 29.00%
and the Actual is	29.50%
then the Variance is	− 0.50% (Negative, subsequently NOT good)

Although such a small Variance is not necessarily alarming, if the Budget is based on a Million Dollar Cost then the Variance is not that small anymore ($5,000.00).

Basic Cost of Goods Sold   by Klaus Theyer C.C.C.

Expressions used: "TODAY" meaning "To Day" - TO DATE means from the beginning of "a chosen" time period until and including TODAY.

MEATS: Due to the high cost of Protein Items, the Cost Percentage is often calculated separately from other food items. However, in order to obtain accurate Food Cost percentage % results, Proteins have to be included in Food purchases.

For daily inventory applications; Today's Closing Inventory becomes Tomorrows Opening Inventory

Method of Calculation: Opening Inventory plus Purchases minus Closing Inventory equals COGS

	Monday	Tuesday	Wednesday	Thursday	Friday	Saturday
OPENING INVENTORY:	1,425.50	1,390.00				
"Group of Proteins"						
+ Meat	335.50	391.30	410.25	613.00	775.25	0.00
+ and Poultry	200.50	65.70	244.75	277.50	325.75	0.00
+ and Seafood	74.50	85.00	222.00	185.50	300.00	0.00
= "Proteins Total"	610.50					
+ Fresh Produce	354.50	155.00	210.10	199.60	410.25	201.50
+ Frozen Vegetable	52.65	125.50	445.90	221.40	390.25	0.00
+ Dairy products	95.35	122.50	117.25	190.50	290.25	90.60
+ Bread/Rolls	80.40	95.40	75.75	95.50	110.25	80.40
+ Dry Goods	220.60	50.60	0.00	336.00	0.00	0.00
= **TOTAL PURCHASES:**	1,414.00					
− **CLOSING INVENTORY:**	1,390.00	855.00	644.00	899.00	622.00	122.50
= **C.O.G.S.:**	1,449.50					
÷ **S A L E S:**	4,300.00	5,500.00	6,215.00	5,898.00	10,222.00	3,333.00
= **DAILY FOOD COST %:**	33.71%					

Total C.O.G.S.: 10,627.50   Total SALES: 35,468.00

"TO DATE" Food Cost Percent % for the SIX day period: _____

Calculate the Cost of MEATS as a Percentage of the TOTAL Purchases:

Total "Proteins" purchased: _____   divided by Total Purchases: _____

equals % _____

Using the same method as above, calculate Daily Proteins Cost Percentage % in comparison to Daily Total Purchases:

Monday	Tuesday	Wednesday	Thursday	Friday	Saturday
43.18%					

Extended C.O.G.S. Calculation
Periodic Product Cost % Calculation
Created by Klaus Theyer C.C.C., inspired by David Jones C.C.C.

Period from: _____   To: _____   Recorders Name: _____

Production/Inventory Area: _____   Product Inventory: _____

	Food Production Area:			**Beverage Production Area:**	
	Opening Inventory ($):	1,500		Opening Inventory ($):	4,750
plus +	Purchase for Period ($):	2,750	plus +	Purchase for Period ($):	2,750
Equals =	Total available for Sale ($):	4,250	Equals =	Total available for Sale ($):	
minus -	Closing Inventory ($):	700	minus -	Closing Inventory ($):	2,000
Equals =	Gross Product C.O.G.S. ($):	3,550	Equals =	Gross Product C.O.G.S. ($):	
plus +	Transfers in Cooking Spirits ($):	250	plus +	Transfers in Food products ($):	150
plus +	Transfers in from other units ($):	50	plus +	Transfers in from other units ($):	50
minus -	Transfers out to Bar ($):	150	minus -	Transfers out to Kitchen ($):	250
minus -	Transfers out to other units ($):	50	minus -	Transfers out to other units ($):	50
minus -	Transfers/Promotions out ($):	100	minus -	Transfers/Promotions out ($):	200
Equals =	Cost of Product consumed ($):	3,550	Equals =	Cost of Product consumed ($):	
minus -	Cost of Employees meals ($):	250	minus -	Cost of Employee beverages ($):	25
Equals =	Actual C.O.G.S. ($):	3,300	Equals =	Actual C.O.G.S. ($):	

Actual Cost percentage calculation:

	Actual C.O.G.S. ($):	3,300		Actual C.O.G.S. ($):	
divided by	FOOD REVENUE	11,500	divided by	BEVERAGE REVENUE	25,000
Equals =	Product Cost percentage (%):	28.70%	Equals =	Product Cost percentage (%):	
	Contribution Margin ($):	8,200		Contribution Margin ($):	

Chapter 2 Revenue and Cost Areas, Cost of Goods Sold (COGS) and Introduction to Budget and Income Statement

The two key reporting documents (instruments)
Externally and Internally (Reporting expressions may change)

Statement of Income and Expenses
For the "ABC" Establishment
For the period ending: yyyy/mm/dd

Revenue - Sales: 100 %	$
Food Sales	$0.00
Beverage Sales	$0.00
Catering Sales	$0.00
Room Sales	$0.00
Miscellaneous Sales	$0.00
Rental Sales	$0.00
Total Sales (Revenue):	**$0.00**
Cost of Product/Rental (COGS)	$0.00
Gross Profit	**$0.00**
Controllable Expenses (Sales related Costs)	$0.00
Overhead/Operating Expenses	$0.00
Labour Expenses (Inc. Benefits)	$0.00
Depreciation (Asset's Loss of Value over Time)	$0.00
Profit/Loss (Net Income/Loss before Tax)	**$0.00**

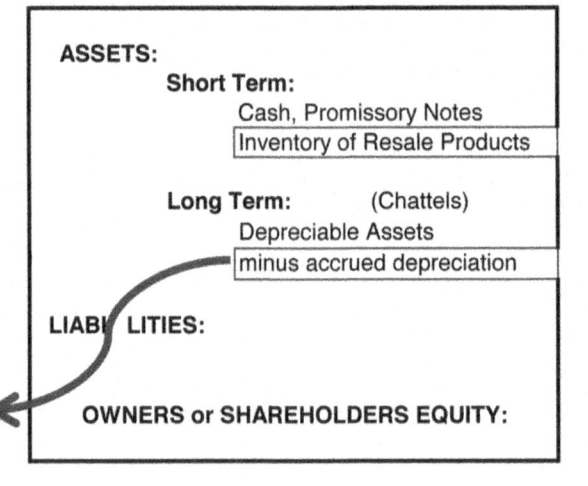

Balance Sheet (Basic)
For the "ABC" Establishment
For the period ending: yyyy/mm/dd

ASSETS:
   Short Term:
      Cash, Promissory Notes
      Inventory of Resale Products

   Long Term: (Chattels)
      Depreciable Assets
      minus accrued depreciation

LIABILITIES:

OWNERS or SHAREHOLDERS EQUITY:

What you should know!
The principle of being in **BUSINESS** is to make a **PROFIT**.
Profit expectations need to be documented using a **BUSINESS PLAN** with a **BUDGET**.
Budget terms vary - from one week - Short Term Budget, to five years - Long Term Budget.
The Business Plan including a Budget is indirectly prescribed by **Canada Revenue Agency**.
Canada Revenue Agency also prescribes the reporting methods and the language used.
(Reporting is based on Common Accounting Principals, which suggest that NO VARIABLE COST
should occur, unless a SALE is made, and in order to make a sale, Product has to be removed from Assets,
(Inventory). In other words, if NO sale was made, NO Variable Cost should have occurred.
There are exceptions to this scenario: Theft, Spoilage, Overproduction, anticipated but not realized sales,
in these cases the product is no longer available for sale and subsequently Cost has occurred.

Balance Sheet (Basic)
For the "ABC" Establishment
For the period ending: yyyy/mm/dd

ASSET:
   Short Term:
      Cash, Promissory Notes
      Inventory of Resale Products

   Long Term: (Chattels)
      Depreciable Assets
      minus accrued depreciation

LIABILITIES:

OWNERS or SHAREHOLDERS EQUITY:

DEPARTMENT Statement of Income and Expenses
For the "ABC" Establishment **KITCHEN**
For the period ending: yyyy/mm/dd

	Revenue - Sales: 100 %	$
+	Food Sales	$0.00
+	Catering Sales	$0.00
+	Miscellaneous Sales	$0.00
+	Rental Sales	$0.00
=	**Total Sales (Revenue):**	**$0.00**
-	Cost of Product/Rental	$0.00
=	**Gross Profit**	**$0.00**
-	Controllable Expenses	$0.00
-	Overhead/Operating Expenses	$0.00
-	Labour Expenses (Inc. Benefits)	$0.00
=	**Profit/Loss**	**$0.00**

DEPARTMENT Statement of Income and Expenses
For the "ABC" Establishment **BAR**
For the period ending: yyyy/mm/dd

	Revenue - Sales: 100 %	$
+	Beverage Sales	$0.00
+	Catering Sales	$0.00
+	Miscellaneous Sales	$0.00
+	Rental Sales	$0.00
=	**Total Sales (Revenue):**	**$0.00**
-	Cost of Product/Rental	$0.00
=	**Gross Profit**	**$0.00**
-	Controllable Expenses	$0.00
-	Overhead/Operating Expenses	$0.00
-	Labour Expenses (Inc. Benefits)	$0.00
=	**Profit/Loss**	**$0.00**

Menu or Selling Price Strategies

The Purpose and Process of Calculating a Selling Price and Associated Costs

To write a menu for a restaurant is the foundation of planning for profit. Although it can be fun to offer all the specialties one always wanted to present to the public, it needs to be taken very seriously so that the offerings not only cover the costs incurred, but also to return a profit.

As previously described, a demographic study of the area is essential to ensure the area will appreciate your offerings and that competitors are not outnumbering your concept.

There Are Really Only Three Venues

Bring a well-known concept (restaurant chain) to the area like a McDonald's, Wendy's, Jack Astor, or Milestones. Alternatively, serve the area with what the majority of inhabitants are able to relate to based on their background, and lastly, to offer something so very unique that it does not depend on the inhabitants of the area, like a specialised restaurant.

In all cases, the description and positioning of menu items play an important role as does the careful pairing of main items and their side dishes and creating a menu that offers a balance of expensive and inexpensive items. These are some of the common steps taken to make the establishment attractive to a wide range of potential customers. This is thoroughly described in my other book *Today's menu, Menu du jour*.

In order to ensure that the calculated sales price of a menu item will generate the desired profit, one must know exactly the various costs involved:

- ▶ Cost of product, including side dishes and garnishes
- ▶ Cost of incidental ingredients like cooking oil and basic seasoning
- ▶ Cost of production labour
- ▶ Energy cost
- ▶ Cost of over production
- ▶ Cost of service, depending on service style
- ▶ Cost of necessary production equipment
- ▶ Cost of storage space and production area

An operator will have a certain expectation for a sale-to-cost ratio, as illustrated in a later example. As a chef, the most important costs to be concerned with are product-related costs and labour cost.

Product cost usually represents a fraction of the selling price. If the selling or menu price would be $20.00 and the cost should be 30 percent of the selling price, then there is $6.00 available for the cost of the product. If the labour cost for the same item is calculated at 25 percent of the selling price, then the preparation and production labour cost cannot exceed $5.00.

This may sound very restrictive and difficult to calculate, but it is a necessary step in planning for profit. With computers and appropriate computer programs, the task is manageable and with tested standard recipes, applied portion control, defined quality of purchased products, inventory control, and careful production and labour scheduling, it is manageable.

The second most common scenario of applied menu price costing is to add all product costs from the standard recipe, including peripheral costs like cooking oil and flour to dust the table, and divide the total cost by the desired cost percentage. For the following example, the total product cost came to $6.25. The desired cost percentage is 25 percent so the selling price should be $25.00 (6.25 ÷ 25% = 25.00). It may seem like a lot of money for a $6.00 item, but one must remember that from the remaining $18.75 labour cost, as well as variable and fixed costs must be covered, and a profit must be made.

Statement of Income and Expenses
For the "ABC" Establishment
For the period ending: yyyy/mm/dd
(with "Costing terms acronyms")

	Revenue - Sales: 100 %	$	Acronym	
+	Food Sales	$0.00	S	
+	Beverage Sales	$0.00	S	
+	Catering Sales	$0.00	S	
+	Room Sales	$0.00	S	
+	Miscellaneous Sales	$0.00	S	
+	Rental Sales	$0.00	S	
=	**Total Sales (Revenue):**	**$0.00**	REV	= Sum of (All Sales)
-	Cost of Product/Rental	$0.00	COGS	= O.I. + P - E.I.)
=	**Gross Profit**	**$0.00**	GP or CM	= (REV - COGS)
-	Controllable Expenses	$0.00	VC	
-	Overhead/Operating Expenses	$0.00	FXC	
-	Labour Expenses (Inc. Benefits)	$0.00	SVC or FXC	
-	Depreciation (Asset Loss of Value over time)	$0.00	FXC	
=	**Profit/Loss (Net Income/Loss before Tax)**	**$0.00**	ALTC	= (GP - VC - FXC - SVC)

S = Sales (without taxes)
REV = Revenue (Accrued Sales)
COGS = Cost Of Goods Sold
GP or CM = Gross Profit or Contribution Margin
VC = Variable Cost (Not Product)
FXC = Fixed Cost
SVC = Semi Variable Cost
ALTC = Alternative Cost
For full text of terms see "Cost Classification" diagram

Introduction to "Budgets" and Budgeting

Budget—from the Old French bougette, diminutive of bouge, small leather bag; from Latin bulga, of Celtic origin meaning little bag; to Middle English bouget, wallet—generally is defined as a list of all planned expenses and revenues. A budget is an important concept in microeconomics, which uses a budget line to illustrate the trade-offs between two or more goods. It is also defined as an itemized summary of estimated or intended expenditures for a given period of time along with proposals for financing them. The total sum of money allocated for a particular purpose or period of time.

A budget, to be meaningful, must be based on realistic, achievable goals and objectives, considering all related factors. A budget could be as simple as dealing with one item—for example, staffing level based on occupancy—or as complex as a business plan. Of course there are many factors to be considered before engaging a calculator.

First, and most important, is the time period. The shortest time period (to be practical) should not be less than one week, and the longest time period not longer than five years. However, it is not unheard of to prepare budgets for one day, or for a longer time span than five years.

Usually, budgets are prepared for all departments within a business, and for different time periods. It is not uncommon to look ahead and determine where the business (financially) should be five years from now. This is usually done with a **long-term** budget. Of course, history has taught us that long-term budgets may be rendered unachievable due to recession or unforeseen circumstances, or, on the contrary, they are too conservative in economic upward trends.

Therefore, every long-term budget should be the guideline for **short-term** budgets. Businesses prepare annual budgets, based on their fiscal year, conforming to the long-term goals and objectives. Once a business has established its **long-term** goals, this becomes the **master** budget. Subsequent **short-term** budgets must remain **flexible** to conform to the long-term goals.

Common Types of Budgets

▲ *Long-term or Master*
▲ *Short-term or Periodic*
▲ *Capital* (balance sheet items: cash flow budget, capital equipment replacement (Asset))
▲ *Operating* (ongoing projection of revenue and expenditures)
▲ *Departmental* (forecasted revenue and expenditures based on one department—for example, food, beverage)
▲ *Master* (most comprehensive, for one year or more (up to five years), including balance sheet and income/expenses from all departments)
▲ *Fixed or Static* (These are based on one level of activity, i.e., revenue)

Estimated expenses are based on this level of revenue. That is, costs (Variable and Fixed) are based on the established average percentages. Once costs are calculated, and sales unexpectedly increase or decrease, it becomes very difficult to make immediate monetary adjustments to this situation.

Simple, but yet a very important equation:

If COST (other than Alternative Cost) is more than Sales, a LOSS will occur.

If COST (other than Alternative Cost) is less than Sales, a PROFIT is achieved.

If Cost (not including Alternative Cost) equals Sales, the "BREAK-EVEN-POINT" has been reached.

EVERY BUSINESS NEEDS TO KNOW AT WHAT LEVEL OF SALES THE "BREAK-EVEN-POINT" WILL BE REACHED

Chapter 2 Revenue and Cost Areas, Cost of Goods Sold (COGS) and Introduction to Budget and Income Statement **27**

▲ *Top-Down*—from a long-term master budget allocation to each department, covering a period of one year, apportioned to one month. Period adjustments are made to conform to the long-term goal.

▲ *Bottom-Up*—from daily departmental sales to weekly-monthly to annual, in order to build a long-term budget.

From Long Term to Departmental Budget (Static - Top - Down)

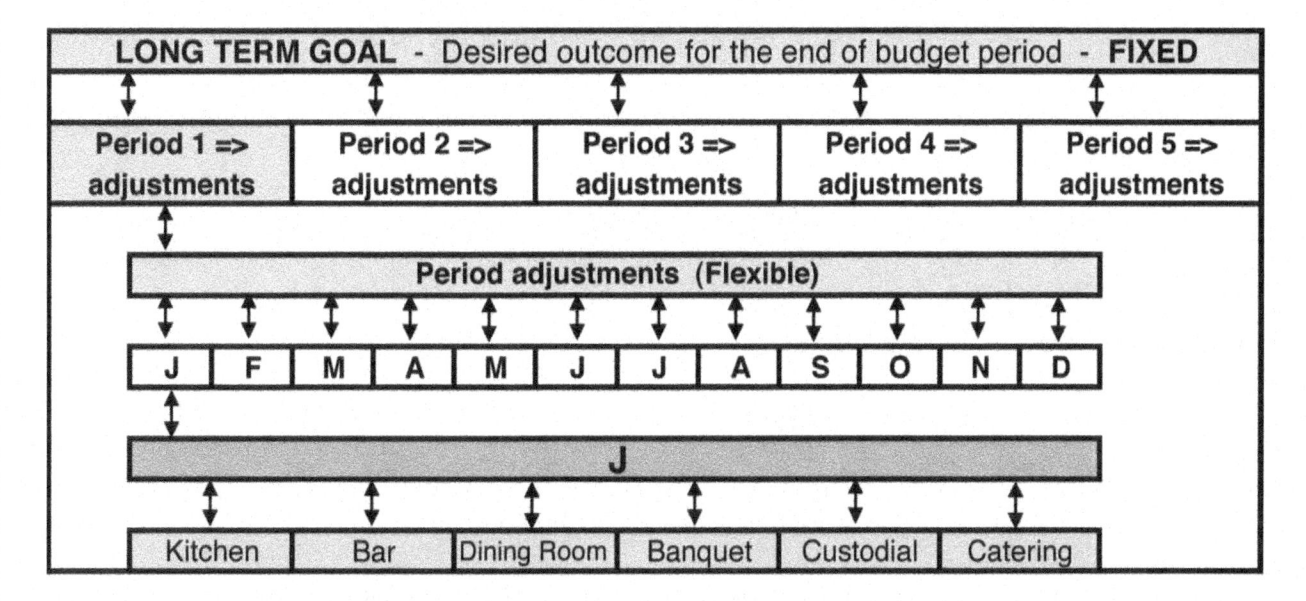

LONG TERM GOAL - Desired outcome for the end of budget period - FIXED
Period 1 => adjustments	Period 2 => adjustments	Period 3 => adjustments	Period 4 => adjustments	Period 5 => adjustments
Period adjustments (Flexible)
J	F	M	A	M	J	J	A	S	O	N	D
J
Kitchen	Bar	Dining Room	Banquet	Custodial	Catering

From Departmental to Long Term Budget (Bottom - Up)

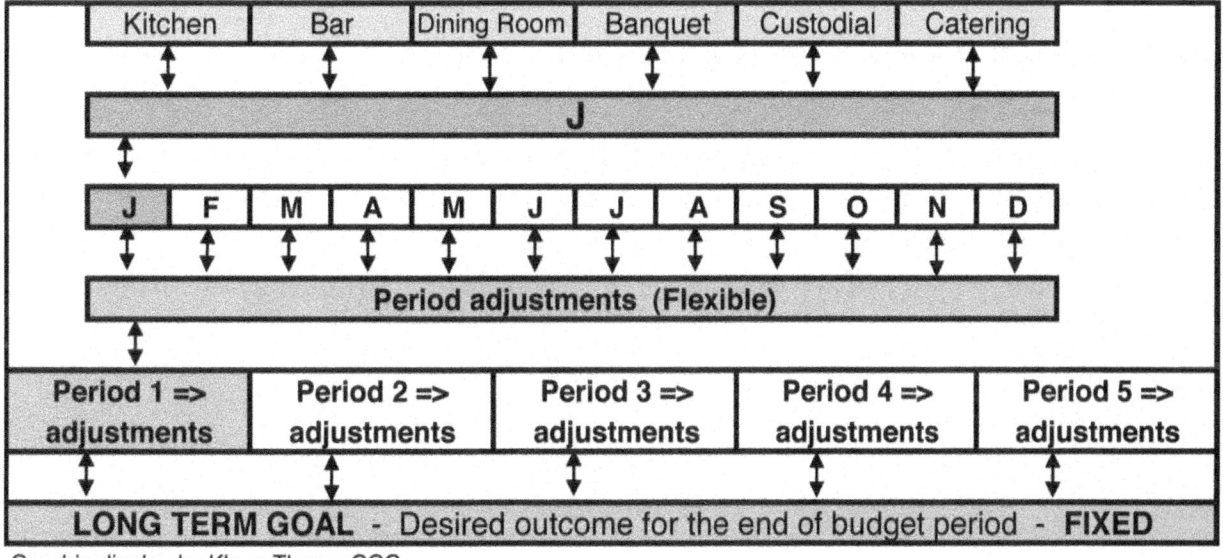

Kitchen	Bar	Dining Room	Banquet	Custodial	Catering
J
J	F	M	A	M	J	J	A	S	O	N	D
Period adjustments (Flexible)
Period 1 => adjustments	Period 2 => adjustments	Period 3 => adjustments	Period 4 => adjustments	Period 5 => adjustments
LONG TERM GOAL - Desired outcome for the end of budget period - FIXED

Graphic display by Klaus Theyer CCC

A Budget Must Be a Realistic Expression of Goals and Objectives in Financial Terms

Budgets are Used

- ▲ To project achievable levels of sales (the increase must at least cover projected inflation)
- ▲ To establish **standards** or **targets** for dollar expenditures
- ▲ To provide a standard against which expenditures can be measured
- ▲ To establish limits for expenditures, and thus to restrict the amounts that can be spent for particular purposes
- ▲ To compare **actual against planned,** analyse the difference **(variances),** and take corrective actions

Note: Budgeting sets not only **goals and objectives;** it may also be **restrictive** and therefore may have **negative connotations,** particularly to middle-management employees. Effects can be frustrating and demoralizing.

"A Budget is a Common Control Technique."

More Common Types of Budgets

- ▲ STATIC — for one level of business activity (Fixed Sales — Fixed Costs)
- ▲ FLEXIBLE — prepared for more than one level of business activity (Adjusted to Sales — Costs)
- ▲ ZBB (Zero-based budgeting) — All budgeted administrative, marketing, property operation and maintenance, energy costs, and general expenses have to be justified by each department.

Types of Budgets for Specific Aspects of Operation

- ▲ Operation Budget — Sales Budget
- ▲ Cash Flow Budget — Capital Equipment — Replacement
- ▲ Repair and Maintenance — Advertising and Promotion
- ▲ Product and Labour
- ▲ Most important is the Operating Budget — it is a forecast of sales and an estimation of costs to earn sales.
- ▲ By extension, the budget suggests the profit that should result after the costs of producing those sales have been met.

Corporate Budget

For years, most companies have taken an inflexible, centralized approach to budget planning and forecasting. But businesses are making big changes in their budget planning and forecasting processes. Once carried out by a CFO (Chief Financial Officer) and accountants, budget planning today has become more of a company-wide effort, with a greater number of managers and employees contributing to the process.

Many companies are striving to combine the traditional bottom-up approach to budget preparation, in which department heads submit budget requests that are combined into a corporate budget, with a top-down approach in which budgets are prepared in conjunction with planned objectives as outlined by management.

Annual budgets were once as unchanging as a statue. More companies now view budgets as living documents subject to revisions on an ongoing basis throughout the year.

	B	C	D	E	F	G	H	I	J	K	L
1	**Budget based on Income Statement**										
2	by Klaus Theyer CCC									Variance Increase/Decrease from THIS to NEXT year	
3					Type of SALE or COST						
4											
5	**Revenue**					This year	%	Next year	%	(+/-) $	(+/-) %
6		Food Sales			Rev/FS	1,500,000	65.79%	1,700,000	68.27%	200,000	13.33%
7		Catering Sales			Rev/FS	360,000		350,000			
8				Total Food Sales	Rev/FS						
9		Beverage Sales			Rev/BS	420,000		440,000			
10			Total Sales, Revenue		REV		100.00%		100.00%		
11											
12	**Cost of Goods Sold**										
13		Meat, Seafood			VC/DVC	298,000		325,000			
14		Fruits, Vegetable			VC/DVC	94,000		114,000			
15		Dairy			VC/DVC	55,000		50,000			
16		Baked Goods			VC/DVC	16,000		20,000			
17		Dry Goods			VC/DVC	245,000		240,000			
18		Total Cost of Food sold (Food COGS)			VC/DVC						
19		Wine Domestic & Imported			VC/DVC	42,400		49,000			
20		Beer Domestic & Imported			VC/DVC	28,500		30,000			
21		Hard Liquor			VC/DVC	22,600		20,000			
22	Total Cost of Beverage sold (Beverage COGS)				VC/DVC						
23			Total COGS		COGS						
24											
25			Gross Profit		GP/CM						
26											
27	**Operating Expenses (Costs)**										
28		Wages (hourly)			VC/SVC	365,000		420,000			
29		Mandatory Benefits (hourly)			VC/SVC	73,000		84,000			
30			Hourly Payroll & related		VC/SVC						
31		Direct Operating expenses			VC	142,000		150,000			
32		Marketing			VC	88,000		92,000			
33		Administrative & General			VC	66,000		70,000			
34			Total Operating expenses		VC						
35											
36	**Fixed Expenses, Overhead, Occupancy Cost**										
37		Wages managerial			FXC	220,000		230,000			
38		Mandatory and other Benefits			FXC	55,000		57,500			
39		Energy & Utility services			FXC	121,000		123,000			
40		Rent/Interest			FXC	87,000		88,000			
41		Depreciation			FXC	80,000		75,000			
42			Total Fixed expenses		FXC						
43											
44			Net Income/Profit/Loss		NIC/P/L						

Chapter 2 Revenue and Cost Areas, Cost of Goods Sold (COGS) and Introduction to Budget and Income Statement

Budget based on Income Statement
by Klaus Theyer CCC

	Type of SALE or COST	This year	%	Next year	%	Variance Increase/Decrease from THIS to NEXT year (+/-) $	(+/-) %
Revenue							
Food Sales	Rev/FS	1,500,000	65.79%	1,700,000	68.27%	200,000	13.33%
Catering Sales	Rev/FS	360,000	15.79%	350,000	14.06%	-10,000	-2.78%
Total Food Sales	Rev/FS	1,860,000	81.58%	2,050,000	82.33%	190,000	10.22%
Beverage Sales	Rev/BS	420,000	18.42%	440,000	17.67%	20,000	4.76%
Total Sales, Revenue	**REV**	**2,280,000**	**100.00%**	**2,490,000**	**100.00%**	**210,000**	**9.21%**
Cost of Goods Sold							
Meat, Seafood	VC/DVC	298,000	16.02%	325,000	15.85%	27,000	9.06%
Fruits, Vegetable	VC/DVC	94,000	5.05%	114,000	5.56%	20,000	21.28%
Dairy	VC/DVC	55,000	2.96%	50,000	2.44%	-5,000	-9.09%
Baked Goods	VC/DVC	16,000	0.86%	20,000	0.98%	4,000	25.00%
Dry Goods	VC/DVC	245,000	13.17%	240,000	11.71%	-5,000	-2.04%
Total Cost of Food sold (Food COGS)	VC/DVC	708,000	38.06%	749,000	36.54%	41,000	5.79%
Wine Domestic & Imported	VC/DVC	42,400	10.10%	49,000	11.14%	6,600	15.57%
Beer Domestic & Imported	VC/DVC	28,500	6.79%	30,000	6.82%	1,500	5.26%
Hard Liquor	VC/DVC	22,600	5.38%	20,000	4.55%	-2,600	-11.50%
Total Cost of Beverage sold (Beverage COGS)	VC/DVC	93,500	22.26%	99,000	22.50%	5,500	5.88%
Total COGS	**COGS**	**801,500**	**35.15%**	**848,000**	**34.06%**	**46,500**	**5.80%**
Gross Profit	**GP/CM**	**1,478,500**	**64.85%**	**1,642,000**	**65.94%**	**163,500**	**11.06%**
Operating Expenses (Costs)							
Wages (hourly)	VC/SVC	365,000	16.01%	420,000	16.87%	55,000	15.07%
Mandatory Benefits (hourly)	VC/SVC	73,000	3.20%	84,000	3.37%	11,000	15.07%
Hourly Payroll & related	VC/SVC	438,000	19.21%	504,000	20.24%	66,000	15.07%
Direct Operating expenses	VC	142,000	6.23%	150,000	6.02%	8,000	5.63%
Marketing	VC	88,000	3.86%	92,000	3.69%	4,000	4.55%
Administrative & General	VC	66,000	2.89%	70,000	2.81%	4,000	6.06%
Total Operating expenses	**VC**	**734,000**	**32.19%**	**816,000**	**32.77%**	**82,000**	**11.17%**
Fixed Expenses, Overhead, Occupancy Cost							
Wages managerial	FXC	220,000	9.65%	230,000	9.24%	10,000	4.55%
Mandatory and other Benefits	FXC	55,000	2.41%	57,500	2.31%	2,500	4.55%
Energy & Utility services	FXC	121,000	5.31%	123,000	4.94%	2,000	1.65%
Rent/Interest	FXC	87,000	3.82%	88,000	3.53%	1,000	1.15%
Depreciation	FXC	80,000	3.51%	75,000	3.01%	-5,000	-6.25%
Total Fixed expenses	**FXC**	**563,000**	**24.69%**	**573,500**	**23.03%**	**10,500**	**1.87%**
Net Income/Profit/Loss	**NIC/P/L**	**181,500**	**7.96%**	**252,500**	**10.14%**	**71,000**	**39.12%**

Depreciation—Capital Cost Allowance and Canada Revenue Agency

The term *depreciation* refers to the "loss of value over time" of an asset. The loss of value is calculated using prescribed "Rates" based on assigned "Classes" as defined by the Canada Revenue Agency (formerly known as Revenue Canada).

Businesses commonly apply the calculated value of the "loss of value over time" against income in order to reduce the taxable income. Depreciation is an FXC Fixed Cost since time cannot be stopped.

Canada Revenue Agency has many rules about depreciation and Capital Cost Allowance (which is the reduction of value of an asset calculated by using a prescribed rate expressed in a percentage) and most commonly the "Diminishing or Declining Balance Method."

The opposite of Depreciation is Appreciation. Appreciation happens when an asset increases its value over time.

Example of Depreciation

Common kitchen equipment (Class 8 – Rate 20% per annum)

Cost of acquisition without GST		2,000.00
First year rule (deduct 50% of cost)		– 1,000.00
	Balance	1,000.00
Year one Capital Cost Allowance (based on 20% rate)		200.00
	Balance	800.00
First year rule deduction added back to asset cost		1,000.00
	Balance	1,800.00
Year two Capital Cost Allowance (based on 20% rate)		360.00
	Balance	1,440.00
Year three Capital Cost Allowance (based on 20% rate)		288.00
Un-depreciated Capital Cost Balance		**1,152.00**

This method is repeated year after year until the equipment is replaced, traded in, sold, or scrapped. If traded in and/or sold and replaced, the trade-in is deducted from the last Balance and the cost of the replacement equipment is added to the remaining value and the depreciation process continues as previously illustrated; however, without the "First year rule calculation."

If the equipment was sold and it was the only or last one in its class (Class 8) — and NOT replaced — a possible Capital gain or a Capital loss may have occurred.

A Capital gain would occur if the equipment was sold for MORE than the Un-depreciated Capital Cost, and a Capital Loss would occur if the equipment was sold for LESS than the Un-depreciated Capital Cost.

The rules about Depreciation and Capital Cost Allowance are rather complex and often confusing, and calculations should be performed by professionals. Canada Revenue Agency lists Classes from 1 to 50 with Sub-Classes and Special Rules with rates from 4% to 100% as well as Fast-Write-Off for Energy efficient and other Special equipment. The *2012 Preparing Your Income Tax Returns* book by C.C.H. a Wolters Kluwer Business book features approximately 110 pages on Capital Cost.

Below is a Capital Cost Allowance example based on the common Canadian Diminishing Balance Method.

Due to the fact that depreciation is normally calculated by accountants, in the following example, the "First-Year-Rule" was purposely omitted.

(Depreciation 2012 Blank) by Klaus Theyer C.C.C.

Depreciation (Capital Cost Allowance) Methods and Examples

Purchased Items NOT intended for sale with a cost over $100.00 cannot be written off as expense but are considered to be an Asset and be depreciated.

Depreciation is the allowable compensation for "Loss of Value" of depreciable Assets over time
Depreciation is the opposite of **"Appreciation"**, in which case the value is increasing. Examples of appreciation would be Art-work, some Alcoholic beverages, Antiques, Real Estate.

Terminology: Beginning of the Year & End of the Year (B.o.Y. and E.o.Y.)
C.C.A. Capital Cost Allowance   **U.C.C.** Un-depreciated Capital Cost (B.o.Y & E.o.Y.)
Depreciation **RATE** in % and AMOUNT   **ACCRUED** (Accumulated) Depreciation
CLASS # (type or group of Asset)   Date of acquisition (Half Year Rule)

The following two methods are prescribed and or acceptable to Canada Revenue Agency (permission to use Straight Line is required); Diminishing Balance and Straight Line Method:

Info needed for Diminishing Balance:

1. Cost of acquisition inc. Delivery, and Financing Cost
2. Cost of installation
3. Allowable Rate (%) of depreciation   **20%**

1.	Cost of acquisition	2,500.00
2.	Cost of Installation	500.00
3.	Rate of depreciation	20.00%

Capital equipment cost (over $100.00) from above:
(including installation)

- C.C.A. — Year 1
- U.C.C.
- C.C.A. — Year 2
- U.C.C.
- C.C.A. — Year 3
- U.C.C.
- C.C.A. — Year 4
- U.C.C.
- C.C.A. — Year 5

Accrued depreciation: _____

U.C.C. after 5 years _____

Info needed for Straight Line:

1. Cost of acquisition inc. Delivery, and Financing Cost
2. Cost of installation
3. Salvage Value at the end of Life expectancy
4. Life expectancy in years

1.	2,500.00
2.	500.00
3.	300.00
4.	5

Capital equipment cost (over $100.00 from above)
(including installation)

S.V. =
U.C.C. - S.V. =

Year 1	C.C.A.
Year 2	C.C.A.
Year 3	C.C.A.
Year 4	C.C.A.
Year 5	C.C.A.

Accrued depreciation: _____

U.C.C. after 5 years _____

(Depreciation 2012 Completed) by Klaus Theyer C.C.C.

Depreciation (Capital Cost Allowance) Methods and Examples

Purchased Items NOT intended for sale with a cost over $100.00 cannot be written off as expense but are considered to be an Asset and be depreciated.

Depreciation is the allowable compensation for "Loss of Value" of depreciable Assets over time
Depreciation is the opposite of **"Appreciation"**, in which case the value is increasing. Examples of appreciation would be Art-work, some Alcoholic beverages, Antiques, Real Estate.

Terminology: Beginning of the Year & End of the Year (B.o.Y. and E.o.Y.)
C.C.A. Capital Cost Allowance   **U.C.C.** Un-depreciated Capital Cost (B.o.Y & E.o.Y.)
Depreciation **RATE** in % and AMOUNT   **ACCRUED** (Accumulated) Depreciation
CLASS # (type or group of Asset)   Date of acquisition (Half Year Rule)

The following two methods are prescribed and or acceptable to Canada Revenue Agency
(permission to use Straight Line is required); Diminishing Balance and Straight Line Method:

Info needed for Diminishing Balance:

1. Cost of acquisition inc. Delivery, and Financing Cost
2. Cost of installation
3. Allowable Rate (%) of depreciation   20%

1.	Cost of acquisition	2,500.00
2.	Cost of Installation	500.00
3.	Rate of depreciation	20.00%

Capital equipment cost	(over $100.00)	from above:
(including installation)	3,000.00	
C.C.A.	600.00	Year 1
U.C.C.	2,400.00	
C.C.A.	480.00	Year 2
U.C.C.	1,920.00	
C.C.A.	384.00	Year 3
U.C.C.	1,536.00	
C.C.A.	307.20	Year 4
U.C.C.	1,228.80	
C.C.A.	245.76	Year 5

Accrued depreciation: 2,016.96

U.C.C. after 5 years   983.04

Info needed for Straight Line:

1. Cost of acquisition inc. Delivery, and Financing Cost
2. Cost of installation
3. Salvage Value at the end of Life expectancy
4. Life expectancy in years

1.	2,500.00
2.	500.00
3.	300.00
4.	5

Capital equipment cost	(over $100.00	from above)
(including installation)	3,000.00	
S.V. =	300.00	
U.C.C. - S.V. =		2,700.00
Year 1	C.C.A.	540.00
Year 2	C.C.A.	540.00
Year 3	C.C.A.	540.00
Year 4	C.C.A.	540.00
Year 5	C.C.A.	540.00

Accrued depreciation: 2,700.00

U.C.C. after 5 years   -

Chapter 3

Essential Math and Applied Culinary Conversions

By Konrad Weinbuch CMC, Humber College ITAL,
School of Hospitality, Recreation and Tourism

Basic Math Refresher

In the Food Service business, like in any other business, it is a primary goal to plan and control costs. This can be achieved using different methods and techniques. But first, the elementary math involved, like decimals, fractions, percentages and conversions must be clearly understood. Conversions, yield calculations, recipe and food costing, all start with basic math. As a Chef or business owner, it can become very costly or even disastrous, to make mathematical mistakes. It is safe to say that it is impossible to be successful as manager, chef or owner, if principals of basic math are not understood and mastered. The following structured explanations and examples, starting with decimal place values, are invaluable for successfully understanding and mastering the essential mathematics and applied culinary conversions.

Decimal Calculations

A decimal is nothing more than a written fraction. To the left of the decimal (dot), we have the integer part, while the fractional part is on the right of the decimal. Decimals are a common style of numbers often found in the food service industry. Here are some examples of the usage and advantages of the decimal value system:

- ▶ Decimals are used to express metric quantities or metric measure
- ▶ Decimal form is used to express currency/money
- ▶ Digital scales use the decimal system to express weight
- ▶ Computer software and calculators use the decimal system
- ▶ Decimals fit into one text line and safe space if compared with fractions
- ▶ It is much easier to compare and evaluate decimals than fractions

Decimal Place Values

The decimal symbol is used to separate the whole part of a number from the fractional of the number

1,000,000	100,000	10,000	1,000	100	10	1	.	0.1	0.01	0.001	0,000,1
millions	hundred thousands	ten thousands	thousands	hundreds	tens	ones	decimal	tenths	hundredths	thousandths	ten thousandths

In North America, a comma is used as divider for thousands, and a decimal for separating whole numbers from the fraction of a whole number. In Europe it is common to use a decimal point to divide the thousands, and a comma to separate the whole number from the fraction. The exact opposite...

Rounding

Rounding is an important math skill. First you have to determine the accuracy of the number. How many "digits" should there be to the right of the decimal? Take the number immediately to the right of the desired decimal place and round down if it is lower than 5, round up if it is 5 or more.

Example: If you desire to round to two decimal places, you must take the number immediately to the right of the second decimal place. If the number immediately to the right of the second decimal place is 5 or more, you must round up, that means that the second decimal place will increase by one number. If the number immediately to the right of the second decimal place is 4 or less, you must round down, that means that the second decimal place stays unchanged.

Example: rounded to two decimal places:

3.245 = **3.25**   5.5443 = **5.54**

rounded to three decimal places:

9.9996 = **10.000**   11.90049 = **11.900**

Exercise: rounded to two decimal places:

2.347 = ☐   6.345 = ☐

rounded to three decimal places:

12.7996 = ☐   1.22455 = ☐

Converting decimals to percent

There are two ways to do so, and neither requires a calculator.

1 ⇒   Multiply the decimal number by 100 and add the % sign

Example: **1.25** multiplied by **100** equals **125**
now add the percentage sign, and you will have **125%**

2 ⇒   Move the decimal two places to the right and add the % sign

Example: **1.25** move the decimal two places to the right, will give you **125**
now add the percentage sign, and you will have **125%**

Example:

2.75 = **275.00%**

Exercise:

1.45 = ☐   0.12 = ☐

0.001230 = ☐   7.7743 = ☐

126.23 = ☐   0.990 = ☐

Converting Percent to decimals:

Again there are two ways, which are basically the opposite of the previous exercise.

1 ⇒ Divide the percentage number by 100 and omit the % sign.

2 ⇒ Move the decimal two places to the left and omit the % sign.

Example:

1     $45\% = \dfrac{45}{100} = $ **0.45**

2   **45%** move the decimal two places to the left, equals **0.45%** now remove the percentage sign and you are left with **0.45**

Exercise:

13% = [ ]   99% = [ ]

2% = [ ]   3560% = [ ]

145% = [ ]   100% = [ ]

Calculating with fractions:

A fraction is an expression in numbers of the relationship of the "part" to the "whole". Fractions are used very frequently in the food service industry. Examples are, but not limited to measuring cups, weight, volume and length. It is common, that recipe units are expressed in fraction form, for example: 1/2 liter, 3/4 bottle, 1/4 pound etc.
We should be aware, that there are three types of fractions:

Numerator = $\dfrac{N}{D}$
Denominator =

⇒ <u>the proper fraction:</u> the numerator is less than the denominator $\qquad \dfrac{1}{2}$

⇒ <u>the improper fraction:</u> the numerator is higher than the denominator $\qquad \dfrac{12}{8}$

⇒ <u>the mixed fraction:</u> a mixed fraction is a combination of a whole number and a fraction $\qquad 2\dfrac{1}{2}$

Always reduce fractions to their "lowest term", that means you have to find the "greatest common divisor", and use it to divide the numerator and the denominator, bringing the fraction to it's lowest term.

Example: $\qquad \dfrac{4}{32} \qquad$ the greatest common divisor is 4 $\qquad \dfrac{4}{32} \div 4 = \dfrac{1}{8}$

Addition of fractions:

When adding fractions, you must have the same/common denominator.
Example:
You have two open bottles of Sherry vinegar, and you would like to combine them. Do you have enough for one complete bottle?

Step 1 $\qquad \dfrac{3}{4} + \dfrac{1}{3} = \ ?$

<u>Calculating the common denominator:</u>
Step 2 $\qquad \dfrac{3}{4} \times \dfrac{3}{3} = \dfrac{9}{12}$

Step 3 $\qquad \dfrac{1}{3} \times \dfrac{4}{4} = \dfrac{4}{12}$

<u>Adding the fraction with the common denominator:</u>
Step 4 $\qquad \dfrac{9}{12} + \dfrac{4}{12} = \dfrac{13}{12} = 1\dfrac{1}{12}$

40 Chapter 3 Essential Math and Applied Culinary Conversions

continued from previous page

Converting to decimals:
Step 5
$$1 + 1 \div 12 = 1 + 0.08333 = 1.08333 = \boxed{1.08}$$

Exercise:

$$\frac{5}{7} + \frac{2}{3} = \frac{}{} + \frac{}{} = \frac{}{}$$

Fraction: ☐ = Decimal: ☐

Subtraction of fractions:

When subtracting fractions, you must perform the multiplications before the subtractions.
First multiply the numerator, then the denominator.

Step 1
$$\frac{3}{4} - \frac{1}{3} = ?$$

Calculating the common numerator and denominator:
Step 2
$$\frac{3}{4} \times \frac{3}{3} = \frac{9}{12}$$

Step 3
$$\frac{1}{3} \times \frac{4}{4} = \frac{4}{12}$$

Subtracting the fractions with common denominator:
Step 4
$$\frac{9}{12} - \frac{4}{12} = \frac{\mathbf{5}}{\mathbf{12}}$$

Converting to decimals:
Step 5
$$5 \div 12 = 0.416666 = \boxed{0.42}$$

Exercise:

$$\frac{9}{8} - \frac{8}{9} = \frac{}{} - \frac{}{} = \frac{}{} =$$

Fraction: ☐ = Decimal: ☐

Multiplication of fractions:

Simply multiply the numerators together then the denominators together.

Step 1
$$\frac{4}{5} \times \frac{2}{6} = \frac{8}{30} = \frac{\mathbf{4}}{\mathbf{15}}$$

Converting to decimals:
Step 2
$$\frac{4}{15} \qquad 4 \div 15 = \boxed{0.27}$$

continued from previous page

Exercise:

						Fraction:	Decimal:
1	$\frac{7}{8}$ × $\frac{8}{9}$	=	———	=	☐	=	☐
2	$\frac{5}{6}$ × $\frac{1}{4}$	=	———	=	☐	=	☐
3	$\frac{2}{3}$ × $\frac{7}{6}$ × $\frac{4}{6}$	=	———	=	☐	=	☐
4	$\frac{1}{2}$ × $\frac{9}{10}$ × $1\frac{2}{8}$	=	———	=	☐	=	☐

Division of fractions:

First convert any mixed numbers into improper fractions. Next invert the second fraction by placing the denominator on top of the numerator. Finally change the division sign, and complete the equation as a multiplication.

Step 1 $\frac{4}{5} \div \frac{2}{6} = $ **?**

Step 2 $\frac{4}{5} \times \frac{6}{2} = \frac{24}{10} = 2\frac{4}{10} = \mathbf{2\frac{2}{5}}$

Converting to decimals:

$2\frac{2}{5} = 2 + 2 \div 5 = \mathbf{2.40}$

Exercise:

								Fraction:	Decimal:
1	$\frac{7}{8} \div \frac{8}{9}$	=	———	×	———	=	———	= ☐	= ☐
2	$\frac{5}{6} \div \frac{1}{4}$	=	———	×	———	=	———	= ☐	= ☐
3	$2\frac{2}{3} \div \frac{7}{6}$	=	———	×	———	=	———	= ☐	= ☐
4	$\frac{7}{8} \div 1\frac{1}{4}$	=	———	×	———	=	———	= ☐	= ☐

Converting fractions into decimals:
First convert any mixed fraction into improper fractions.
Then, divide the numerator by the denominator.
Example:

$$2 \frac{3}{4} = \frac{11}{4} = 11 \div 4 = \boxed{2.75}$$

Exercise:

$$3 \frac{7}{8} = \boxed{} \qquad 5 \frac{9}{12} = \boxed{}$$

Converting decimals to fractions:
Using the Decimal Place Value Chart, express the number as a decimal.
Translate the decimal number into a fraction and reduce to the lowest term.
Example:

$$0.85 = 85 \text{ hundredths} = \frac{85}{100} = \frac{17}{20}$$

Exercise:

1.45 = ☐   0.68 = ☐   2.35 = ☐

3.25 = ☐   1.88 = ☐   4.44 = ☐

Adding and Subtracting Weights and Measures

Calculating with weights and measures is probably the most common form of basic math in the food service industry.

Place Values, Columns in the Decimal System

100000s	10000s	1000s	100s	10s	1s
3	1	2	7	9	0

= 312,790

Carrying forward when Adding Numbers

Lets say, you add 7 + 8 = 15, you will write 5 in the Ones column, then you carry the 1 forward to the Tens column and so on...

Example and Exercise:

```
    1 5           1 1            1
  + 2 4         6 6          1 0 9
  = 3 9       + 9 8        + 3 7 7
              = 1 6 4      = 4 8 6


  1 1
  1 7 9         1 7 7 7      1 2 9 9 9
+ 2 5 6       + 6 8 5 7    + 9 9 8 8 7
=             =             =
```

Borrowing when Subtracting Numbers

When subtracting 9 from 27, (27 - 9 = 18), because 7 is smaller than 9, you cannot subtract 9 from 7.
Therefore, you will have to borrow 1 from the Tens column, making it 17 and leaving only 1 in the Tens column.
Now subtract the 9 from 17, and write 8.
In the Tens column subtract 0 from 1 and write 1.
The Result will be 18.

Example and Exercise:

```
                                      2 3
      1                               1 1
   2̸ 7         8 5        3 4 3     3̸ 4̸ 3
  -   9      - 3 4      - 1 8 6    - 1 8 6
  = 1 8      = 5 1      =          = 1 5 7
```

44 Chapter 3 Essential Math and Applied Culinary Conversions

Exercise continued

1	2	3	4
377 -299 =	2889 -1299 =	1333 -999 =	9811 -8998 =

Adding and Subtracting Weights and Measures, Metric and US

Adding and subtracting mixed units

Very often we have to calculate with mixed units, like liters and milliliters for recipe production and quantities.

Let's say you have 17 liters and 850 milliliters of Gazpacho in one pail, and 7 liters and 600 milliliters in another pail.

How much Gazpacho do you have altogether?

1 liter	=	1000	milliliters
1 kg	=	1000	grams

Example:

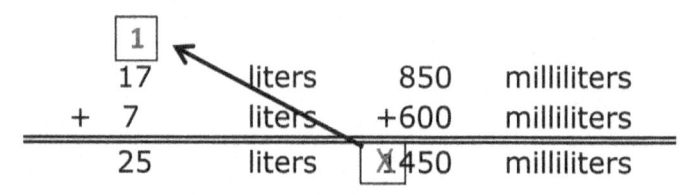

```
      [1]
    17    liters      850   milliliters
 +   7    liters    +600   milliliters
    ─────────────────────────────────
    25    liters    1450   milliliters
```

Take the thousands (1000ml) away from the milliliters, convert them to liters and "carry" the result to the liters.

The other way around would be, if you have 17 liters and 850 milliliters of Gazpacho, and you need 7 liters and 900 milliliters for lunch service.
How much Gazpacho should you have left?

```
                                           6 → 1
  17 liters   850 milliliters          1X̶ liters   850 milliliters
  -7 liters   -900 milliliters    =    -7 liters   -900 milliliters
  ─────────────────────────────         ─────────────────────────────
  10 liters   -50 milliliters           9 liters   950 milliliters
```

Because 850ml is smaller than 900ml, you will have to "borrow" from the liter column.

Exercise:

1
```
    29 liters    500 milliliters
   +7 liters    900 milliliters
   ──────────────────────────
       liters       milliliters
```

2
```
    99 liters    850 milliliters
  +19 liters    900 milliliters
   ──────────────────────────
       liters       milliliters
```

3
```
    98 kg    450 grams
   -19 kg    700 grams
   ──────────────────
       kg       grams
```

4
```
    69 kg    765 grams
    -9 kg    550 grams
   ──────────────────
       kg       grams
```

Exercise continued

5

112 liters	850 milliliters
-26 liters	500 milliliters
-7 liters	900 milliliters
liters	milliliters

6

15 kg	850 grams
+29 kg	630 grams
+37 kg	720 grams
kg	grams

7

125 liters	730 milliliters
-18 liters	150 milliliters
-26 liters	500 milliliters
-7 liters	900 milliliters
liters	milliliters

8

15 kg	210 grams
+2 kg	375 grams
+17 kg	610 grams
+31 kg	390 grams
kg	grams

9

112 liters	750 milliliters
-14 liters	125 milliliters
-3 liters	300 milliliters
-36 liters	200 milliliters
-21 liters	850 milliliters
liters	milliliters

10

5 kg	650 grams
+11 kg	175 grams
+9 kg	290 grams
+19 kg	590 grams
+27 kg	780 grams
kg	grams

US gal	=	1 US gallon = 4 quarts = 8 pints = 16 cups = 128 fl oz
US qt	=	1 US quart = 2 pints = 4 cups = 32 fl oz
US pt	=	1 US pint 2 cups = 16 fl oz
US cup	=	1 US cup = 8 fl oz = 16 tablespoons = 48 teaspoons
US fl oz	=	1 US fluid ounce = 2 tablespoons = 6 teaspoons
lbs	=	1 pound = 16 ounces
oz	=	1 ounce

Example:

98 lbs	12 oz		98 lbs	12 oz
+19 lbs	15 oz	=	+19 lbs	15 oz
117 lbs	**27 oz**		**118 lbs**	**11 oz**

convert 27 oz to lbs (=1lbs , 11oz), carry or add the 1 lbs to the lbs column, and write 11 oz in the oz column.

54 lbs	12 oz		54 lbs (3)	12 oz (16)
-37 lbs	15 oz	=	-37 lbs	15 oz
17 lbs	-3 oz		16 lbs	13 oz

when subtractring a larger number from a smaller number, you must "borrow". Borrow 1lbs, convert it to ounces, and add the 16 ounces to the ounces column and regroup.

46 Chapter 3 Essential Math and Applied Culinary Conversions

Exercise:

11

	19 lbs	9 oz
	+31 lbs	15 oz
	lbs	oz

12

	26 lbs	11 oz
	-17 lbs	13 oz
	lbs	oz

13

	9 lbs	12 oz
	+19 lbs	7 oz
	+67 lbs	15 oz
	lbs	oz

14

	54 lbs	3 oz
	-19 lbs	7 oz
	-27 lbs	15 oz
	lbs	oz

15

	14 lbs	1 oz
	+18 lbs	14 oz
	+15 lbs	12 oz
	lbs	oz

16

	61 lbs	7 oz
	-18 lbs	10 oz
	-32 lbs	15 oz
	lbs	oz

17

	3 gal	1 qt	1 pt	1 cup
	+6 gal	2 qt	0 pt	1 cup
	+11 gal	3 qt	1 pt	1 cup
	gal	qt	pt	cup

18

	24 gal	3 qt	1 pt	1 cup
	-8 gal	1 qt	1 pt	0 cup
	-5 gal	1 qt	1 pt	1 cup
	gal	qt	pt	cup

19

	10 gal	3 qt	0 pt	1 cup	7 floz
	+3 gal	3 qt	1 pt	1 cup	6 floz
	+9 gal	3 qt	0 pt	1 cup	5 floz
	gal	qt	pt	cup	floz

20

	18 gal	2 qt	1 pt	1 cup	4 floz
	-6 gal	2 qt	1 pt	0 cup	3 floz
	gal	qt	pt	cup	floz

21

	10 gal	3 qt	0 pt	1 cup	6 floz
	+6 gal	1 qt	1 pt	0 cup	6 floz
	+9 gal	3 qt	0 pt	1 cup	7 floz
	gal	qt	pt	cup	floz

22

	29 gal	3 qt	1 pt	1 cup	6 floz
	-10 gal	3 qt	0 pt	1 cup	7 floz
	gal	qt	pt	cup	floz

Percent and Percentages

　　　　　　　　　Per　　=　　"For (each)"
　　　　　　　　　Cent　 =　　Hundred

When confronted with percent or percentage, always ask yourself percent/percentage of what?

Percent means the ratio/relationship of one number to 100.
Therefore 10% stands for 10 parts from every 100.

- % The expression "35 percent of Canadians like to drink beer" means that 35 people out of a group of hundred Canadians like to drink beer.

- % To find a percentage of any given number, you simply multiply.

- % In mathematics, the word **"of"** means to **multiply**

Example:
　　Half of the twenty apples were rotten means:

$$\frac{1}{2} \;=\; 1 \div 2 \;=\; 0.50 \;\times\; 20 \;=\; \boxed{10}$$

- % If 35% of Canadians like to drink beer, how many "beer lovers" can we expect from a group of 500 Canadians?

Example:　　　35 ÷ 100 = 0.35
　　　　　　　　 0.35 x 500 = 175

- % The pay cheque of $950.00 was increased by 8 percent. How much is the pay increase?

Example:　　　8 ÷ 100 = 0.08
　　　　　　　　 0.08 x 950 = 76.00

The Old (=100%), plus or minus a percentage of the Old equals the New

- % The dinner bill is $ 27.50 tax included. What will that bill be if 15% graduities are added?

Example:
27.50	=	100%
?	=	15%
?	=	115%
115.00 ÷	100	= 1.15
27.50 x	1.15	= 31.63

continued from previous page

%   The price for beef tenderloin increased by 36% in the last 3 years. Today's price is $28.50 per kg.
What was the price per kg three years ago?

Example:

28.50	=	136%	(100% + 36%)
?	=	100%	

136%	÷	100	=	1.36	
28.50	÷	1.36	=	<u>20.96</u>	

%   As a longtime customer you receive a rebate of 18% on your Gym membership. Your membership rate was $720 a year before the rebate, what will your new membership rate be?

Example:

720.00	=	100%
− rebate	=	18%
?	=	82%

82	÷	100	=	0.82	
720.00	×	0.82	=	<u>590.40</u>	

%   You increased the selling price for NY steak from $16.50 to $18.50. What is the percent increase?

Example:

18.50	=	? %			
16.50	=	100%			
18.50	−	16.50	=	2.00	
2.00	÷	16.50	=	0.1212	= <u>12.12%</u>

Exercise:

1   Yesterday's sales were $1,950.00. You plan to increase yesterday's sales by 19%. What will the sales <u>increase</u> be?

2   Using the information from # 1. Unfortunately you didn't achieve the planned sales increase today. Sales decreased by 19% instead.
What are today's sales?

continued from previous page

3 The price of fuel has increased by 78% since 10 years ago.
Today's price is $1.29 per liter. What was the price 10 years ago?

4 Due to overstock, the price for live lobster decreased by 27%.
Today's price is $7.55 per lbs. What was the price before the decease?

5 Last week the price for a case unsalted butter was $57.50.
This week's price is $63.80. What is the <u>percent</u> increase?

6 The F&B Mngr. plans to increase the selling price for the "table d'hôte" menu by 18%. Currently the table d'hôte sells for $31.50.
What will the new selling price be?

$31.50 = 100 %
= 118 %

7 The food cost for last year's "Mother's Day" buffet was $18,550.00
This year's food cost was $20,245.00
What is the percentage of the increase?

$18,550.00 =
$ increase = ? %

9.14 %

8 Today there was a beautiful chef's knife on sale for $175.00,
a price reduction of 35%.
What was the price of the chef's knife before it went on sale?

Conversions
What and Why?

In Food and Beverage production most commonly it is QUANTITIES which need to be converted:
   From One Weight Unit to another:
   From Lbs or Oz to Kg or Gr or any combination thereof...
   From One Volume Unit to another:
   From Fluid Ounce, Pint, Quart, Gallon to Milliliter, Deciliter or Liter, not to mention Cup (3 different ones), Teaspoons and Tablespoons, as well as from/to Metric, US or Imperial...

Complete the following exercises using the information provided, and the data from the conversion chart.

3 decimal places for liters and Kg, 2 decimal places for all remaining calculations

Volume measurements

From Metric Volume to US Volume Measurements and vice versa

US fl Ounces to milliliters

Ladles
Example: ladle size; 7 oz x 29.6ml = 207.2 ml
The most common sizes for ladles are :

   8 oz = 3.36 ml
   6 oz = _____ ml
   4 oz = 41.98 ml
   2 oz = _____ ml

How many liters of soup will you need for 150 portions, if you serve one 6 oz ladle of soup per portion? [____]

Wine glass size
Example: glass size is 7 oz x 29.6ml = 207.2 ml
   bottle size is 750 ml ÷ 207.2 ml = 3.62 glasses.
The international standard for wine bottles is 750ml, how many glasses of wine can you serve from one bottle if the glass volume is:

   6 oz = [____] glasses
   5 oz = [____] glasses
   4 oz = [____] glasses

US Cups to liters to milliliters

In the food service industry we are used to use three different sizes of cups:
- 1 US Cup   237 ml
- 2 Imp. Cup   227 ml
- 3 Metric Cup   250 ml

However, the most common cup is the US cup.

If a recipe for risotto yields 10 portions, and asks for 4.5 US cups of chicken stock. How many **ml** of chicken stock will you need for 25 portions?

Example: 4.5 UScups x 237ml = 1066.5 ml   [   ] ml
               1066.5 ml ÷ 10 portions x 25 portions

               (÷ 1000)   How many liters?   [   ] ltr

Exercise:

You have 18 liters of chicken stock, how many portions of risotto can you produce with it?   [   ]

US Pints to liters, to milliliters

1 pint equals 0.47 liters. To calculate how many pints are in 1 liter, all you have to do is to divide 1 liter by 0.47.

1 pint equals 473 ml, therefore if you want to calculate how many milliliters are in one pint, all you have to do is to multiply the pints by 473.

Example: 1 liter ÷ 0.47 = 2.13 pints
               3 pints x 473 = 1419 ml

Exercise:

12.5 ltr	=	[ ] pints	3 pints	=	[ ] liters
7.8 ltr	=	[ ] pints	7.5 pints	=	[ ] liters
19.5 ltr	=	[ ] pints	25.5 pints	=	[ ] liters

4 pints	=	[ ] ml
7.5 pints	=	[ ] ml
12.5 pints	=	[ ] ml

US Quarts to liters, to milliliters

1 quart equals 0.95 liters. To calculate how many quarts are in 1 liter, all you have to do is to divide 1 liter by 0.95.

1 quart equals 946 ml, therefore if you want to calculate how many milliliters are in one quart, all you have to do is to multiply the quarts by 946.

52 Chapter 3 Essential Math and Applied Culinary Conversions

continued from previous page

Example: 1 liter ÷ 0.95 = 1.05 quarts
3 quarts x 946 = 2838 ml

Exercise:

2.5 ltr	=	2.31 quarts	5 quarts	=	4.75	liters
6.7 ltr	=	2.6 quarts	8.7 quarts	=	8.27	liters
21.3 ltr	=	0.75 quarts	11.5 quarts	=	10.93	liters

1.7 quarts	=	1.	ml
8.4 quarts	=	709	ml
17.2 quarts	=	16271.2	ml

US Gallons to liters, to milliliters

1 gallon equals 3.8 liters. To calculate how many liters are in 1 gallon, you must divide the gallons by 3.8. If you want to convert gallons into liter,
you must multiply the gallons by 3.8, or divide the gallons by 0.264.
1 gallon equals 3784 ml, therefore if you want to calculate how many milliliters are in one gallon, all you have to do is to multiply the gallons by 3784.

Example: 1 ~~liter~~ (gallon) ÷ 0.264 = 3.8 (3.788) ~~gallons~~ (Liters)
2 gallons x 3.8 = 7.6 liters
3 gallons x 3784 = 11352ml

Exercise:

2.5 ltr	=	0.66 gallons	3.2 gallons	=	12.16	liters
6.7 ltr	=	1.769 gallons	11.7 gallons	=	44.	liters
21.3 ltr	=	5.26 gallons	4.9 gallons	=	18.62	liters

1.2 gallons	=		ml
5.9 gallons	=		ml
11.3 gallons	=	42946	ml

Weight Measurements

Ounces to grams   Grams to ounces
Steaks

The weight for steaks is most commonly advertised in ounces, before cooking. Therefore you must convert in order to find out their metric weight.

Example: one 7 Oz steak = 7 x 28.35 = 198.45 Gr
210 Gr ÷ 28.35 = 7.41 Oz

continued from previous page

Exercise:
Steak size:

8 oz	=		grams	170 Gr	=	6	oz
10 oz	=		grams	200 Gr	=	7	oz
14 oz	=	396.9	grams	240 Gr	=	8.5	oz
16 oz	=	453.6	grams	220 Gr	=	76.8	oz
6 oz	=	170.1	grams	300 Gr	=	10.6	oz

Pound to ounces, ounces to pounds
There are **16** ounces in a pound, therefore you must multiply by **16** if you want to convert pounds into ounces, and vice versa, you must divide by 16 if you want to convert ounces into pounds.

Exercise:

2.5 lbs	=	40	Oz	18 Oz	=	1.25	lbs
1.75 lbs	=	28	Oz	46 Oz	=	2.88	lbs
2.25 lbs	=	36	Oz	6 Oz	=	0.38	lbs

Kilogram to pounds, to ounces
1 Kg equals 2.205 lbs, therefore if you want to convert Kg into pounds you must multiply be 2.205. If you desire to convert pounds to Kg, you must divide the pounds by 2.205.
Another method to convert Kg into pounds is, to divide the Kg by 0.454.
To convert pounds into Kg, you can also multiply the pounds by 0.454.
1 Kg equals 35.3 ounces. If you desire to convert Kg to Oz, just multiply Kg by 35.3. If you want to convert Oz into Kg, you must divide Oz by 35.3.

Example: 3 Kg x 2.205 = 6.615 lbs

8 lbs ÷ 2.205 = 3.628 Kg
2 Kg x 35.3 = 70.6 Oz
49 Oz ÷ 35.3 = 1.388 Kg

Exercise:

3.4 Kg	=	7.5	lbs	3.2 lbs	=	1.45	Kg
6.7 Kg	=	14.8	lbs	7.7 lbs	=	3.49	Kg
11.9 Kg	=	26.2	lbs	15.1 lbs	=	6.85	Kg
1.9 Kg	=	66.07	oz	65 oz	=	1.84	Kg
5.9 Kg	=	208.7	oz	41 oz	=	1.16	Kg
0.7 Kg	=	24.71	oz	32 oz	=	0.81	Kg

Pounds and ounces to grams

1 pound equals 454 gr. If you convert pounds to grams, you must multiply the pounds by 454. If you desire to convert grams to pounds, you must divide the grams by 454.

1 ounce equals 28.35 gr. In order to convert ounces to grams you must multiply the ounces by 28.35. To convert grams to ounces, just divide the grams by 28.35.

Example: 2 lbs x 454 = 908 gr

1200 gr ÷ 454 = 2.64 lbs
5 oz x 28.35 = 141.75 gr
220 gr ÷ 28.35 = 7.76 oz

Exercise:

1.5 lbs	=	681 gr	800 gr	=	1.76 lbs
0.75 lbs	=	3 gr	1750 gr	=	3.85 lbs
9.2 lbs	=	4176.8 gr	12500 gr	=	27.53 lbs
6 oz	=	170.1 gr	325 gr	=	11.46 oz
18.5 oz	=	529.47 gr	480 gr	=	16.93 oz
27 oz	=	765.45 gr	1250 gr	=	44.0 oz

Temperature measurements, from Fahrenheit to Celsius and vice versa

Fahrenheit is the temperature measurement used in the USA, and therefore most kitchen equipment in Canada is calibrated in Fahrenheit.
32 degrees F is the freezing point, while the boiling point of water is defined to be 212 degrees F (depending on altitude).
The Celsius temperature scale (also known as centigrade), is the most popular method to measure temperatures, and it is used all over the world, because of it's accuracy. 0 degree C is the freezing point, and the boiling point of water is defined at 100 degrees C (depending on altitude).
There are 2 basic formulas to convert from one temperature scale to another.

From Fahrenheit to Celsius: (°F-32) ÷ 9 x 5 = °C
or (°F-32) ÷ 1.8 = °C

From Celsius to Fahrenheit: (°C x 9 ÷ 5) + 32 = °F
or (°C x 1.8) + 32 = °F

Exercise:

425 °F	=	°C	4 °C	=	39.2 °F
245 °F	=	118.3 °C	60 °C	=	140 °F
130 °F	=	54.4 °C	220 °C	=	428 °F

Length Measurements in the kitchen

Most common US Standard Lengths
Inches   =   25.4 Mm, or 2.54 Cm
Feet   =   304.8 Mm, or 30.5 Cm, or 0.3 Mtr
Yards   =   91.4 Cm, or 0.91 Mtr

Most common Metric Standard Lengths
Millimeters   =   0.04 inch
Centimeters   =   0.39 inch
Meters   =   39.4 inch, or 3.28 ft, or 1.09 Yd

Exercise:

7.5 inch	=		Mm	0.8 Mtr	=		inch
12 inch	=		Cm	1.5 Mtr	=		Ft
36 inch	=		Mtr	3 Mtr	=		Yd
75 Mm	=		inch	4 Ft	=		Mtr
45 Cm	=		Ft	2.5 Yd	=		Cm
4 Mtr	=		Yd	1250 Mm	=		Mtr

From Hours, Minutes to Seconds

Actually we distinguish between the 12 hour clock and the 24 hour clock (Military Time, Zulu Time, GMT Greenwich Mean Time). While several countries worldwide use the 24 hour clock, written and spoken from 0.00 hours to 24.00 hours, most countries use the 12 hour clock mainly in spoken time, and the 24 hour notation is written. With the 12 hour clock, we use phrases like in the morning, in the afternoon, in the evening and at night. The terms a.m. and p.m. are seldom used outside English speaking countries. Here in Canada we are used to both clocks. We use the 24 hour clock mainly as "digital" time, and the 12 hour clock as written and spoken time. AM meaning "Ante Meridiem," from midnight until noon. PM meaning "Post Meridiem," from noon until midnight. It can cause confusion to use the terms 12 a.m. and 12 p.m., because neither is accurate. Better use 12 noon and 12 midnight, when clarity is required. Airlines, railroads and other companies use terms like 12:01 a.m. at the beginning of the day, and 11:59 p.m. for the end of it.

It is very common to define time in fractions of an hour, like ¼ hour, ½ hour, ¾ hour, 1½ hours and so on . . . Mistakes are made, because one whole hour is divided into 60 minutes and not into 100 units (cents) as we are used to from one dollar.

Example:

¼ hour = 60 minutes x 0.25 = 15 minutes

1½ hours = 60 minutes x 1.5 = 90 minutes

Calculating labour cost:

A Prep cook is paid $16.50 per hour, and it takes him 35 minutes to prepare the recipe for risotto (30 portions). What is the labour cost for the total recipe?

$16.50 ÷ 60 x 35 = $9.63

Exercise:

What would the labour cost be for "coq au vin", if the cook's hourly wage is $18.75, and if it takes him 1 hour and 10 minutes to prepare the dish?

The standardized time to prepare a recipe of 50 liters of "celery cream soup" is 55 minutes. What is the labour cost if the prep cook's hourly wage is $18.90?

The prep cook worked 6 days last week. Unfortunately the hours marked on the "sign in-sign out" sheet were all mixed.
Exactly how many hours did the prep cook work last week?

Monday	6¼ hours
Tuesday	7.5 hours
Wednesday	7 hours and 45 minutes
Thursday	7 hours 40 minutes
Friday	6.5 hours
Saturday	off
Sunday	4 hours 20 minutes

(two decimals)

Recipe conversion

1. Convert the following recipe into metric
2. Adjust the recipe to yield 50 portions
3. Calculate the total weight for 15 port. in metric
4. Calculate the total weight for 50 port. in metric

Lobster, Spinach and Artichoke dip

Yield 15 portion		15 Portion metric	50 Portion metric
4 1/4 oz	Lobster meat		
1 lbs	Spinach, blanched, refreshed and dry		
3 oz	Butter, unsalted		
1/2 oz	Cloves, Garlic, minced		
1/3 cup	AP Flour		
1 cup	Milk, whole		
1 cup	Cream 35%		
1 tbsp	Lemon juice		
3 oz	Double smoked bacon		
3/4 cups	Cheddar Cheese, grated		
1/2 cup	Oka Cheese, small dice		
7 oz	Artichokes, jar		
3 oz	Parmesan cheese		
2 tsp	Kosher Salt		
1/2 tsp	Pepper, black ground		
Total weight in grams ======>			

Some useful information:

1 tsp salt	7 gram
1 tsp pepper	3.5 gram
1 cup flour	145 gram
1 cup cheddar	120 gram
1 cup Oka cheese	130 gram
1 ounce	28.35 gram
1 pound	454 gram
1 cup liq.	230 gram
1 tbsp liq.	15 gram

Recipe conversion

1. Convert the following recipe into metric
2. Adjust the recipe to yield 50 portions
3. Calculate the total weight for 15 port. in metric
4. Calculate the total weight for 50 port. in metric

Lobster, Spinach and Artichoke dip

Yield 15 portion		15 Portion metric	50 Portion metric
4 1/4 oz	Lobster meat		401.63
1 lbs	Spinach, blanched, refreshed and dry		1,513.33
3 oz	Butter, unsalted		
1/2 oz	Cloves, Garlic, minced		47.25
1/3 cup	AP Flour	48.33	
1 cup	Milk, whole	230.00	
1 cup	Cream 35%	230.00	
1 tbsp	Lemon juice	15.00	
3 oz	Double smoked bacon		
3/4 cups	Cheddar Cheese, grated	90.00	
1/2 cup	Oka Cheese, small dice	65.00	
7 oz	Artichokes, jar	198.45	
3 oz	Parmesan cheese	85.05	
2 tsp	Kosher Salt	14.00	
1/2 tsp	Pepper black ground	1.75	
Total weight in grams	=====>		5,787.82

Some useful information:

1 tsp salt	7	gram
1 tsp pepper	3.5	gram
1 cup flour	145	gram
1 cup cheddar	120	gram
1 cup Oka cheese	130	gram
1 ounce	28.35	gram
1 pound	454	gram
1 cup liq.	230	gram
1 tbsp liq.	15	gram

Conversions Worksheet 1 Metric, Imperial, US

All calculations should be to a minimum of 2 decimal places

1   You have produced **18.000** liters of Pheasant Consommé
For the banquet you will need **120** portions of **5** oz US each.
Do you have enough? Yes/No
Exact portion count please

2   You have produced **18.000** liters of Wild Mushroom cream soup
You will have to serve **125** portions of **6** oz Imperial each
Do you have enough? Yes/No
Exact portion count please

3   The standard baking trays measure 18" x 26" x 1" high
How many 1" x 1½" x 1" brownies can you cut from this tray
considering trimmings of **10%** percent?
Total number of brownies?

4   You would like to produce **95** pieces of 1" x 2" x 2" high brownies
How many baking trays will you have to prepare?
Number of whole trays?   mathematical exact answer

5   You are in charge of a BBQ party for **300** people
on average they will consume **50** single patty burgers
150 double patty burgers
100 triple patty burgers
1 portion of Caesar salad per guest
1½ cups of coffee per person

Note:
a head of lettuce yields **5** portions of salad
each hamburger needs **4** slices of tomatoes
each tomato yields **9** slices
a coffee package yields **8** brewed cups
for each coffee you will need **2** creamers-milk & **1½** envelopes of sugar

How much/many do you have to buy?
hamburger patties   coffee packages
lettuce heads   creamers-milk
tomatoes   sugar envelopes

Don't forget to pack the stir-stix and napkins..

Conversions Worksheet 2 Metric, Imperial, US

Calculate the mathematical correct answer.
Each answer should be given with two decimal places, except liters and kilograms, which should be expressed with three decimal places.

1   1 bottle of red wine contains **750** ml
you will host a banquet for **420** people, and each one will receive
2 ½ glasses of red wine **4** oz US (is the glass size).
How many glasses per bottle ? [ ]
How many bottles do you have to order for the upcoming event ? [ ]

2   For the same banquet you serve **8** oz New York Strip loin Steaks
Your butcher calculates a trimming and portioning loss of **20%** percent
How many oz of strip loin do you have to order? [ ] oz
How many lbs do you have to order? [ ] lbs
How many Kg will you have to order? [ ] Kg
If each strip loin weighs **4.200** Kg
How many strip loins have to be ordered? [ ]

3   The same banquet menu indicates, that each guest will receive
one **6** oz Imp. Portion of consommé. The apprentice
informs you, that there are **75.000** liters of consommé in stock.
Will it be enough to serve **420** customers Y/N [ ]
How many Imp. Oz are needed ? [ ]
How many Imp. Gallons will be required ? [ ]
How many liters of consomme are needed ? [ ]

4   The **420** guests will receive **3** slices of French baguettes
per person. Each slice is cut **2.5** cm thick.
The baker informs you, that each baguette is **3** feet long.
How many French baguettes do you have to order, considering a
10% percent trimming loss. # of [ ] French baguettes?

5   You instructed the Chef de partie to cook all the strip loin steak to
an internal temperature of **125** degrees Fahrenheit
Unfortunately, his thermometer is in Celsius.
To what degree Celsius should the steaks be cooked? [ ]

Chapter 3 Essential Math and Applied Culinary Conversion

Quick Conversion Factors for Kitchen and Bar   by Klaus Theyer CCC   June 2013   Page

NOTE: Significance of conversions should be **limited to 4 decimal** places.

U.S. VOLUME Units for accurate conversion multiply Units times factor for Metric				For simple Recipe conversion (SRC) use:
one (1) unit x factor equals = Metric				
1	Tsp	4.928365563	Ml	5
1	Tbsp	14.78509669	Ml	15
1	Fl Oz	29.5701934	Ml	29.6
1	Cup	0.2365615470	Ltr	0.24
1	½ pint	0.23656155	Ltr	0.24
1	Pint	0.473123094	Ltr	0.47
1	Quarts	0.9462461880	Ltr	0.95
1	Gallons	3.784984752	Ltr	3.8

VOLUME (US Liquid Fluid)

1 US fl Oz = 29.57 Ml. 1 US Gal = 4 Qrt or 8 Pnt or 128 Fl Oz.

1 US Gal = 3.785 Ltr or (SRC 3800 Ml)

1 US fl Oz x 0.960764769 = 1 Imp fl Oz

or 1 US fl Oz x 0.961 = 1 Imp fl Oz

1 Ltr = 10 Dl = 1000 Ml = 33.818 US fl Oz

1 Us fl Oz = 2 Tbls of liquid. 4 US fl Oz = 1/2 Cup. 8 US fl Oz = 1 Cup.

3 Tsp = 1 Tbls, 1 Tbls = 1/16 of a US Cup, 4 Tbls = 1/4 US Cup,

8 Tbls = 1/2 US Cup, 1/2 Lb (8 oz) of Butter = 1 Cup,

1 Lbs of Butter = 2 Cups

2 US Cups = 1 Pnt, 2 Pnt = 1 Qrt, 4 Qrt = 1 US Gal or 3.785 Ltr

MIXED VOLUME Units for accurate conversion multiply Units times factor for Metric				For simple Recipe conversion (SRC) use:
one (1) unit x factor equals = results				
1 US	Tsp	0.1666666667	US fl Oz	0.17
1 US	Tbsp	0.5000000000	US fl Oz	0.5
1	Ml	0.0338178377	US fl Oz	0.034
1	250 Ml	8.454459425	US fl Oz	8.500
1	Ltr	33.8178376894	US fl Oz	33.82
1	Ltr	2.1136148556	US Pnt	2.11
1	Ltr	1.056807428	US Qrt	1.06
1	Ltr	0.2642018569	US Gal	0.264

QUICK BAR measurement conversions:

1	Imp Oz Shot	28.5	Ml
1	US Oz Shot	29.57	Ml
1 1/2	Imp Oz Shot	42.6	Ml

	Metric Ml	US fl Oz	Imp fl Oz
1 Glass	148	5	5.2
1 Glass	177	6	6.25
1 Btl	187	6.3	6.6
1 Btl	341	11.5	12
1 Btl	500	16.91	17.6
1 Btl	750	25.4	26.4
1 Btl	1,000	33.81	35.2
1 Btl	1,500	50.72	52.8
1 Keg	20,000	676.28	703.9

IMPERIAL VOLUME Units for accurate conversion multiply Units times factor for Metric				For simple Recipe conversion (SRC) use:
one (1) unit x factor equals = Metric				
1	Tsp	3.625116000	Ml	5
1	Tbsp	14.500464000	Ml	15
1	Fl Oz	28.410000000	Ml	28.4
1	Cup	0.2272800000	Ltr	0.23
1	½ pint	0.284100000	Ltr	284
1	Pint	0.568200000	Ltr	0.57
1	Quarts	1.136400000	Ltr	1.14
1	Gallons	4.546000000	Ltr	4.55

VOLUME (Imperial Liquid Fluid)

1 Imp fl Oz = 28.413 Ml. 1 Imp Gal = 4 Qrt = 8 Pnt = 160 Fl Oz,

1 Gal = 4.546 Ltr or (SRC = 4550 Ml)

1 Imp fl Oz ÷ 1.0408375 = 1 US fl Oz or, 1 Imp fl Oz ÷ 1.041 = 1 US fl Oz

1 Ltr = 10 Dl = 1000 Ml = 35.195 Imp fl Oz

1 US fl Oz = 29.574 Ml minus 1 Imp fl Oz (28.413 ml) = 1.161 Ml,

hence the US fl Oz is 1.161 Ml, or (4.088%) larger than the Imp fl Oz

Quick Conversion Factors for Kitchen and Bar

Page 2

NOTE: Significance of conversions should be **limited to 4 decimal** places.

by Klaus Theyer CCC June2013

FLUID Units abbreviations:

Tsp	Teaspoon
Tbsp	Tablespoon
Ml	Milliliter
Dl	Deciliter
M cup	Metric cup
Ltr	Liter
US fl Oz	US fl ounce
US Cup	Cup
US Gal	US Gallon
US Qrt	US Quart
US Pnt	US Pint
Imp fl Oz	Imperial fl ounce
Imp Cup	Imp cup
Imp Gal	Imperial Gallon
Imp Qrt	Imperial Quart
Imp Pnt	Imperial Pint
Btl	Bottle

LENGTH Units abbreviations:

Mm	Millimeter
Cm	Centimeter
Mtr	Meter
Km	Kilometer
Inch "	Inch
Ft '	Foot
Yd	Yard
Mi	Mile

NM   is a Nautical Mile

Temperature definition **& conversion:**

C = Celsius   F = Fahrenheit

To Convert From **F** to **C**
(F - 32) ÷ 9 x 5   or (F - 32) ÷1.8
To Convert From **C** to **F**
(C x 9 ÷ 5) + 32   or (C x 1.8) + 32

Common C to F conversions:

-40	-40
0	32
100	212
121	250
149	300
177	350
191	375
204	400
232	450
260	500
288	550
315.5	600

SOLID Weight abbreviations:

Gr	Gram
Dkg	Decagram
Kg	Kilogram
Oz	Ounce
Lbs	Pound

	C	F
Room temperature	21.11	70.0
Body temperature	36.8	98.2
Absolute zero (0)	-273.15	-459.7
Boiling	100	212.0
Freezing	0	32.0

Quick Conversion Factors for Kitchen and Bar   by Klaus Theyer CCC   June 2013   Page 3
NOTE: Significance of conversions should be **limited to 4 decimal** places.

MIXED Volume Units for accurate conversion multiply Units times factor for Results				For simple Recipe conversion (SRC) use:
one (1) unit x factor equals = results				
1	Tsp	0.1276000000	Imp fl Oz	0.13
1	Tbsp	0.5104000000	Imp fl Oz	0.5
1	Ml	0.0351988736	Imp fl Oz	0.04
1	250 Ml	0.0351988736	Imp fl Oz	8.80
1	Ltr	35.1988736360	Imp fl Oz	35.20
1	Ltr	1.7599436818	Imp Pnt	1.76
1	Ltr	0.8799718409	Imp Qrt	0.88
1	Ltr	0.2199929602	Imp Gal	0.22

LENGTH Units - for accurate conversion Multiply units times factor for Result			
one (1) unit x factor equals = results			
1	Mm	0.04	Inch "
1	Cm	0.39	Inch "
1	Mtr	39.4	Inch "
1	Mtr	3.28	Ft '
1	Mtr	1.09	Yd
1	Km	0.06	Mi
1	Km	0.54	Nautical NM
1	inch "	25.4	Mm
1	inch "	2.54	Cm
1	inch "	0.03	Mtr
1	foot '	0.3	Mtr
1	Yd	0.91	Mtr
1	Mi (land)	1.61	Km
1	Nautical NM	1.85	Km

WEIGHT Units for accurate conversion multiply Units times factor for Result				For simple Recipe conversion (SRC) use:
one (1) unit x factor equals = results				
1	Oz	28.34952312	Gr	28.35
1	Gr	0.035273962	Oz	0.035
1	Lb	0.45359237040	Kg	0.454
1	Lb	453.5923704	Gr	454
1	Kg	2.2046226199	Lb	2.205
1	Kg	35.2739619558	Oz	35.3
1	Metric Ton	1.102311311	US Ton	1.1
1	US Ton	0.9071847399	Metric Ton	0.91

WEIGTH Conversion Summary
1 Kg = 100 Dkg or 1000 Gr
1 Lbs - 16 Oz
A Metric Ton = 1000 Kg which converts to 1.1 US Ton
A US Ton = 907.2 Kg which **converts to 0.91 Metric Ton**

LENGTH Conversion Summary
Mm = Millimeter, Cm = Centimetre, Mtr = Meter, Km = Kilometer
1 Cm = 10 Mm, 1 Mtr = 100 Cm = 1000 Mm, 25.4 Mm = 1 Inch "
Inch " = Inch, Ft ' = Foot (feet), Yd = Yard, Mi = Mile, NM = Nautical Mile
12 Inch " = 1 Ft, 3 Ft = 1 Yd, 5280 Ft = 1 Mi, 1 Mi = 1760 Yd

Sales, Cost, Cost %, formulae, by Klaus Theyer CCC

Explanation of abbreviations:
S.P. = Selling Price,   **C** = Cost,
C % = Cost percentage,
COGS = Cost Of Goods Sold,
R or Rev = Revenue,

Cost → Cost % → S.P. → Cost

The "3" basic formulas to calculate either Cost, Selling Price or Cost percentage:
(If your calculator has a % key and if you use it you may omit the x 100)

COST ÷ COST % = S.P.   S.P. × COST % = COST

COST ÷ (S.P. x 100) = COST %   COST × Factor = S.P.

Common Yield, A.P., U.P., L, E.P., Y, %, $, formulae:

Explanation of abbreviations:
Yield = Edible remains of As Purchased   **A.P.** = As Purchased
U.P. = Usable remains of As Purchased   **E.P.** = Edible Portion
L = Loss, difference between A.P. And Edible Portion or Yield
Y = Yield, Consumable or Edible Portion   **%** = Percentage
$ = Value   The $ or % could apply to any descriptor above

E.P. or U.P. ÷ (A.P. x 100) = Yield %   A.P. × Yield % = E.P.

E.P. or U.P. ÷ Yield % = A.P.   A.P. $ ÷ Yield % = E.P. $

E.P. $ × Yield % = A.P. $ A.P. $ ÷ E.P. Weight = E.P. $

L or U.P. ÷ A.P. = L or U.P. %   A.P. $ ÷ E.P. Count = E.P. Item $

A.P. Weight × Yield % = E.P. Weight

Chapter 4

Yield Calculations

Yield

An expression used to identify the edible/consumable remains by adjusted weight and adjusted cost of As Purchased products.

▶ **A.P. (As Purchased)**
Usually expressed as: Cost – Quantity (Weight – Volume – Pieces)
Quality and Percentage %

▶ **A.P.** is considered to be 100% (the whole thing)

▶ **U.P. (Usable Portion)**
Refers to pre-prepared or trimmed and uncooked or to-be-cooked and not deboned product (e.g., Ham, Leg of Lamb)
Usually expressed as:
Percentage % – Cost – Quantity (Weight – Volume – Pieces) and in Quality.

▶ **E.P. or Yield (Edible Portion - Consumable product)**
Usually expressed as:
Percentage % – Cost – Quantity (Weight – Volume – Pieces) and in Quality.
The Edible Portion is the consumable remains of a product. The E.P. may be the same as the A.P., in which case the A.P. and the E.P. (Yield) is 100%.
Conversely, if the A.P. product is being pumped, marinated, larded or barded, baked or steamed, or is a Pasta or Rice product, then the E.P. (Edible Portion) may be larger or more in volume/weight than the A.P. product. In these situations it is advisable for Cost calculations to accept the A.P. Cost as the E.P. Cost, or as illustrated in the Line Cost example, calculation of the Yield adjusted cost or quantity.

▶ **Loss**
The difference between A.P. and E.P. is loss.
Usually expressed as:
Percentage % – Cost – Quantity (Weight – Volume – Pieces) and in Quality.

66 Chapter 4 Yield Calculations

A **Loss** of product may occur due to: pouring, mixing, spillage, spoilage, and/or due to trimming, cooking, condensing, boning, dehydration, slicing, carving, chilling, freezing, etc.

For mathematical purposes, it is most beneficial to know the **Yield** and the **Loss** expressed **as a percentage** %. Knowing the percentage will allow you to complete all necessary Yield and Cost and Yield and Weight calculations.

NOTE: Yield calculations **are not** necessary if the **A.P.** weight and **Dollar** amount is apportioned into consumable units. For example, a Strip loin weighs 4.5 kg and costs $62.00 – trimmings (loss) equals .5 kg; 20 steaks are cut from it, so cost per steak is: $62.00 ÷ 20 steaks = $3.10 per steak (Unit cost).

Recipe Yield is the term used for the quantity, portions, or units to be expected if the recipe is followed accurately.

Yield Calculations within a Recipe Example

▶ **INFO:** Purchased bag of Onions A.P. 40 lbs at a Cost of $30.00. The recipe calls for 10 kg peeled Onions. The Loss of peeling is usually 10%. How many lbs of Onions need to be peeled (with or without crying)?

▶ Facts needed for calculation:
A.P. Weight (40 lbs)   A.P. Cost ($30.00)
Loss % (10%)   Yield % (?)

Follow these Steps:

▶ **FIRST:** Covert A.P. Weight to Recipe Unit Weight (R.U.)
lbs × 0.4536 = kg 40.00 × 0.4536 = 18.144 kg (A.P.)

▶ **SECOND:** Let's calculate the Yield percentage by subtracting the Loss in kg from the Purchased kg and then divide the result by the A.P. kg and multiply the result by 100 to achieve the Yield percentage:
18.144 − 1.814 = 16.3296 (E.P. kg) ÷ 18.144 =.090 × 100 = 90% (Y %)

▶ **THIRD:** Calculate the Usable Portion, which is also the Yield, by multiplying the A.P. kg by the Yield percentage.
18.144 × 90% = 16.3296. I hope you noticed that you just made two different calculations, both yielding the same result. It would also have been sufficient to subtract the known Loss % from the A.P., which is always 100% to obtain the Yield percentage (90.00%).

▶ **FOURTH:** Knowing the Yield percentage, divide the U.P. weight (10.00 kg) by the Yield % to obtain the amount of Onions that have to be peeled. 10.00 kg (U.P.) ÷ 90.00% (Y %) = 11.11 kg (A.P.)

In math, there is often more than one method of calculation to achieve the same result. For accuracy, I recommend to complete necessary calculations in more than one way.

In general and in the following example, when calculating **Average (AVG)** Percentages—and **NOT only for Yield calculations**—the calculations should always be based upon **Totals;** that is, the Total U.P. (Usable Portion) weight is divided by the Total A.P. (As Purchased) weight, times 100 to arrive at the **Average Usable Portion Yield** percentage of 86.667% (A.V.U.P.Y.%), Ditto for the

E.P.Y.%. The Total E.P. kg is divided by the Total A.P. kg to calculate the Average Yield percentage (A.V.Y %). **Do not** calculate the A.V. Y.% or the A.V. U.P. % by adding the percentages and dividing them by the number of units tested.

Here are the most common formulas pertaining to yield calcualtion.

A complete set of often used formulas can be found at the end of Chapter 3.

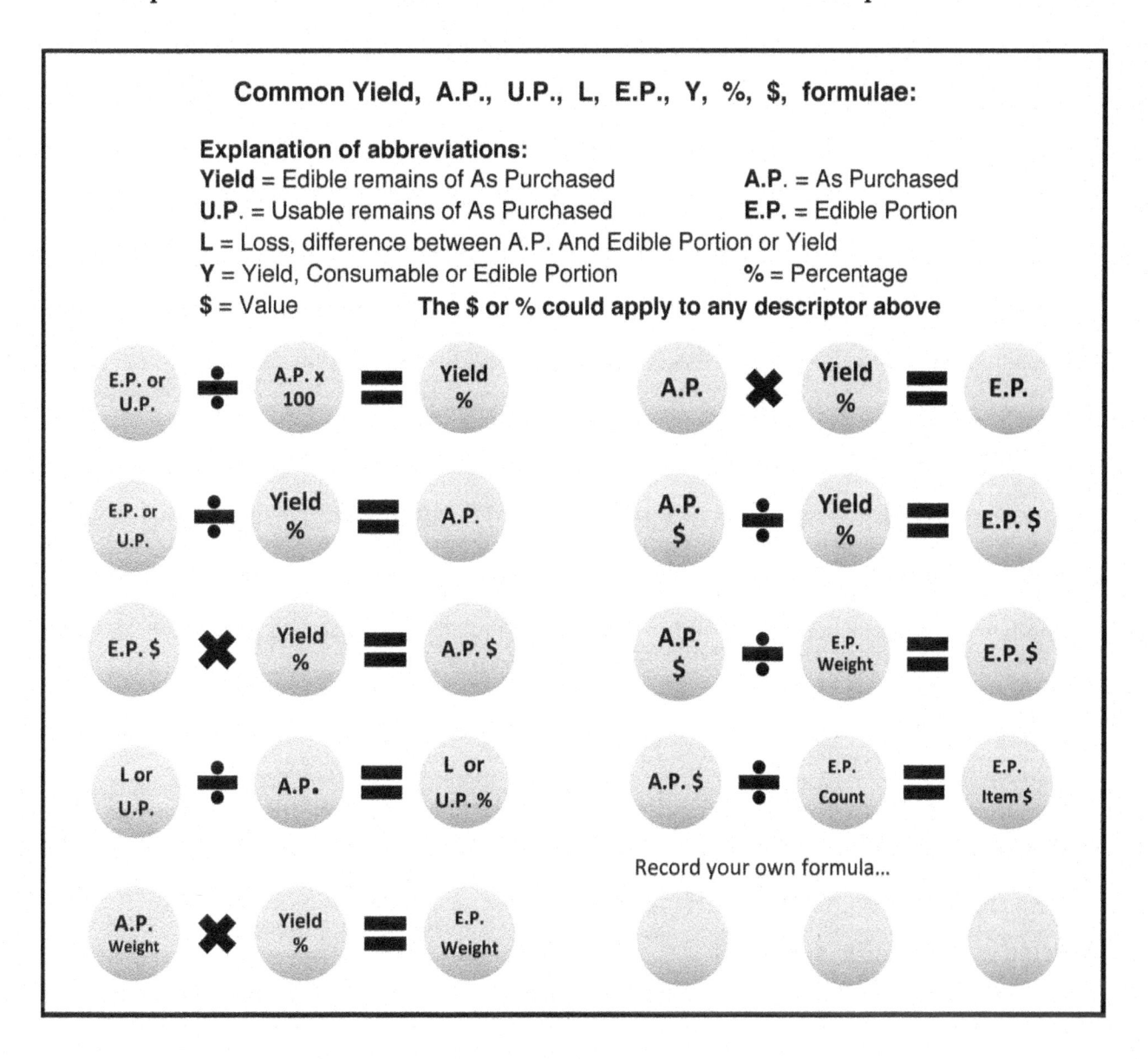

Common Yield, A.P., U.P., L, E.P., Y, %, $, formulae:

Explanation of abbreviations:
Yield = Edible remains of As Purchased   A.P. = As Purchased
U.P. = Usable remains of As Purchased   E.P. = Edible Portion
L = Loss, difference between A.P. And Edible Portion or Yield
Y = Yield, Consumable or Edible Portion   % = Percentage
$ = Value   **The $ or % could apply to any descriptor above**

E.P. or U.P. ÷ A.P. x 100 = Yield %

A.P. ✕ Yield % = E.P.

E.P. or U.P. ÷ Yield % = A.P.

A.P. $ ÷ Yield % = E.P. $

E.P. $ ✕ Yield % = A.P. $

A.P. $ ÷ E.P. Weight = E.P. $

L or U.P. ÷ A.P. = L or U.P. %

A.P. $ ÷ E.P. Count = E.P. Item $

Record your own formula...

A.P. Weight ✕ Yield % = E.P. Weight

Average Yield Percentage (Butcher Test)

Prior to selecting a supplier for meat(s) products, a Yield test should be conducted to establish the average shrinkage (Loss) and Yield based on supplied Quality.

A.P. (kg) Weight	Trim Loss (kg)	U.P. (kg)	U.P. Yield %	Cooking Loss (kg)	E.P. Yield (kg)	E.P. Yield %
10.00	1.50	8.50	85.00	2.00	6.50	65.00
9.50	1.20	8.30	87.37	2.00	6.30	66.32
9.75	1.20	8.55	87.69	1.80	6.75	69.23
Total: 29.25	Total: 3.90	Total: 25.35	Average: 86.667	Total: 5.80	Total: 19.55	Average: 66.838

To carry the previous example a step further by calculating the Yield ADJ (Adjusted) Dollar, add the following information:

Purchase one was $12.50 per kg, Purchase two was $12.75 per kg, and Purchase three was $12.60 per kg. Calculate the Total Purchase Cost by multiplying 10 x 12.50 + 9.50 x 12.75 + 9.75 x 12.60 = $368.98. Divide this result by the Total A.P. weight and divide the result by the Y %.

$368.98 ÷ 29.25 kg = $12.61 ÷ 66.838% = $18.87. Of course, the same result would have been calculated by diving Total Cost A.P. by the E.P. kg.

$368.98 ÷ 19.55 kg = $18.87. Once again, in math there is often more than one method of calculation to achieve the same result. For accuracy it is recommend that necessary calculations are completed in more than one way.

Another method of calculating Yield Adjusted Cost (Y.A.C.) is the **Yield Factor method.** Using the example provided, the Y.A.C. is $18.87 and the A.P.$ was $12.61.

Y.A.C. $18.87
A.P.$ $12.61 equals the factor (multiplier) 1.4964.

If there would be an increase in the A.P.$ (New Cost $12.75), multiply the New Cost with the Factor and, voila, you have the new Y.A.C. or Edible Portion Cost: $12.75 x 1.4964 = $ 19.08. This method saves you from re-doing the Butchers tests averages. This method will not be accurate if there is a change in the product or cooking method resulting in a higher or lower yield.

Following is a Butcher Yield Test for Cooks

An actual Butcher Yield test would focus on the usable/sellable muscle in proportion to Bones, Fat, Sinew, Collagen, as well as reworkable and other trimmings to the total carcass.

There are Yield calculation sheets available on my webpage: *www.menuforprofit.com*

Chapter 4 Yield Calculations 69

Butcher Yield Test (from WebPage) by Klaus Theyer CCC — Highlighted area are input fields.

Name of tester: _____   Date of test: _____

Name of Product tested: Strip Loins Canada Prime

Grade: Prime   Origin: Canada (Alberta)

NOTE: All calculation must be to no less than two decimal places!

Supplier:	A.P. Weight in Kg	A.P. Cost per Kg	Total Cost	Prep/Trim Weight in Kg	(U.P.) Prepped Weight	Prep Loss %	(U.P.) Yield % Prior to Cooking	Cooking loss @ %	Cooking loss Kg	Yield (E.P.) weight	Yield %	Yield $ per Kg
A	7.2	$16.80		0.80				10.94%				
B	7.3	$16.80		0.90				12.50%				
C	7	$17.75		0.60				12.03%				
D	6.9	$17.90		0.40				10.00%				
Totals:								XXXXXX				
Actual or Aver:												

Average Cost of 1 Kg (E.P.): _____   The average Yield percentage % is: _____

The best Yield % is: _____   Supp. ? ___   The best Yield Kg cost is: _____

Based on the best Yield $ per Kg Cost:

Cost of a 180 gramm E.P. portion is: _____
The cost for all other ingredients (Side Dishes) is: 1.95
Portion - Plate/Line Cost is: _____   If Selling Price is => $22.00
Selling price based on a 25.00% Cost is _____   What is the actual Cost percentage:? _____

Butcher Yield Test (from WebPage) by Klaus Theyer CCC — Highlighted area are input fields.

Name of tester: _____   Date of test: _____

Name of Product tested: Strip Loins Canada Prime

Grade: Prime   Origin: Canada (Alberta)

NOTE: All calculation must be to no less than two decimal places!

Supplier:	A.P. Weight in Kg	A.P. Cost per Kg	Total Cost	Prep/Trim Weight in Kg	(U.P.) Prepped Weight	Prep Loss %	(U.P.) Yield % Prior to Cooking	Cooking loss @ %	Cooking loss Kg	Yield (E.P.) weight	Yield %	Yield $ per Kg
A	7.2	$16.80	$120.96	0.80	6.4	11.11%	88.89%	10.94%	0.70	5.70	79.17%	$21.22
B	7.3	$16.80	$122.64	0.90	6.4	12.33%	87.67%	12.50%	0.80	5.60	76.71%	$21.90
C	7	$17.75	$124.25	0.60	6.4	8.57%	91.43%	12.03%	0.77	5.63	80.43%	$22.07
D	6.9	$17.90	$123.51	0.40	6.5	5.80%	94.20%	10.00%	0.65	5.85	84.78%	$21.11
Totals:	28.40	$69.25	$491.36	2.70	25.70			XXXXXX	2.920	22.78		$86.30
Actual or Aver:	7.100	$17.31	$122.84	0.675	6.43	9.51%	90.49%	11.36%	0.730	5.70	80.21%	$21.58

Average Cost of 1 Kg (E.P.): $21.58   The average Yield percentage % is: 80.21%

The best Yield % is: 84.78%   Supp. ? D   The best Yield Kg cost is: $21.11

Based on the best Yield $ per Kg Cost:

Cost of a 180 gramm E.P. portion is: 3.80
The cost for all other ingredients (Side Dishes) is: 1.95
Portion - Plate/Line Cost is: 5.75   If Selling Price is => $22.00
Selling price based on a 25.00% Cost is 23.00   What is the actual Cost percentage:? 26.14%

Chicken Yield   by Konrad Weinbuch CMC

After de-boning a whole chicken, weigh and calculate the percentage of each individual chicken part in relation to the whole chicken.

Add the weight of all the chicken parts to determine the total weight and the total percentage.

				%
A.P.	Whole chicken	1680	gram	100.00%
	1 Leg	275	gram	16.37%
plus	1 Breast	262	gram	15.60%
plus	1 Thigh	145	gram	8.63%
plus	1 DrumStick	120	gram	7.14%
plus	1 Supreme	252	gram	15.00%
plus	2 Wing Lollipops	66	gram	3.93%
plus	Bones, trimmings	560	gram	33.33%
equals	Total	1680	gram	100.00%

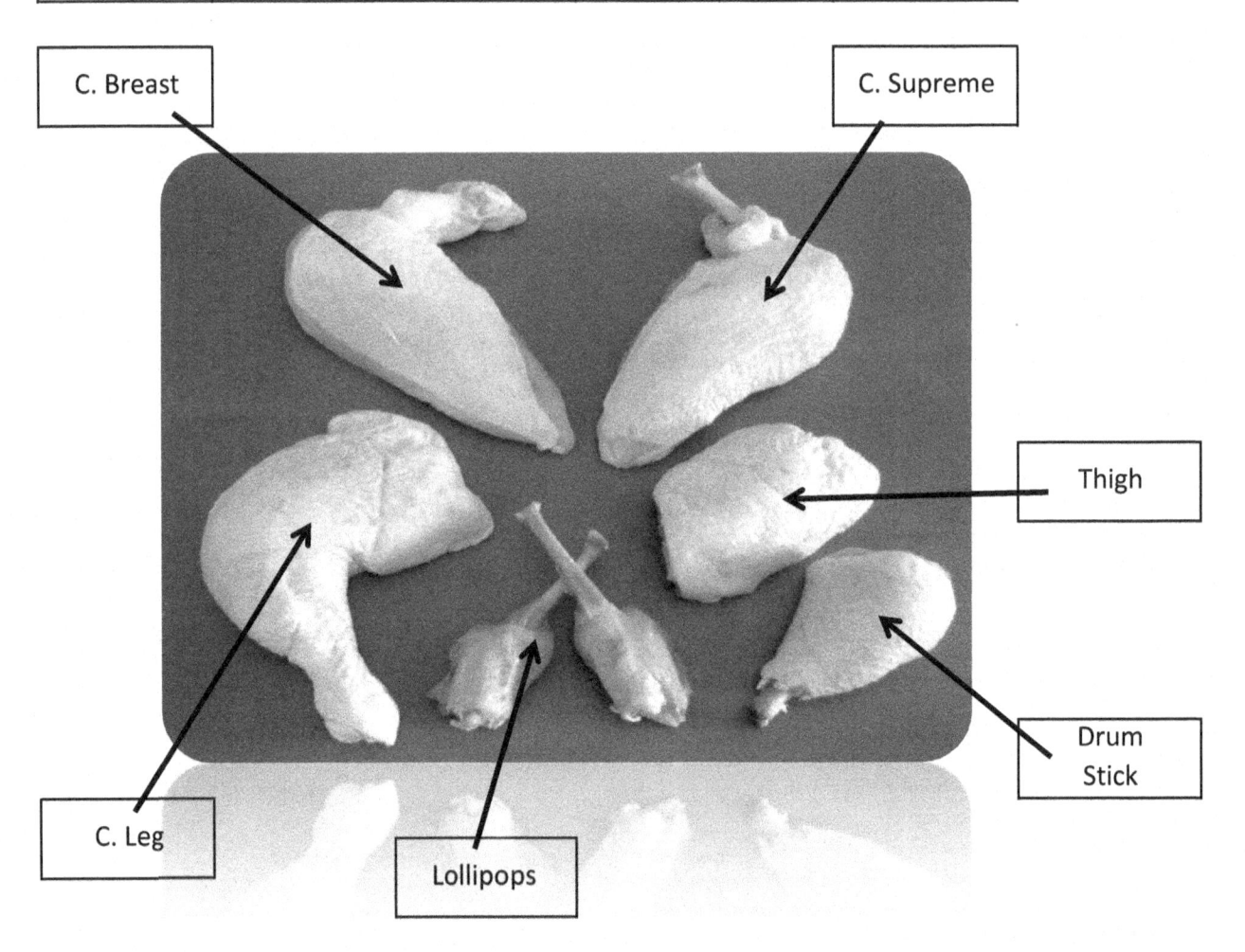

Complete Chicken Yield
by Konrad Weinbuch CMC
From A.P through U.P. to E.P.

For a light business lunch function, you will need to prepare | 250 | club sandwiches. For each sandwich you need | 110 | Gr of perfectly roasted and de-boned chicken meat. But before you start, you should calculate the Yield percentage, which will allow you to order the exact amount of chicken (Kg) needed.

	weight (Gr)	percent
1 Whole Chicken A.P.	1750	
Cooking loss	390	
2 U.P. 1 after roasting		
3 boning loss 1	295	
4 U.P. 2 partially boned		
5 boning loss 2	175	
6 E.P. perfectly cooked and de-boned		
Total loss		

How many Kg of whole chicken do you need to order for this function? _____ Kg

How many Kg of whole chicken are required if the function increases to 375 guests? _____ Kg

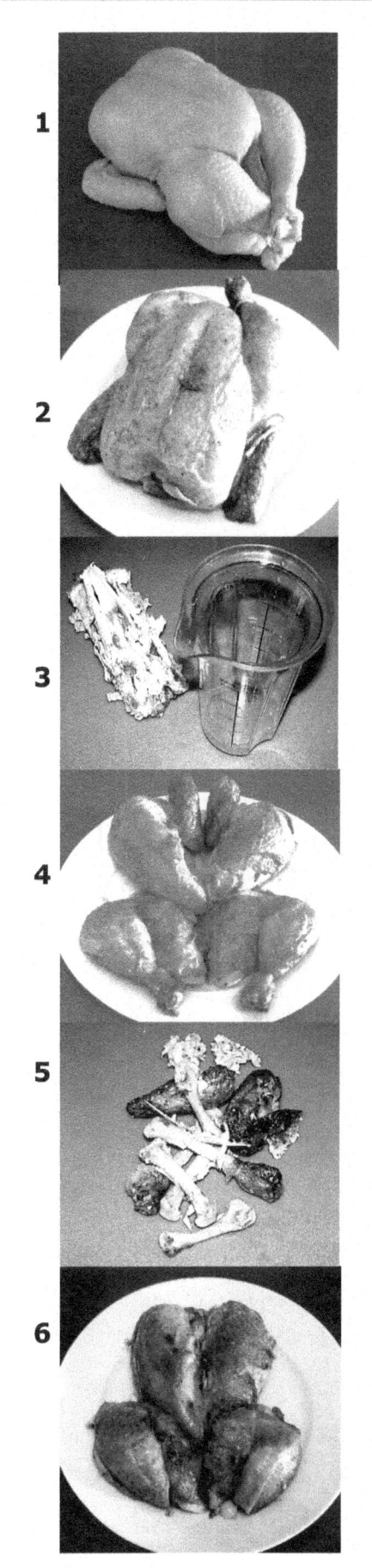

Complete Chicken Yield
by Konrad Weinbuch CMC

From A.P through U.P. to E.P.

For a light business lunch function, you will need to prepare **250** club sandwiches. For each sandwich you need **110** Gr of perfectly roasted and de-boned chicken meat. But before you start, you should calculate the Yield percentage, which will allow you to order the exact amount of chicken (Kg) needed.

	weight (Gr)	percent
1 Whole Chicken A.P.	1750	100.00%
Cooking loss	390	22.29%
2 U.P. 1 after roasting	1360	77.71%
3 boning loss 1	295	16.86%
4 U.P. 2 partially boned	1065	60.86%
5 boning loss 2	175	10.00%
6 E.P. perfectly cooked and de-boned	890	50.86%
Total loss	860	49.14%

How many Kg of whole chicken do you need to order for this function? **54.073** Kg

How many Kg of whole chicken are required if the function increases to **375** guests? **81.110** Kg

Butcher's Yield Test 2
by Konrad Weinbuch CMC

Product tested: Canada AAA strip loin
Final product: Strip loin roast

A.P. Cost per Kg	$17.80	$17.55	$18.15	$18.45		
Supplier	A	B	C	D	Total weight	Average
A.P. weight (kg)	6.550	7.280	7.750	5.880		**6.865**
Meat juices loss	0.200	0.215	0.280	0.190	**0.885**	
U.P. 1 (kg)			7.470			
Trimming loss	1.840	1.860	1.910	1.550	**7.160**	
U.P. 2 (kg)	**4.510**					**4.854**
Roasting/cooking loss (kg)	1.120	1.380	1.460	1.040		
U.P. 3 (kg)		**3.825**				
Portioning loss (kg)	0.520	0.650	0.730	0.440		**0.585**
Yield weight (kg)			3.370			
Yield %	43.82%				XXX	
Loss weight (kg)				3.220		
Loss %				54.76%	XXX	
Yield adjusted cost per Kg			$41.74		XXX	

Best yield percentage ☐   Best yield adjusted cost per kg ☐

1. Using the strip loin with the best <u>yield adjusted cost per kg</u>, what is the cost for a portion weighing **180** grams E.P.? ☐

2. What would the Selling price be, with a **29%** Food cost? ☐

3. If the selling price is **$23.20** what would the food cost % be? ☐

Butcher's Yield Test 2   by Konrad Weinbuch CMC

Product tested: Canada AAA strip loin
Final product: Strip loin roast

A.P. Cost per Kg	$17.80	$17.55	$18.15	$18.45		
Supplier	A	B	C	D	Total weight	Average
A.P. weight (kg)	6.550	7.280	7.750	5.880	27.460	6.865
Meat juices loss	0.200	0.215	0.280	0.190	0.885	0.221
U.P. 1 (kg)	6.350	7.065	7.470	5.690	26.575	6.644
Trimming loss	1.840	1.860	1.910	1.550	7.160	1.790
U.P. 2 (kg)	4.510	5.205	5.560	4.140	19.415	4.854
Roasting/cooking loss (kg)	1.120	1.380	1.460	1.040	5.000	1.250
U.P. 3 (kg)	3.390	3.825	4.100	3.100	14.415	3.604
Portioning loss (kg)	0.520	0.650	0.730	0.440	2.340	0.585
Yield weight (kg)	2.870	3.175	3.370	2.660	12.075	3.019
Yield %	43.82%	43.61%	43.48%	45.24%	XXX	43.97%
Loss weight (kg)	3.680	4.105	4.380	3.220	15.385	3.846
Loss %	56.18%	56.39%	56.52%	54.76%	XXX	56.03%
Yield adjusted cost per Kg	$40.62	$40.24	$41.74	$40.78	XXX	$40.85

Best yield percentage **45.24%**   Best yield adjusted cost per kg **$40.24**

1. Using the strip loin with the best <u>yield adjusted cost per kg</u>, what is the cost for a portion weighing **180** grams E.P.? **$7.24**

2. What would the Selling price be, with a **29%** Food cost? **$24.98**

3. If the selling price is **$23.20** what would the food cost % be? **31.22%**

Yield Exercise — AAA Strip loin roast
by Konrad Weinbuch CMC

The butcher was asked by the chef to order AAA strip loins for Saturday's dinner function. Each guest will receive a portion of **170** Gr of strip loin roast and **290** guests are expected at the function. How many Kg of AAA strip loin should the butcher order for this function?

(3 decimals for Kg, 2 decimals for %)

		weight Kg	percent
1	A.P. Strip loin in bag	7.380	
	Meat juices	0.215	
2	U.P. 1 Strip loin unpacked		
3	trimming loss	1.860	
4	U.P. 2 trimmed strip loin		
	cooking loss	1.380	
5	U.P. 3 Strip loin after cooking		
6	Portioning loss	0.650	
7	E.P. Perfectly roasted sliced Strip loin		

How many Kg of AAA strip loin will the butcher have to order for this function? _____ Kg

If the function increases to **465** guests How many Kg of AAA strip loin will the butcher have to order _____ Kg

How many Kg of AAA strip loin are required if the portion size is **0.155** Kg, and **395** guests are expected? _____ Kg

Chapter 5

The Standard Recipe—Unit and Unit Cost

Standard Recipes are essential to establish, and subsequently to maintain, consistency in quality standards, by product description, quantities used, method of preparation, equipment and small ware needed, presentation-plating standard, quantities produced, portion or quantity yield, production time allotted, and method of costing applied.

The use of Standard Recipes is one way of ensuring that when repeat customers place an order, they will receive what they have been accustomed to, time after time.

The Standard Recipe I developed and refined with the input of my industry colleagues is a living document which currently features two pages; **Recipe Input & Costing Page**—for the name and other core information of the recipe, for identifying the ingredients and quantity used, the purchase and cost information, the yield percentage, labour hours, yield portions and ultimately the "Portion Cost." It also features selling price calculation scenarios. The second page, the **"Methods & Presentation Page"** carries necessary information from the first page forward and has two input areas: Method of preparation and an area to place a picture or graphic. A third page is currently in the planning stages which would contain Nutritional information.

Use this link to download the blank form or to look at some of the samples available:

http://menuforprofit.com/mfp_cc_files/Standard_Recipe_Read_Me.pdf

The ROW numbers and the COLUMN letters are for easy reference. If you look at the Recipe online or downloaded you will notice small triangular red tabs. Once you "Mouse-over" them a help note/menu will open. Please follow the instructions.

Standard_Recipe_2013.xlsx – Copyright 2013 © by Klaus Theyer, c/o E.T. Service

READ ME FIRST document

Dear Reader;

The **Standard_Recipe_2013.xlsx** is protected against accidental formula alterations. It is designed to be used with MS Excel and was developed for **food and/or a beverage menu items**. The recipe form and a few sample recipes which are posted on my website at www.menuforprofit.com are available to anyone, free of charge, as long as the disclaimer is accepted by the user. http://www.menuforprofit.com/costcontrol/recipeforms.asp

The fundamental structure has been adopted from the original handwritten document format which was developed some 40 years ago. Over the years it was converted from a one page handwritten document to become a very versatile two page computerized document. The (**Method & Presentation page**) is intended for the production area, and the (**Recipe Input & Costing page**) for administrative purposes, like deciding on the quality and quantity standards of products to be used, and for cost control.

The blank or white cells are input areas and should be used and completed as needed. Almost every cell or group of cells of this Workbook has a **help-menu** attached which **should be read and followed**. A conversion table with the most commonly used conversion measurements and methods is also appended for your convenience. (A full **conversion table** can be retrieved from the **Download Area**). The appended "Measurement acronyms from the dropdown list" should be adhered to, to achieve standardized and/or comparable results. The headers for the different groups of input areas have been lightly coloured to illustrate the relationship between them. All result areas are in light yellow.

The bottom part of the **Method & Presentation page** offers **Additional Selling Price calculation scenarios** to calculate the most appropriate Selling Price based on either the desired **Cost Percentage**, or the desired **Gross Profit**, or the **Prime Cost** percentage. You may also calculate the projected **Product Cost Percentage** % based on the selected **desired Selling Price**. All pertinent information entered from the **Recipe Input & Costing page** will automatically carry forward to the partially unprotected **Method & Presentation page** to enter the method of preparation in the designated **TEXT BOX** area and to import a picture or graphic into the assigned **Highlighted Area**, using the Home, and Insert tab.

The Recipe form has been field tested and performed flawlessly as expected. Once you have tried the recipe and you noticed an error, typo or malfunction, or have a suggestion for improvements, I would sincerely appreciate hearing from you.

Contact email: etservice1978@gmail.com   Many thanks and I hope you enjoy working with this new standard recipe form.

PS: Remember to save each created recipe with a different file name.

Klaus Theyer CCC

I recommend that you look at the completed recipe samples prior to completing one on your own.

Recipe Summary

Although, the recipe may look intimidating at first glance, it is easily completed by using a step-by-step approach, completing the input areas and by following the suggestions in the automatic "help" windows.

Each page of the recipe can be printed independently from the other pages.

Notes about the recipe (all pages): If information needs to be changed or updated, you may edit the field by locating the cell-pointer (cursor) on that field and pressing the F2 key; text can now be easily edited without retyping. Numerical values and percentages should be typed over.

PLEASE DO NOT CUT, COPY, AND PASTE FROM ONE CELL TO ANOTHER.
THIS MAY CAUSE INCORRECT RESULTS IN THE COSTING PAGE.

Chapter 5 The Standard Recipe—Unit and Unit Cost

STANDARD RECIPE FORM

Please enter text and values in white (unprotected) cells/areas only. Do not copy from one cell to another as this may change the embedded formulas.
All pertinent information should be entered on Page 1 of 1 before insertion of Picture or Method of preparation on Page 2 of 2

		Page 1 of 2
RECIPE NAME:	Enter Recipe Name	
OUTLET NAME:	ABC	
SOURCE or Reference or URL used for Recipe:		RECIPE NUMBER: 123
PORTION Size/Weight /Volume described =>	6	DATE: Month Year
		RECIPE CATEGORY: Insert Direct Labour Requirements:
RECIPE PORTIONS in ##		Production time in minutes # # 10
		Average Labour Hour Cost $ $18.00
		Calculated labour cost: $3.00

Measurement acronyms from drop-down list

BG	BG for Bag
BTL	BTL for Bottle
BUNCH	BUNCH for herbs or bundled Veg.
CRT	CRT for Carton/Box
CUP	CUP for standard 8 Oz US or 237 Ml
DKG	DKG for Dekagram (1 DKG = 10 Grams)
DL	DL for Decilitre or Deciliter
GR	GR for Grams
IMPCUP	IMPCUP for 8 Oz Imp Cup or 227 Ml
IMPFLOZ	IMPFLOZ for Imperial Fluid Oz
IMPGAL	IMPGAL for Imperial Gallon
IMPP	IMPP for Imperial Pint
IMPQ	IMPQ for Imperial Quart
KG	KG for Kilogram
LBS	LBS for pounds
LTR	LTR for Liter or Litre
MCUP	MCUP for Metric Cup for 250 Ml
ML	ML for Millilitre or Milliliter
OZ	OZ for Solid weight
PC	PC for Piece
SLC	SLC for Slice
TBL	TBL for Table Spoon (3 TSP or 15 Ml)
TSP	TSP for Tea Spoon (5 Ml)
TT	TT for "to taste"
Unit	for items measured-counted in Units
USFLOZ	USFLOZ for US fluid Oz
USG	USG for US Gallon
USP	USP for US Pint
USQ	USQ for US Quart
WDG	Wedge

"AS PURCHASED" / "A.P. Converted to R.U." / "YIELD CALCULATIONS"

Describe the Ingredients used in this recipe in common Recipe Units (R.U.) as detailed and practical as needed	R.U. "RECIPE UNIT" Recipe Units used in ## only	Recipe Units in weight volume/size	A.P. Package content I.e. Pieces Bag, Case	A.P. Cost $ of A.P. # of Units	A.P. Package content Converted to Recipe Units # Unit #	Insert Yield % below (as needed)	Yield adjusted Cost $ Weight/Vol.	Yield adjusted Weight or Volume	Calculated Recipe Unit Cost $	Recipe Units used from "D"	Extended Recipe Cost in $
Sample Item	KG	pkg	4 LBS	$16.50	1.82 KG	85%	19.41	1.5	10.6893	1 KG	10.689

RECIPE SUB-TOTAL ===> 10.689

ADD: Ice-Solce-Overproduction percentage here ===> 10% 1.069

TOTAL RECIPE COST ===> 11.758

DIVIDED by Recipe Portions # from (C6) 6

EQUALS PORTION COST OF 1.96

Input desired SELLING PRICE => $7.95 GROSS PROFIT 5.99

PORTION COST % BASED ON SELLING PRICE 24.65%

Standard Recipe Form design /revision by Klaus Tenter CCC, F.T. Service © 2012, www.menuforprofit.com H by Karen M. Naik, FT /Learning Professional/ Number College

Additional Selling Price Calculation Scenarios:

This Cost percentage creates a Selling Price of $ 5.04 28.0%

To Calculate the Selling Price based on a Desired Cost Percentage, enter the Cost % here ===> $ 7.00

and a Gross Profit of

To Calculate the Cost Percentage based on a Desired Selling Price, enter the Selling Price $ here ===> $ 7.95

This Selling Price created a Cost Percentage of 24.65% and a Gross Profit of $ 5.99

To Calculate the Selling Price based on a Desired Gross Profit, enter the GP Amount $ here ===> $ 5.00

Based on this Expected GP the Selling Price should be $ 6.96 and the Cost Percentage will be 28.16%

Recipe prepared or Updated by:

Total Recipe Cost INCLUDING Labour Cost 14.76

Portion Cost INCLUDING Labour Cost 2.46

Selling Price based on Desired Prime Cost percentage. Enter % ==> 45% 5.47

80 Chapter 5 The Standard Recipe—Unit and Unit Cost

Please enter text and values in white (unprotected) cells/areas only. Do not copy from one cell to another as this may change the embedded formulas.

STANDARD RECIPE FORM
All pertinent information should be entered on Page 1 of 1 before insertion of Picture or Method of preparation on Page 2 of 2

RECIPE NAME:	Enter Recipe Name					RECIPE NUMBER:	123		Page 1 of 2
OUTLET NAME:	ABC					DATE:	Month Year	RECIPE CATEGORY:	
SOURCE or Reference or URL used for Recipe:								Insert Direct Labour Requirements:	
PORTION Size/Weight/Volume described =>								Production time in minutes # #	10
RECIPE PORTIONS IN ##	6							Average Labour Hour Cost $	$ 18.00
								Calculated labour cost:	$ 3.00

	Describe the ingredients used in this recipe in common Recipe Units (R.U.) as detailed and practical as needed	R.U. "RECIPE UNIT"		A.P. "AS PURCHASED"			"A.P. Converted to R.U."	"YIELD CALCULATIONS"		Calculated Recipe Unit Cost $	Recipe Units used from "D"	Recipe Units used from "E"	Extended Recipe Cost in $
		Recipe Units used in volume/size	Recipe Units in weight	A.P. Package content i.e. Pieces Bag, Case	A.P. Package Cost $ of A.P.	A.P. Units in $	A.P. Package content Converted to Recipe Units #	Insert Yield % below	Yield adjusted Weight or Volume				
						Unit #	Weight/Volu.	(as needed)	Cost $				
1	Sample Item	1	KG	pkg	4 LBS	$ 16.50	1.82	KG	85%	19.41	10.6893	1	KG	10.689
2														
3														
...														
35														

Standard Recipe Form design/revision by Klaus Thever CCC, E.T. Service © 2012, www.menuforprofit.com & by Karen M. Nair, IT/Learning Professional, Humber College

ADD: Ice-Spice-Overproduction percentage here ===> | | 10% | 1,069
RECIPE SUB-TOTAL ===> | | | 10.689
TOTAL RECIPE COST ===> | | | 11.758
DIVIDED by Recipe Portions # from (C6) | | | 6
EQUALS PORTION COST OF | | | 1.96

Additional Selling Price Calculation Scenarios:

To Calculate the Selling Price based on a Desired Cost Percentage, enter the Cost % here ==> | 28.0% |
This Cost percentage creates a Selling Price of | $ 7.00 | and a Gross Profit of | $ 5.04 |

To Calculate the Cost Percentage based on a Desired Selling Price, enter the Selling Price $ here ==> | $ 7.95 |
This Selling Price created a Cost Percentage % of | 24.65% | and a Gross Profit of | $ 5.99 |

Input desired SELLING PRICE => | $7.95 | GROSS PROFIT | 5.99
PORTION COST % BASED ON SELLING PRICE | | 24.65%

To Calculate the Selling Price based on a Desired Gross Profit, enter the GP Amount $ here ==> | $ 5.00 |
Based on this Expected GP the Selling Price should be | $6.96 | and the Cost Percentage will be | 28.16% |

Total Recipe Cost INCLUDING Labour Cost | | 14.76
Portion Cost INCLUDING Labour Cost ==> | | 2.46

Recipe prepared or Updated by: | | Selling Price based on Desired Prime Cost percentage, Enter % ==> | 45% | 5.47

Standard Recipe Form design/revision by Klaus Theyer CCC, E.T. Service © 2012, www.menuforprofit.com & by Karen M. Nair, IT/Learning Professional, Humber College

STANDARD RECIPE NAME:	Enter Recipe Name		OUTLET NAME:	ABC
DATE:	Month Year	RECIPE PORTIONS:	6	

PORTION Size/Weight/Volume described =>   0

Ingredients used from Recipe Input Page:

	Sample Item	1	KG
1			
2			
3			
4			
5			
6			
7			
8			
9			
10			
11			
12			
13			
14			
15			
16			
17			
18			
19			
20			
21			
22			
23			
24			
25			
26			
27			
28			
29			
30			
31			
32			
33			
34			
35			

TEXT BOX for Method of preparation:

1. Measure, treat and prepare ingredients with respect and care
2. Follow the method of preparation
3. Follow the picture for presentation/service

Highlighted Area below is the assigned area for a presentation Photo or Illustration:

NOTE: Use the **Insert Tab** and select Picture or Object.

Recipe prepared or Updated by:	0	DATE:	Month Year

STANDARD RECIPE FORM

Please enter text and values in white (unprotected) cells/areas only. All pertinent information should be entered on Page 1 of 1 before insertion of Picture or Method of preparation on Page 2 of 2. Do not copy from one cell to another as this may change the embedded formulas.

RECIPE NAME:	Cream of celeriac soup		RECIPE NUMBER:	123		Page 1 of 2
OUTLET NAME:	ABC		RECIPE CATEGORY:			
SOURCE or Reference or URL used for Recipe:	CULN 241 Topic 5		DATE:	June 2013		Insert Direct Labour Requirements:
PORTION Size/Weight/Volume described =>	3600 ml = 18 portions, 200 ml each					Production time in minutes ##	40
						Average Labour Hour Cost $	$ 18.00
Additional Selling Price Calculation	18					Calculated labour cost:	$ 12.00

	Describe the ingredients used in this recipe in common Recipe Units (R.U.) as detailed and practical as needed	Recipe Units used in # # only	Recipe Units in weight volume/size	A.P. Package Units i.e. Pieces Bag, Case	A.P. "AS PURCHASED" Package content # of Units	A.P. Cost $ of A.P.	A.P. Unit #	"A.P. Converted to R.U." A.P. Package content Converted to Recipe Units # Weight/Volu.	Insert Yield % below (as needed)	"YIELD CALCULATIONS" Yield adjusted Cost $	Yield adjusted Weight or Volume	Calculated Recipe Unit Cost $	Recipe Units used from 'D'	Recipe Units used from 'E'	Extended Recipe Cost in $
1	celeriac (celery root)	750	GR	LBS	1 LBS	$ 3.75	454.00	GR	70%	5.36	317.8	0.0118	750	GR	8.850
2	cooking onions	300	GR	BG	50 LBS	$ 24.00	22,700.00	GR	82%	29.27	18,614.0	0.0013	300	GR	0.387
3	leeks, large	300	GR	LBS	1 LBS	$ 2.83	454.00	GR	68%	4.16	308.7	0.0092	300	GR	2.750
4	butter, unsalted	150	GR	CRT	25 LBS	$ 102.50	11,350.00	GR	98%	104.59	11,123.0	0.0092	150	GR	1.382
5	A.P. Flour	60	GR	BG	20 KG	$ 19.78	20,000.00	GR	98%	20.18	19,600.0	0.0010	60	GR	0.061
6	chicken stock	1800	ML	LTR	1 LTR	$ 0.60	1,000.00	ML	100%	0.60	1,000.0	0.0006	1800	ML	1.080
7	cream 35%	225	ML	LTR	1 LTR	$ 4.42	1,000.00	ML	100%	4.42	1,000.0	0.0044	225	ML	0.995
8	kosher salt		TT					TT						TT	
9	white ground pepper		TT					TT						TT	
10	sugar		TT					TT						TT	
11															
12	for sachet														
13	parsley sprig, with stems, roughly chopped	80	GR	Bunch	3 OZ	$ 1.39	85.05	GR	100%	1.39	85.1	0.0163	80	GR	1.307
14	fresh thyme sprig, with stems, roughly chopped	40	GR	Bunch	2 OZ	$ 1.75	56.70	GR	100%	1.75	56.7	0.0309	40	GR	1.235
15	bay leafs		TT					TT						TT	
16	pepper corns		TT					TT						TT	

RECIPE SUB-TOTAL ===>			18.046
ADD: Ice-Solvo-Overproduction percentage here ==>		10%	1.805
TOTAL RECIPE COST ===>			19.851
DIVIDED by Recipe Portions # from (C6)			18
EQUALS PORTION COST OF			1.10
Input desired SELLING PRICE ==>		$7.95	
PORTION COST % BASED ON SELLING PRICE			13.87%
		GROSS PROFIT	6.85
Total Recipe Cost INCLUDING Labour Cost			31.85
Portion Cost INCLUDING Labour Cost ==>			1.77
Selling Price based on Desired Prime Cost percentage. Enter % ==>		45%	3.93

Additional Selling Price Calculation Scenarios:

This Cost percentage creates a Selling Price of	$	3.94	28.0%
To Calculate the Selling Price based on a Desired Cost Percentage, enter the Cost % here ==>			2.84
To Calculate the Cost Percentage based on a Desired Selling Price, enter the Selling Price $ here ==>	$	6.50	
This Selling Price created a Cost Percentage % of		16.97%	5.40
		and a Gross Profit of	
To Calculate the Selling Price based on a Desired Gross Profit, enter the GP Amount $ here ==>	$	5.00	18.07%
Based on this Expected GP the Selling Price should be	$	6.10	
		and the Cost Percentage will be	

Recipe prepared or Updated by: Konrad Weinbuch CMC

Standard Recipe Form design/revision by Klaus Tenge CCC, E.T. Service © 2012. www.menuforprofit.com & by Karen M. Nair, IT/Learning Professional, Humber College

Standard Recipe Form design/revision by Klaus Theyer CCC, E.T. Service © 2012, www.menuforprofit.com & by Karen M. Nair, IT/Learning Professional, Humber College

STANDARD RECIPE NAME:	Cream of celeriac soup		
DATE: June 2013	RECIPE PORTIONS:	18	OUTLET NAME: ABC

PORTION Size/Weight/Volume described => 3600 ml = 18 portions, 200 ml each

Ingredients used from Recipe Input Page:

1	celeriac(celery root)	750	GR
2	cooking onions	300	GR
3	leeks, large	300	GR
4	butter, unsalted	150	GR
5	A.P. Flour	60	GR
6	chicken stock	1800	ML
7	cream 35%	225	ML
8	kosher salt		TT
9	white ground pepper		TT
10	sugar		TT
11			
12	for sachet		
13	parsley sprig, with stems, roughly chopped	80	GR
14	fresh thyme sprig, with stems, roughly chopped	40	GR
15	bay leafs		TT
16	pepper corns		TT
17			
18			
19			
20			
21			
22			
23			
24			
25			
26			
27			
28			
29			
30			
31			
32			
33			
34			
35			

TEXT BOX for Method of preparation:

Heat the butter in a small sauce pan, and sweat the celeriac with the onions and the leeks, without colouring
Add the flour (prepare a roux), continue sweating the vegetables with the flour
Add the hot chicken stock while stirring continuously
Bring to a boil, reduce to simmer, add the sachet and season
Simmer for 30 minutes, remove the sachet, and puree in the bar blender, until very smooth
Return to the sauce pan, bring up to simmer, add the cream and adjust the seasoning

Highlighted Area below is the assigned area for a presentation Photo or Illustration:

NOTE: Use the **Insert Tab** and select Picture or Object.

Recipe prepared or Updated by: Konrad Weinbuch CMC	DATE: June 2013

Unit and Unit Cost

A UNIT may be defined as the smallest dividable amount of the whole.

Example

A 1 litre bottle contains 1000 ml, hence the UNIT would be 1 millilitre. This may not be a very practical approach when it comes to gathering ingredients for a recipe; however, for cost calculation purposes it is the most accurate method of calculation.

Example

One (1) litre (L) bottle of Brandy costs $40.00; hence, one millilitre (ml) will cost $00.04. If you use 25 ml (5 US Teaspoons) in the recipe, then the **Extended Cost** (Unit Cost × Number of Units used) is $1.00.

In Cost Control, a UNIT may have a different meaning. An assembled Plate of Food as promoted on the menu or a completed Drink is also one unit for the purpose of calculating how many items were sold or prepared for Sale. If you were to buy eggs, in cartons of 180 (6 trays × 30 each) or in cartons of 12, one egg would be ONE UNIT.

If you were to buy Sugar in a 40 kilogram (kg) bag, then the Smallest Dividable Amount would be ONE GRAM. If, however, you are in a large production situation, and recipes require a minimum of 1 kg, then of course the Smallest Dividable Amount for your operation would be 1 kg. For accuracy purposes, if practical, I suggest that you use the Smallest Dividable Amount in all your calculations.

Then there is the Unit of Labour Cost—it is important to allocate the appropriate Cost of Labour to calculate Costs. For example, food production should use the Food Production Staff average Labour Hour Cost including Cost of Benefits to calculate the total cost of food produced, which is then divided by the number of usable portions to establish the portion (Unit) cost.

Should you or your working environment still be stuck on Imperial or U.S. measurements, then of course the Metric examples based on the System International (SI) need to be converted. For your convenience you will find a conversion table in the Tools and Workshops Section of this publication.

Chapter 6

Additional Important Costs (Hidden, Surrounding, Plate and Line Cost)

Calculating of Menu Item Cost

Moving away from management's point of view (considering all "Profit Centres") focusing on the operational aspects, let's look at the production areas (Kitchen/Bar). Controlling COST starts by identifying and calculating the COST of items offered on the menu.

A great deal of research based on Demographics, Competition, Popularity, Practicality, and Profitability has gone into the selection of specific menu items; hence it is imperative to know the accurate cost of each item offered for sale to establish a Selling Price within the target Profit expectation. The following chart identifies Production costs, and these costs are to be transferred on to a "Standard Recipe" using the Ice, Spice, Overproduction, Waste allowance provision.

Menu Items Costs' Consideration

PRIMARY COSTS
Products, Ingredients - Direct, Indirect Labour

SECONDARY COSTS
Accompaniments - Side dishes - Garnishes

HIDDEN COSTS
Cooking method, Cooking supplies, Condiments
Product quality, Cooking equipment....

MENU ITEM COST

- ▶ **Direct Cost:** Cost of Product used and Service rendered.
- ▶ **Variable Cost or Sales-related Cost:** Amenities, Condiments, etc....
- ▶ **Indirect Costs:** Cleaning material, Linen and Uniform rental, Equipment maintenance, etc. These types of Costs are Variable Costs as they relate to Sales and are often referred to as Operating Costs.
- ▶ **Overhead Cost:** Fixed Costs, such as Rent, Mortgage, Utilities and Insurance, Décor (flowers or candles on table), and in most cases Labour Cost, including Benefits.
- ▶ **Semi-Variable Cost:** Total Labour Cost (fixed and variable, full-time and part-time employees), including Benefits.
- ▶ **Alternative Cost:** Expected Profit in Cost Calculations and Budgeting.
- ▶ **Capital Cost:** (Capital investment, any item not for re-sale costing more than $100.00) Cost occurring for buildings, building material, chattels, and equipment. Canada's Revenue Agencies view any Building addition, Chattel, or Equipment Cost over $100.00 as Capital Cost, and therefore can only be partially (by means of depreciation) written off against Income.
- ▶ **Daily Food Cost:** Is calculated by dividing actual Cost of product used to make the Sales (Opening Inventory + Purchases − Closing Inventory) divided by Sales (Revenue) times 100 = Daily Food Cost percent %.
- ▶ **Historical Cost:** Cost occurred in a comparable time frame. That is, last year's Mothers Day Sales/Cost. This information is very useful for planning purposes.
- ▶ **Planned Cost:** Historical and/or other Cost information applied—Projected Cost.
- ▶ **Theoretical Cost:** Cost calculation based on Standard recipes (portions) not considering leftovers, wastage, over-production. Theoretical Cost must be compared to Actual Cost to establish the existence of a Variance that could be positive or negative—in either case it must be closely monitored.
- ▶ **Ideal Cost:** Ideal Food or Beverage Cost is usually an Average Cost Percentage, based on Menu offerings that are achieving anticipated Profit.
- ▶ **Total Cost:** Accrued (accumulated) Cost within a specific time frame.
- ▶ **Advertising and Promotional Cost:** Cost occurring to Advertise and Promote your business to potential customers. Cost of Food and Beverage is allocated to the corresponding production areas and compensated for by crediting inventory with the value of the product used.
- ▶ **Staff Meal Cost:** This Cost is handled similar to the Advertising and Promotional Cost.

Line and Plate Cost

A plate presented to a customer is usually an assembly of the main item (protein), side dishes (starch and vegetable), and perhaps a garnish (edible or inedible).

The combined cost of these ingredients are referred to as **Plate or Line Cost**. For a simplified costing approach, calculate the cost of each and all side dishes and garnishes. Divide this sum by the number of items used in this calculation, resulting in the Average Cost of one Side dish/Garnish. Calculate the portion protein cost, add the cost of the number of Side dishes/Garnishes used based on the Average Cost, and you just calculated the Line-Plate Cost for this item.

Plate Cost = # of Side-dishes × Average Line Cost + Protein Cost

Easy enough? Yes. Accurate enough? Your decision!

LINE or Basic Cost with Plate Cost - Book 2013

Please calculate the LINE cost for using the following information!

Conversion facts:

1 oz	28.375	grams
1 lbs	0.4536	kg
1 lbs	453.6	grams
1 Kg	2.2050	lbs
1 lbs	16	oz

4	Side dishes

Calculations must be extended/rounded to 3 decimal places

#	AP info	convert to R.U. portion size		R.U.#	A.P. $	Yield %	Portion Size		Cost of additional ingredients used $	Total Cost
1	Carrots - Bag	20	kg		22.00	93%	1.5	oz	0.15	
2	Spinach - Bag	0.5	kg		2.05	75%	2	oz	0.10	
3	Cauliflower	5	lbs		5.50	85%	60	gr	0.15	
4	Green Beans	1	kg		7.50	92%	2	oz	0.20	
5	Broccoli	2	kg		7.00	85%	2	oz	0.20	
6	Brussel Sprouts	2	lbs		6.50	90%	60	gr	0.15	
7	Potatoes	50	lbs		18.50	85%	60	gr	0.15	XXXXXX
8	Tomatoes Tray 24 pc	24	pc	XXXXXX	XXXXX	XXXXX	XXX		XXXXXX	XXXXXX
	1 Tomato = 8 wedges	8	wdg		14.00	95%	2	wdg	0.05	
9	Rice Bag	5	lbs		6.75	250%	25	gr	0.10	
10	Pasta	5	lb		6.00	150%	30	gr	0.15	

Total =>
Avg. =>

Total Cost of Line Items?	
Average Cost of Line Item?	
Avg. Line Cost Item x	4
+ Main Item portion cost	
= Plate Cost	
Cost percentage is:	32%
Selling Price is:	

by Klaus Theyer C.C.C.

Chapter 6 Additional Important Costs (Hidden, Surrounding, Plate and Line Cost) 87

88 Chapter 6 Additional Important Costs (Hidden, Surrounding, Plate and Line Cost)

LINE or Basic Cost with Plate Cost - Book 2013

by Klaus Theyer C.C.C.

Please calculate the LINE cost for **4** Side dishes using the following information!

Conversion facts:

1 oz	28.375	grams
1 lbs	0.4536	kg
1 lbs	453.6	grams
1 Kg	2.2050	lbs
1 lbs	16	oz

Calculations must be extended/rounded to 3 decimal places

	AP info	convert to R.U.		R.U.#	A.P. $	Yield %	Portion Size		Cost of additional ingredients used $	Total Cost
1	Carrots - Bag	20	kg	705.60	22.00	93%	1.5	oz	0.15	0.200
2	Spinach - Bag	0.5	kg	17.64	2.05	75%	2	oz	0.10	0.410
3	Cauliflower	5	lbs	2268.00	5.50	85%	60	gr	0.15	0.321
4	Green Beans	1	kg	35.28	7.50	92%	2	oz	0.20	0.662
5	Broccoli	2	kg	70.56	7.00	85%	2	oz	0.20	0.433
6	Brussel Sprouts	2	lbs	907.20	6.50	90%	60	gr	0.15	0.628
7	Potatoes	50	lbs	22680.00	18.50	85%	60	gr	0.15	0.208
8	Tomatoes Tray 24 pc	24	pc	XXXXXX	XXXXX	XXXXX	XXX		XXXXXX	XXXXXX
	1 Tomato = 8 wedges	8	wdg	192.0	14.00	95%	2	wdg	0.05	0.204
9	Rice Bag	5	lbs	2268.0	6.75	250%	25	gr	0.10	0.130
10	Pasta	5	lb	2268.0	6.00	150%	30	gr	0.15	0.203

Total Cost of Line Items?			3.398
Average Cost of Line Item?		Avg. =>	0.340

Avg. Line Cost Item x	4	1.36
+ Main item portion cost		6.80
= Plate Cost		8.16
Cost percentage is:		32%
Selling Price is:		25.50

Avg. => 3.40
0.34

Chapter 7

Demographics, Popular Selling Price Methods and Calculations

Feasibility Study
Will the theme and concept be profitable based on the selected demographic area?

Although a very important function, it is best left to experts because of the complexity and possible errors in interpretation.

Demographic Study
The study of a specific area, location and its population for various evaluation purposes.

The result of this study should reveal the statistical information of populations with reference to size, density, distribution and vital statistics as well as the ability (of the current market) to expand or decline.

Demographics are prepared for many different reasons. For the purpose of establishing a restaurant or other food service establishment, the following is perhaps the most important information about the population. The research process is referred to as **psychographics** or **customer profiling**:

- Age
- Ethnic origin
- Household type
- Marital status
- Occupation
- Income and disposable income
- Number of vehicles per family
- Who are my potential customers?
- Would they fit my planned concept?
- Where are my customers coming from?
- What do they have in common?
- What activities are they participating in/patronizing?
- Other related data

Chapter 7   Demographics, Popular Selling Price Methods and Calculations

What is my personal knowledge of the area?

The following information is evaluated for estimating the success (feasibility) of a specific type of establishment:

- What is the potential of a population increase in this area?
- What could be my share of the market? (Based on direct or indirect competition)
- What is the mix of residential, commercial, and/or manufacturing properties?
- Does this area have any attractions?
- Public transportation, ease of access, parking?
- How much area do I need for the planned business to succeed?
- How many potential customers could be attracted by the planned concept?

And perhaps most important for planning a specific type of establishment is the knowledge of **disposable income**.

Sample Demographic—Toronto West, Cloverdale Mall

INFORMATION AT A GLANCE

Strategically located next to a highway this mall is a well-established community centre, with a wide selection of strong performing fashion, specialty, and service retailers.

Type of Center: single level, enclosed
Number of Stores: 105 stores and services
GLA of Center: 380,000 square feet
Parking: 1917 parking stalls

Demographic Profile—Trade Area: 5 km radius

2006 Trade Area Population: 240,406
2010 Trade Area Projected Population: 276,467; anticipating a 15% increase

Ethnicity: (Top Five Single Responses)

English*	59.8%	Polish	9.6%
Italian	9.2%	Portuguese	5%
Ukrainian	3.9%		

*English includes: Canadian, English, British, Irish, Scottish, Welsh origins

Age Breakdown (in Years):

0 to 4	6%
5 to 19	17%
20 to 24	6%
25 to 34	15%
35 to 44	13%
45 to 54	13%
55 to 64	10%
65 to 74	10%
75 & over	6%

2006 Estimated Average Household Income in Trade Area: $79,108

2010 Estimated Average Household Income in Trade Area: $89,037 based on a 3% annual increase.

Estimated weekly traffic: 90,000 shoppers per week (annual average)

Based on the listed facts, what type of restaurant could be opened in the mall? A lot more information is needed. However the provided information, although being a crude assessment of the area, is a good overview.

Aerial view of Toronto. © Andy A., 2011. Used under license from Shutterstock, Inc.

Once the demographic study is completed, the psychographic and competitive analysis as well as the feasibility study indicate that based on the selected theme and concept, the expected profit is achievable.

A **competitive analysis** or **comparative analysis** will help you realize who your competition might be. Although competition is healthy since it provides an opportunity for price-value relationship and promotion of quality product, I believe it is important to differentiate your establishment's image and/or offerings from the competition to avoid direct competition.

In a competitive environment a business must excel in comparison to the competition to be successful.

Share the Market—Market Shares

It has become very popular for competitive establishments to congregate within a few blocks from one another, attracting customers to this area and giving them the opportunity to decide which one to patronize.

A list of potentially direct and indirect competitive establishments in alphabetical order:

Asian restaurant: Buffet or table service, specializing in cuisines from the Asian region, including China, Japan, Malaysia, Thailand, Vietnam.

Australian restaurant: Offers a menu characterized by fresh seasonal produce and dishes that reflect trends in Australian cooking, in an informal setting.

Bistro Restaurant: The term *bistro* is sometimes interchanged with *café*. A bistro in its true sense is actually a **café** that offers full meals and service and often features an outdoor patio.

Brasserie: see Bistro Restaurant

Breakfast Restaurant: Specializing in providing breakfast at least six days per week and/or all-day breakfast.

Buffet Restaurant: Often featuring ethnic specialities, especially popular are Oriental, Italian, and Mexican buffets.

BYO Restaurant: Restaurant and bistro that are or not wine/liquor licensed, allowing customers to bring their own alcoholic beverages. Corkage is usually charged to cover the labour cost and glassware use.

Café: A café is a casual restaurant with an unhurried atmosphere that may or may not offer table service. Customers order their food from a counter and serve themselves or are served. A café menu traditionally offers things such as coffee, espresso, pastries, sandwiches or light meals. A popular feature of a café is that it often features outdoor seating.

Casual Dining: Offers comfortable atmospheres and has mid-range prices.

Caterer: Caters on-site or off-site and may provide **personal chef services**.

Coffee Shop: Provides coffee, tea, pastries, snacks and casual meals during day time.

Concessions: Operate in conjunction with other activities such as sporting events, local festivals, or may be seasonal in nature and operate at public parks and pools. Menus are limited and food preparation is simple. Toronto recently licensed concessions; food carts named "Toronto a la cart," which offer ethnic specialities.

Delicatessen: Operation offering foods intended for immediate consumption. The main product line is normally luncheon meats, cheeses, and preserved fish products. Offerings include sandwiches, soups and salads, crudites and party trays. Most foods are precooked prior to delivery. Preparation of food products is generally simple, but can also be exclusive and exquisite, catering to the wealthy.

Eatertainment Restaurant: A phrase coined for restaurants that rely heavily on entertainment to attract customers, often not focusing on repeat customers and quality food preparation. (Hard Rock Cafe, Planet Hollywood) see also **Restaurant in a Theatre**

Ethnic Restaurant (see **Specialty Restaurant**): Ranges from quick-service to upscale. Menus usually include North American versions of ethnic dishes and/or authentic ethnic foods often offering kosher and/or Halal products.

European Restaurant: Specializing in cuisine from a country or region of Europe.

Family Restaurant: Offers a varied menu, including children's menu, and targeted to the family dining market and children. Since they charge reasonable prices, they appeal to seniors. They have fast service falling between quick service and full-service restaurants.

Fast Casual Dining: One example of a successful current trend. Fast casual is slightly more upscale than fast food. Fast casual restaurants offer disposable dishes and flatware, but their food tends to be presented as more upscale, such as gourmet breads and organic ingredients. Open kitchens are popular with fast casual chains, where customers can see their food being prepared.

Fast Food: Operations that specialize in one or two main entrees such as hamburgers, pizza or chicken. These operations may also provide salad and/or ice cream service. Preparation of food products is generally simple and often involves deep-fried food products.

Fine Dining Restaurant: Provides a formal, structured dining experience at the high end of the market. Also referred to as "white tablecloth dining."

French Restaurant: Specialising in French cuisine (although it falls into the European category, it is honourably mentioned separately due to France's long history in organising, standardising, and modernising classical cooking).

Full Service Restaurant: Operations that offer complete and varied menus for breakfast, lunch and dinner. It has multiple entrees for each meal period, which may include soups, salads and/or desserts. Preparation of food products is often complex and involves multiple steps. Most full-service operations will provide customer seating and may include liquor service (Milestones, Montana, Jack Astor, Outback, just to name a few).

Game Restaurant: Common as in Europe where the gaming and subsequent hunting laws are quite different than in North America. In North America all game to be sold in a restaurant must come from a controlled farming environment. Hunted game may only be served for fundraising purposes.

Ice Cream Parlour: Originated in Europe, evolved to also serve drinks and coffees besides the selection of different homemade ice creams in a similar make up as a café. Usually not found in its traditional style in North America, except in Italian areas of larger cities. North American substitutes, usually without any seating, are places like Baskin-Robbins, Dairy Queen, Ben & Jerry's.

Indian Restaurant: Specializing in regional or general Indian cuisine.

Mexican Restaurant: Specializing in Mexican or Tex-Mex cuisine.

Mobile Unit: Operations that operate from mobile vans, push carts or trailers selling food items (potentially hazardous). The operations may be somewhat seasonal in nature. Food service may be limited with most of the complex food preparation taking place in a commissary. See also **Concession.**

Pizza Restaurant: Pizza is the primary menu feature.

Pub: Short for public house, pubs date back hundreds of years to Europe, especially Great Britain. Pubs have a timeless appeal for their laid-back atmosphere. Brewpubs offer beer made in-house, as well as a wide selection of other beers and ales. Pubs can offer full menus, as well as appetizers.

Raw Food Restaurant: A new trend to be watched—food and juices are processed and served in their raw stages, usually made from organically grown products.

Restaurant (Children): Catering specifically to kids. See also **Family Restaurants.**

Restaurant in a Brewery: Restaurant within or adjacent to the premises of a brewery, most commonly trying to pair its beers with carefully selected entrees. See also **Restaurant in a Winery.**

Restaurant in a Hotel: Offering one or more in-house dining facilities ranging from cafeteria style to a "Signature Restaurant."

Restaurant in a Motel/Motor Inn/Guesthouse: Restaurants within a motel/motor inn/guesthouse offering in-house dining.

Restaurant in a Pub/Hotel/Club/Tavern: Restaurant located within a pub/hotel/club/tavern offering in-house dining ranging from snack-bar to casual, to fine dining and banquets.

- **Restaurant in a Resort:** A restaurant located within a resort, offering an in-house dining experience influenced by the theme of the resort.
- **Restaurant in a Spa:** Dining facility within a spa expected to serve healthy food choices.
- **Restaurant in a Theatre:** Theatre with dinner prior to the show, usually self-serve buffets. See also **Entertainment Restaurant.**
- **Restaurant in a Winery:** Restaurant within or adjacent to the premises of a winery, most commonly trying to pair its wines with carefully selected entrees. See also **Restaurant in a Brewery.**
- **Seafood Restaurant:** Specializing in seafood; offers a wide array of fish and shellfish prepared in a variety of ways.
- **Specialty Restaurant:** (also see **Ethnic Restaurant**) Specializing in a particular multicultural or religious cuisine not specifically accommodated by any other listed categories (vegetarian, vegan, etc.).
- **Steak House, Restaurant:** Red meat is primary focus. Usually offering salad bars and other items such as poultry, seafood and pasta. Most menu offerings are à la carte including side dishes.
- **Sushi or Oyster Bar:** Usually located within a restaurant, supermarket, or delicatessen, serving raw and specialty seafood items.
- **Themed Restaurant:** Part of a chain or franchise that has a distinctive, deliberate and consistent themed image or brand (Red Lobster, Jack Astor, Olive Garden, Mr. Greek, Rainforest Cafe, etc.).
- **Vegetarian/Vegan Restaurant:** Specializing in serving vegan and/or vegetarian dishes.
- **For some extravagantly themed restaurants visit:** http://weburbanist.com/2008/08/10/15-of-the-strangest-themed-restaurants-from-buns-and-guns-to-cannabalistic-sushi/

As you may be able to appreciate, each of the before mentioned establishments will have their own expectation of profit, associated sales and costs.

Popular Selling Price Methods and Calculations

In order to establish a *Selling Price* many important factors need to be considered. As seen from the preceding Demographic study, Psychographics and Completive analysis, it is important to select the appropriate Theme and Concept for the area and offer competitive Selling prices.

Themes and Concepts

The Process of Establishing Themes and Concepts

Basically there are three types of restaurant styles:

1. *Fast food or quick service*—Offering limited menu items that can be prepared quickly. These locations often feature eat in, take-out areas, and drive-thru windows.

2. *Mid scale or family type*—Offer full meals at a medium price that customers perceive as "good value." They can be full service, buffets, or limited service establishments with customers ordering at the counter and having their food brought to them.

3. *Upscale or fine dining*—Offer high-quality cuisine at high-end prices. They usually provide well-trained service, a maître d', often a sommelier, and feature a high quality of ambience.

What kind/type of restaurant to open is a complex decision, based on many factors: How does this establishment fit into your, or the corporate, business plan? What are the primary focuses? What are the goals and objectives? Should it be part of a chain, have its own identity, be franchised or a sole proprietor, unique, extravagant, exclusive, or accommodating to the majority of potential customers **(based on demographics)**?

Once these important decisions have been made, everything that follows will need to conform—from the dining room layout and design, the kitchen and bar, catering and take-out, to what type of menu(s), and the number of people needed to cover all positions and shifts.

Many things need to be decided upon selecting your restaurant's concept. Perhaps an important question to ask is: "What kind of restaurant would I want to eat in every day? The final selection of the concept must instill confidence and comfort to you, investors, suppliers, and all other creditors.

An equally important question to ask is: **"What kind of restaurant is sustainable in this demographic area?"** Most populated areas have established restaurants and, subsequently, there is competition. The type of competition identified through a **competitive analysis** might be difficult to avoid altogether; perhaps the best way to beat the competition is to offer something different than the existing establishments.

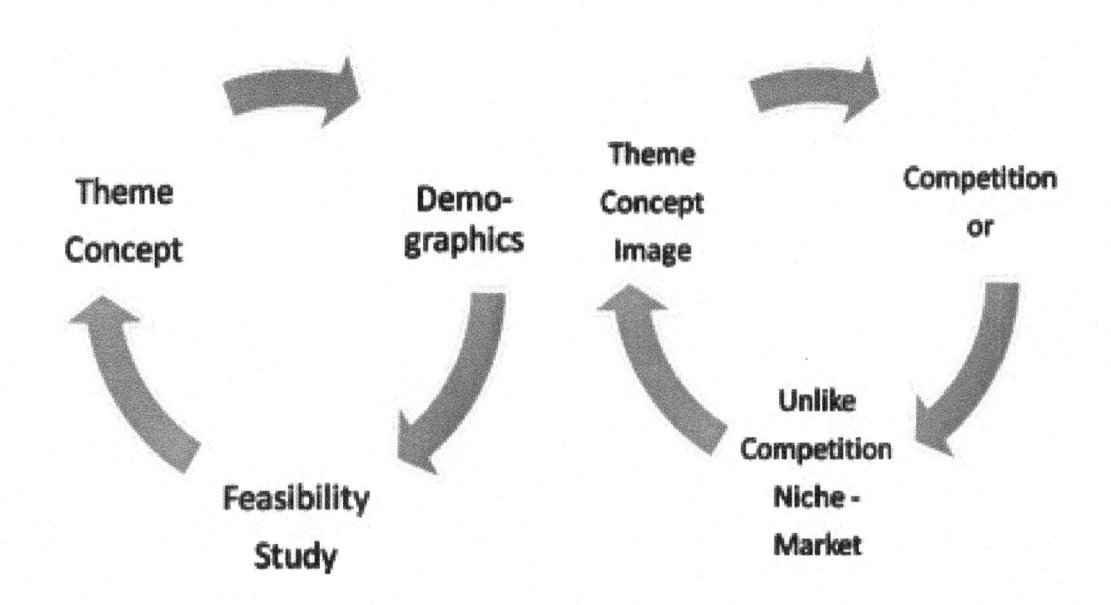

Theme Concept → Demographics → Theme Concept Image → Competition or Unlike Competition Niche-Market → Feasibility Study → Theme Concept

If the demographic area already has one or several Oriental restaurants, perhaps instead of opening a Chinese or Thai restaurant, a Malaysian or Vietnamese theme would not be a **"head-on competition"**; however, it potentially would attract the same clientele as the Chinese or Thai establishment.

Another example: if there is already a strong presence of Italian restaurants, a Mediterranean restaurant encompassing specialities from all the Mediterranean countries—which would be different enough not to be a head-on competition—may attract a larger cluster of potential customers.

Concept Considerations

The Potential Customer Base

Downtown office employees will most likely go to a nearby place for lunch but will eat dinner in the area where they live or go home to come back to the city for an evening out.

Suburban residents will most likely be going to town (suburban downtown area or next larger cities downtown) for an evening out but will stay in the neighbourhood for an everyday meal.

The Type of Eatery

Will there be a need or sensible reason to have one, or all, of the various licences to serve alcoholic beverages? Will the type of customer you are serving be able to drink alcoholic beverages—office workers, students, adolescents, families? Is the eatery specialized through its appearance—type or style—to serve a specific type of customer? That is, fast food, fine dining, family type, tourist attraction, catering, institutional, etc.

Atmosphere

The theme and concept, its make-up and menu must be a reflection of the atmosphere or, in reverse, must create an atmosphere.

Customers will have a perception prior to entering the establishment of "what they should expect" based on the name, make-up, advertising, and decor of the building, and subsequent to entering will either be neutral, satisfied, pleasantly surprised, or disappointed.

Their expectations of the offerings, documented on the menu(s), the personality of the staff, followed by the quality, taste, and presentation of the menu items and the availability of appropriately matching beverage selection and the perceived value of this expectation will further influence their feeling of neutrality, satisfaction, being pleasantly surprised, or disappointment.

Workforce

As previously mentioned the type of establishment and the result of a feasibility study will ultimately determine the requirement for labour needs. Should the open positions be staffed by trained, qualified and experienced staff or are trainable and inexperienced workers sufficient?

The type of eatery does commit to a certain level of service that customers expect—from someone who flips hamburgers to an executive chef who directs a brigade of chefs and cooks; from counter or buffet service to tableside cooking; from a beverage menu to a sommelier. In each situation, there is a tremendous difference in training, qualifications, expertise, and subsequent remuneration.

Cost of "Type" of Business

Although it is not within the mandate of this book, I do want to mention that the type of eatery will strongly determine the business costs, as well as the cost of developing that business. If it is a franchise, the popularity of the franchise sometimes out-values the structural cost; that is, it might be less costly to build the actual building than to purchase the franchise rights including the theme, concepts, its popularity and perceived future earning power.

Concept Checklist

A restaurant concept is the result of combined characteristics:

- ▶ Physical establishment—type of eatery
- ▶ Type of potential customer
- ▶ Unrestricted menus vs. limited menus
- ▶ Eat in, take out, delivery
- ▶ Caterings, in house, on location, personal chef services
- ▶ Atmosphere
- ▶ Level of service and expertise
- ▶ Among many more considerations

Your **concept** should be different enough to clearly separate your idea from the competition.

The clarity of your concept is very important. If your concept is not understood or sounds too extravagant or out-of-place it may not attract the customers you would like to have.

To introduce a new concept can carry high advertising costs, and it may take longer than anticipated for customers to buy into the concept.

Great care must be taken when pricing your menu items. Competition indirectly dictates the menu prices and, unless your dishes are quite different than the competitors, potential customers may not be prepared to pay more than what the competition is charging.

A menu must be designed with attractive and popular menu items that should be easily cross-utilized to minimize waste and to limit the need for storing a great variety of different products.

Every perishable product purchased, ideally, should be able to be utilized in at least two different menu offerings or menu items that differentiate themselves through diverse cooking methods. The same raw product should transform into different dishes using a variety of cooking methods.

Additionally, offered menu items should be priced not only on product cost but also considering the actual labour involvement. From a labour perspective, it is a lot cheaper to grill a steak than to prepare an open-faced sandwich, while a steak will yield a much higher menu selling price.

Available equipment should be considered when planning menu items so that equipment and workspace is available, fully utilized, and not overloaded. Overloading equipment could cause delays in preparation and unexpected waiting time for customers. Offering "au gratin" dishes without a salamander could cause considerable problems.

You researched the concept, evaluated all considerations, did your feasibility study and are ready to settle for a specific location when your real estate broker calls you with a new listing you previously did not consider—a great restaurant opportunity, in a great location, in a high traffic area. You must ensure that your concept is compatible with the area of this new location. If the population in this new area is different than the assessed area, you should obtain new demographic data to verify that your concept will still work or make the necessary changes.

Menu or Selling Price Strategies

The Purpose and Process of Calculating a Selling Price and Associated Costs

To write a menu for a restaurant is the foundation of planning for profit. Although it can be fun to offer all the specialties one always wanted to present to the public, it needs to be taken very seriously so that the offerings not only cover the costs incurred, but also to return a profit.

As previously described, a demographic study of the area is essential to ensure the area will appreciate your offerings and that competitors are not outnumbering your concept.

Key Terms

Throughout this publication you have been confronted with many Cost/Profit-related terms that are not unique to the hospitality industry. In any industry specific expressions are being used to convey and discuss business matters in a professional manner. These expressions do change over time and new expressions are being coined frequently. What used to be Room Service is now often referred to as In-Room Dining.

The term Retained Earnings has been shortened to Retention by some users. If attention is paid to what is said or written, terminology conversion is not that difficult to decipher.

Let's look at the term **Planned**. In order to plan something, a considerable thought process is usually followed: **Plans** fulfill a **Desire**. **Anticipation** is used in the planning process. **Target**(s) is/are being identified. **Goals** are being set. **Standards** are being established based on perceived **Ideals**. This process is being **documented**.

A **Projection Forecast** is being prepared (in financial terms, a **Budget**).

The **Budgeted Forecast** is compared with the **Actual** results, and any **Difference** (**Variance**), positive or negative, is being identified and analysed for **Corrective** Actions (**Adjustments**) and for future planning.

Being COST Conscientious:

"In order to be conscientious, one must understand and acknowledge."

One must constantly be on the look-out for COST.

Recognize, monitor, and control planned Cost,

and look-out for Cost occurring that is not planned.

COST is usually expressed as a **FRACTION** of Sale.

Sale or Revenue is always 100%

The FRACTION of Sale or Selling Price is commonly expressed as a Cost Percentage of Sale. The equation to calculate a Derived Cost percentage is: Product Cost (or Cost of Sale), divided by Selling Price (or Sale), times 100 equals Cost percentage.

Example:
Food or Beverage Sale is $10.00.
Cost of Food or Beverage Sale is $4.00.
$ 4.00 ÷ $10.00 = .40 × 100 = 40.00% (Food or Beverage Cost percentage)
C ÷ S (R) × 100 = C %

The Same Formula Applies for Labour Cost Percentage

Selling Price calculation based on Cost percentage: **C ÷ C % = S.P.**
Cost calculation based on S.P. and C %: **S.P. × C % = Cost**
Cost % based on Cost and S.P.: **C ÷ S.P. × 100 = C %**

The aforementioned three formulas are the most often used formulas in Planning for Cost, Selling Prices and Cost Control.

The Factor Method

Selling Price Calculations Using the Factor Method

The Factor method is similar to the percentage method; however, instead of a percentage, a fraction is used based on percentages. Assuming that what you wish to sell (Selling Price) equals 100% or the number 100, the factor is calculated by dividing the percentage into 100. Example: The cost is $5.00, the desired percentage is 28%, 100 divided by 28 equals 3.571. To calculate a selling price using the Factor method, multiply Cost × Factor ($5.00 × 3.571 equals $17.855). In comparison, using the most common method, Cost divided by Cost % ($5.00 divided by 28% equals $17.857). The difference between the two calculations is due to the rounding of decimal places.

	A	B	C	D	E	F	G	H	I	J	K
1	Pricing Factors and/or Multiplier Table (expand to your own use):										
2	Example # 1: 100 divided by 55 equals Factor 0.067 (for accuracy purposes do not round)										
3											
4		100%	/	Cost %	Factor	Cost %	Factor	Cost %	Factor	Cost %	Factor
5	1	100%	÷	15	0.067	21	0.048	27	0.037	33	0.030
6	2	100%	÷	16	0.063	22	0.045	28	0.036	34	0.029
7	3	100%	÷	17	0.059	23	0.043	29	0.034	35	0.029
8	4	100%	÷	18	0.056	24	0.042	30	0.033	36	0.028
9	5	100%	÷	19	0.053	25	0.040	31	0.032	37	0.027
10	6	100%	÷	20	0.050	26	0.038	32	0.031	38	0.026
11	7	100%	÷								
12	8	100%	÷								
13	9	100%	÷								
14	10	100%	÷								

Other Methods of Calculating Selling Prices

▶ **Based on Competition:** Not advisable to use, unless it is a very similar type of operation. Every business will have their unique costs. Business One may have a large amount to invest and subsequently a small mortgage with a small amount of interest to be paid every month in comparison to Business Two who had a smaller capital base to draw from and subsequently a larger mortgage and, because of that, a higher monthly fixed cost. Labour cost very often varies from one establishment to another — one may be family operated while the other depends solely on hired help and may subsequently have a higher labour cost.

- **Based on Uniqueness of Product:** A rare occurrence in our shrinking world of hospitality.
- **Based on Tradition:** No longer affordable in the ever-changing economy and subsequently no longer applicable.
- **Based on What the Market Will Support:** Everybody has a monetary threshold when it comes to "dining out"-related spending, depending on personal needs and circumstances. Caution: If you are able to lower your menu prices in a bad economy, customers may think you are actually overcharging them when times were good.
- **Based on Loss Leader Principle:** Attract customers by offering menu items at a lower than-usual price in the hope that they will consume more regular-priced items. This is a common retail practise.
- **Based on Operator's Profit Expectation:** Self-explanatory — Sometimes not possible because of competition.

Cost Behaviour as Business (Sales) Volume Changes

Demonstrated with two scenarios:

- **Scenario One:** Employees scheduled for normal business based on reservations with unexpected guests arriving in larger or fewer numbers than anticipated.

Staff Schedule Numbers #	Staff Schedule Value $	# of expected Customers	Ratio # Customer to Staff	Ratio $ per Customer	Change in # of Customers	Ratio $ per Staff	Ratio $ per Customer
12	$1,344.00	150	12.5	$8.96	180	15	$7.47
12	$1,344.00	150	12.5	$8.96	120	10	$11.20

- **Scenario Two:** Changes of Overhead cost per unit if more or less units than expected are being sold.

Average Overhead Cost per Month $	Average number of Units Sold per month #	Average Overhead Cost per Unit $	Change to: +/– Number of Units Sold #	Change to +/– Dollar per Unit	Difference +/– Positive Negative
$2,000.00	20,000	$00.10	25,000	$00.08	180
$2,000.00	20,000	$00.10	17,000	$00.12 ($00.11765)	($00.02)

Gross Profit Pricing

Gross Profit (Sales minus COGS) is an Income Statement calculation and expression that can also be applied to individual menu items (Selling Price minus Product Cost). Remaining costs include: Alternative, Fixed, and Semi-Variable Costs.

To apply this method, you must establish the Average Gross Profit for each Menu Item (Gross Profit divided by Number of Customers served).

Once this figure has been established, it is used as a basis for calculations.

Example: Gross Profit is $150,000.00. Number of Customers served during this period were 30,000. The Gross Profit per customer is $5.00. Cost of Product is $1.25.

(Gross Profit of $150,000.00 divided by 30,000 Customers equals Average Gross Profit per Customer.)

Once the Average Gross Profit has been established, the pricing method is quite simple. The Selling Price is calculated by adding the Average Gross Profit and the Cost of Product ($5.00 plus $1.25 equals SP $6.25). This method is particularly useful to achieve an appropriate Selling Price if the calculated menu items have a vast difference in cost.

Gross Profit Pricing example/comparison
by Klaus Theyer C.C.C.

Name of Item	Recipe Cost $	Desired Cost %	Calculated Selling Price $	Gross Profit $ expectation	Calculated Selling Price $	Menu Price $	Actual Cost %
Beef Consommé	0.87	20%	4.35	5.00	5.87	6.00	14.50%
Vegetable Soup	0.95	20%	4.75	5.00	5.95	6.00	15.83%
Birds Nest Soup	1.75	20%	8.75	5.00	6.75	8.00	21.88%
Spaghetti	1.75	30%	5.83	5.00	6.75	9.00	19.44%
Pastrami Sandwich	1.25	30%	4.17	5.00	6.25	8.00	15.63%
Beef Steak	4.00	30%	13.33	5.00	9.00	14.00	28.57%
Lobster	8.00	30%	26.67	5.00	13.00	20.00	40.00%

In the example provided, different Desired Cost percentages were applied for the different menu items (groups). It is quite common to apply different percentages for offered items (groups), such as Appetizers, Soups, and Salads; Main Courses and Desserts; and Beverages.

At this point, I believe I have covered the most popular methods of Selling Price calculations; however, as more books are read about this topic, you will be confronted with more methods. Following are names and short explanations of methods to be considered.

- **Variable Cost Pricing:** Grouped menu items using different Cost percentages to calculate Selling Prices.
- **Combined and Product Cost and Labour Cost Pricing:** Similar to Prime Cost Pricing, exact Product Cost and exact Labour Cost (instead of percentages) for the produced menu item is used for calculation.
- **All and/or Actual Cost Pricing:** (Not common in Food Service): This method requires accurate and up-to-date Actual Cost information for the whole operation (Product Cost, Labour Cost, Operating Cost and Alternative Cost (Profit)).

All Costs are added and divided by the number of items produced, resulting in Selling Price for this item.

Cost Plus Pricing (Simplified Method)

Similar to Gross Profit Pricing. Management calculated the Average Cost for each patron and the Desired Profit for each patron; by adding the two numbers and the Product Cost, the Selling Price has been established.

(Formulae: Total Fixed Cost divided by Number of Units Sold equals Fixed Cost Per Unit Sold plus Units VC plus Profit expectation equals Selling Price. (FXC ÷ Number of Units Sold = FXC per Unit + VC + Profit = S.P.))

One Selling Price Method

This method of applying a Fixed Selling Price for each item in a group of items is often applied to menu offerings, such as Soups, Salads and Desserts; main course groups such as Pasta, Fish, Veal and Beef; and beverages such as domestic beers, imported beers, domestic wines, imported wines, etc. This method discourages the consumer from selecting menu items based on their budget and allows them to pick and choose from same-priced items within a category.

Market or Seasonal Pricing

Based on availability and demand for product. Some products are only available for a limited period of time due to growing or harvesting seasonality and production limitations; for example, White Asparagus (high season May to June) or Beaujolais Nouveau, which is annually released at one minute past midnight on the third Thursday of November from little villages and towns in France.

Psychological Method (Odd and Prestige), Competitive Pricing

Psychological Pricing is intended to influence the customers' perception of the actual price of a product. Two common forms of psychological pricing are **odd/even pricing** and **prestige pricing.**

http://www.businessdictionary.com/definition/odd-even-pricing.html

The Psychological pricing method is based on the belief that certain prices or price ranges are more appealing to buyers. This method involves setting a price in odd and/or even numbers (just under round even numbers) such as $19.95 instead of $20.00.

Originally, this practice was meant to prevent pilfering of cash by forcing a cashier to open the cash register (to pay change to the customer) and thus register the transaction. Although not conclusively supported by any research findings, its proponents claim that the consumers see a $19.95 price as "just above $10.00" and not as "just below $20.00."

A buyer will pass along the price as being lower than it is either because they recall it being lower than the even number or they want to impress others with their success in obtaining a good value. For instance, in our example, a buyer who pays $29.95 may tell a friend they paid "a little more than $20" for the product when in fact it was much closer to $30.00.

Prestige Pricing

Another psychological effect, called prestige pricing, points to a strong correlation between perceived product quality and price. The higher the price the more likely customers are to perceive it as being higher quality compared to a lower-priced product. (Although there is a point at which customers will begin to question the value of the product if the price is too high.) In fact, the less a customer knows about a product the more likely they are to judge the product as being of higher quality based on only knowing the price. Prestige pricing can also work with odd/even pricing as marketers, looking to present an image of high quality, may choose to price products at even levels (e.g., $10.00 rather than $9.95). Read more:

http://www.businessdictionary.com/definition/odd-even-pricing.html#ixzz11GYezM42

On the next page is a formulae table which contains the most often used cost-calculation formulas applied in our industry.

Sales, Cost, Cost %, formulae, by Klaus Theyer CCC

Explanation of abbreviations:
S.P. = Selling Price,   **C** = Cost,
C % = Cost percentage,
COGS = Cost Of Goods Sold,
R or Rev = Revenue,

The "4" basic formulas to calculate either Cost, Selling Price or Cost percentage:

(If your calculator has a % key and if you use it you may omit the x 100)

$$\text{COST} \div \text{COST \%} = \text{S.P.}$$

$$\text{S.P.} \times \text{COST \%} = \text{COST}$$

$$\text{COST} \div (\text{S.P.} \times 100) = \text{COST \%}$$

$$\text{COST} \times \text{Factor} = \text{S.P.}$$

Chapter 8

Purchasing, Receiving, Storing, Inventory and Inventory Costing—Simplified

Edited by Eric Nadeau, Acheteur Regional, Quebec & Ottawa—
Regional Buyer, Quebec & Ottawa

Fairmont Le Reine Élizabeth—Fairmont The Queen Elizabeth Hotel,
900 Boul. René Lévesque Ouest, Montréal, QC, H3B 4A5, Canada

The **"Theme"** and **"Concept"** of the establishment will lead to purchasing "Standards"

The industry readily accepts the four "W's" of purchasing;

"WHY" *(need)*

"WHAT" *(item)*

"WHEN" *(date & time needed)*

"WHERE" *(from)*

Purchasing is based on standards specific to the individual establishment or chains. Every individual establishment is unique in their needs; hence they will have different standards based on their theme and concept. Just by looking at the different types of establishments, one can imagine the different fare being offered and the different products being procured.

"WHAT"

Each of the illustrated food service establishments have considerably different offerings on their menus and subsequently need different products to serve their customers' needs and expectations.

"WHY"

Because there is a **"Need."** By offering Food and Beverage items on the respective menu(s), a justifiable need is created that allows for procurement of these items.

From the two **"Bills of fare"** groups—Food and Beverage "Standard Recipes" are being created.

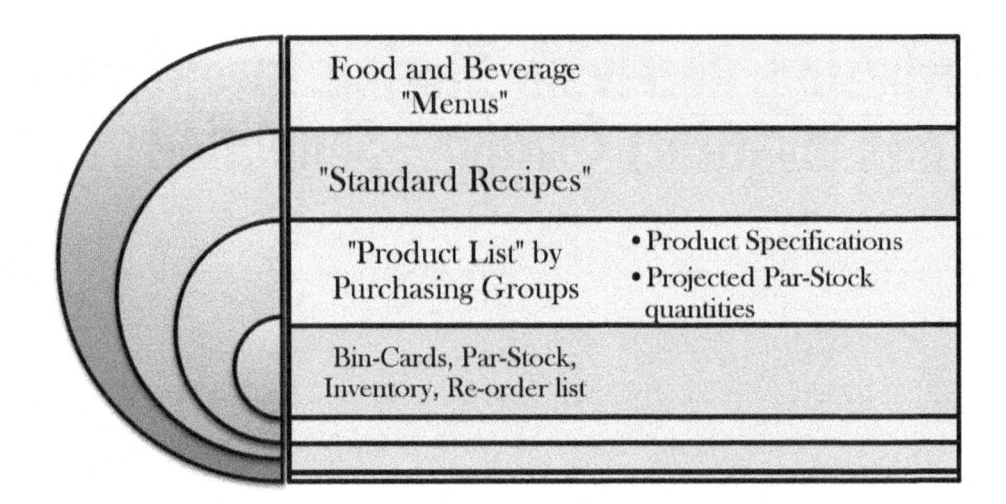

Food and Beverage "Menus"

"Standard Recipes"

"Product List" by Purchasing Groups
- Product Specifications
- Projected Par-Stock quantities

Bin-Cards, Par-Stock, Inventory, Re-order list

All offered menu items should be derived from cost-extended standard recipes. The products identified on these recipes need to have clearly defined standards of quality. **This is achieved by completing a "Purchase Specification Form."**

The purpose of a Product specification form is to document the expected standard for products based on all or some of the listed criteria. This form(s) may also be used, in a summary format, and referred to as a market or call sheet sorted into the food groups or potential suppliers for each food group. Example: Rice would be Dry goods.

Sample

Name or description of item. Example: Beef Rib-Eye—NAMP (National Association of Meat Purveyors), CMC (Canadian Meat Council) 112.

- ▲ **Package—Size—Dimensions:** Insulated Cardboard, N/A, N/A.
- ▲ **Weight—Volume—Count—Pieces:** Four to a case, Vacuum packed, 3.9 to 4.1 kg each
- ▲ **Place of Origin:** Canada or U.S.
- ▲ **Grade—Canadian or Equivalent:** Canada AAA from Angus, or Sterling Silver or Blackwell Cattle. Canada AAA would compare to USDA Choice.
- ▲ **Quality description:** Aged for a specific number of days. Dry-aged.
- ▲ **Purchasing quantity:** Two cases per week
- ▲ **Price per unit (expected):** $10.50 per kg
- ▲ **Rebate expected:** 2% for COD and 2% for orders exceeding $1500.00 within four weeks
- ▲ **Value considerations/adjustments:** N/A (This scenario applies in most cases to products prepared and/or packaged to your specification—such as dressings, marinades, condiments, toiletry, beverages. Due to the custom labelling/packaging there might be an upcharge that makes it necessary to consider its **value and potential benefit**.)

Product Specification Form:	
Name:	
Brand Name:	
Package type/material:	
Pkg. Size-Dimension:	
Weight-Volume-Count-Pieces:	
Place of Origin:	
Grade: Canadian or equivalent:	
Quality defined/described:	
Additional Information:	
Purchasing Quantity:	
Purchasing Frequency Daily/Weekly/Monthly:	
Rebate expected based on volume (# &/or $):	
Value Consideration (Own label):	

FOR INTERNAL USE ONLY: (Sent to Supplier)	A	B	C	D
A:				
B:				
C:				
D:				

Other description examples could include:

- ▶ The product purchased being a cucumber; should it be straight or curved?
- ▶ If the product is a strip loin or a filet, if not the whole, is it a centre cut?
- ▶ If the product is a whole strip or filet, how much fat is to be trimmed?
- ▶ If the product is boned-filleted fish, has the bone been added back for weighing?

"WHEN" and "WHERE"

The last two of the **"4 W's"** in purchasing refer to **TIME** and **WHERE** the product should be purchased.

The less time there is to look for competitively priced items, based on purchase specifications, the more likely it is to pay a premium price for it. Worse, it may not be obtainable when needed.

The task to find reputable suppliers follows some established procedures that are being challenged by the availability of "One-stop-buying" for most of, if not all, of your required products.

Note: On the bottom of the "Product specification form" there is a check-box for sending the "Spec" to Supplier A, B, C, or D for a price quotation. Once an answer is received it is recorded on a "Market" or "Call-sheet," aiding in the decision process of selecting specific suppliers for the type of comparable product. Most suppliers no longer participate in this rather time-consuming method of quoting prices item-for-item; instead, they will supply you with their product list identifying the type, quality, and cost of products they carry.

Purchasing from Multiple Vendors

The established way of purchasing requires you to compare prices and other conditions from at least three different potential suppliers (vendors) based on your purchase specifications and to buy from two or more different suppliers.

Advantages

- ▶ Ability to negotiate based on competitive offers.
- ▶ Selection of best supplier for specific products.
- ▶ Simplified credit/debit procedures.
- ▶ Personalized service from knowledgeable vendor representative.

Disadvantages

- ▶ Frequency of different deliveries.
- ▶ Various credit arrangements.
- ▶ Considerable amount of time invested in ordering, tracking and receiving products and monitoring each vendor's invoice due dates.
- ▶ Possibly more expensive if purchased from a small supplier.

Purchasing from One-Stop Vendors

In comparison, one-stop vendors may not provide a selection of different levels of quality products within one group of products. Due to the many varieties one-stop vendors carry, the representative may not have the intimate product knowledge you expect. However, the benefit is simplified accounting—one vendor, one credit arrangement, and one invoice—rather than credit and debit procedures adhering to acceptable accounting principles involving considerable paperwork.

Note: Recently some One-stop vendors have and are merging with small suppliers to be able to offer specialty items or products they are unable to warehouse themselves; i.e., GFS purchased or is working together with companies specializing in portioned meat and fish products. SYSCO purchased or is working together with Produce companies to be able to comply with customers' requests.

Both scenarios have obvious advantages and disadvantages—you must decide which is the most suitable method accommodating your needs.

The Purchasing Process

Needed products are identified by departments using Requisitions. These documents are forwarded to Stores/Purchasing office. They will be collated and sorted into Purchasing groups. Suppliers/Vendors are being selected by "Searching the market" using a "Market/Call" sheet, which contains the following info:

Product Category	Vendor "A"	Vendor "B"	Vendor "C"	Purchase from:
Product Name:	Co$t	Co$t	Co$t	A, B or C

The decision of who to buy from is NOT solely based on price: Other factors to be taken in consideration include credit arrangements, reputation of supplier, sanitary conditions, ability to deliver when needed, accessibility, discounts, services (salesperson, computer software, equipment), etc.

Upon selection of a Vendor, a P.O. (Purchase Order) with a unique number (unwritten contract) and specified shipping instructions is issued to the Vendor.

All Purchase Orders (P.O.) should bear a unique number. This number is issued by the Purchaser. By issuing a P.O. # you are entering into an unwritten contract, which, in simple terms, has the following meaning: The Vendor agrees to fill the order "as ordered" based on the supplied purchase specifications and shipped within the stipulated time frame. The authorized Purchaser agrees to receive the shipped goods, provided that they are "as ordered," and to pay for them on time. A P.O. # may be issued with each individual order or as a "Blanket" order for a period of time with one specific supplier.

Upon receipt and examination of the ordered goods, the Invoice is compared to the P.O. for accuracy in quantity, quality and price of the items shipped. If everything is "as ordered" the Invoice is signed by the authorized receiver and the products are directed to the appropriate areas (Requisitioner—Storage—Production—Sales).

If there are discrepancies between the P.O. and Invoice, a Credit or Debit note, as appropriate, must be issued (Accounting procedure).

A Credit note, issued by the Vendor's representative (Driver), allows the Vendor to Credit your account with the value (Cost) of the returned goods.

A Debit note, issued by the Purchaser/Receiver, allows the Vendor to Debit your account for goods that were shipped to you but were not ordered by you or were not on your invoice, but you decided to keep them.

All transactions (Date, Time, Invoice #, P.O. #, Credit/Debit notes) are recorded on a **Receiving Summary Sheet.** This receiving summary sheet and all Invoice #, P.O. #, Credit/Debit notes are sent to the Accounting department for timely payment, and copies are being sent to Stores/Purchasing for reconciliation/control.

Helpful Steps "Prior" to Selecting a Purveyor/Vendor

- ▶ Check Vendor's premises for sanitary standards
- ▶ Make a "credit check" (especially when considering contract buying)
- ▶ Make reference calls
- ▶ Meet sales representative—your first link to new products
- ▶ Discuss suitable credit arrangements
- ▶ Verify delivery conditions and frequency
- ▶ Specify conditions for substitutions of products

Helpful Steps "After" Selecting a Purveyor

- ▶ Monitor delivery terms and times
- ▶ Periodic "re-checking" of premises for sanitary standards
- ▶ Encourage visits of sales representative to provide samples and discuss new products
- ▶ Establish a list of persons with "ordering" authority to avoid duplicate orders
- ▶ Establish acceptable ordering methods; that is, issuance of P.O.#, telephone orders from identified authorized individuals only

- Establish a list of persons with "signing" authority for Invoices and "Debit notes"
- Do periodic checks to verify quality as specified and quantity as ordered
- Do periodic market price checks for price comparison with other suppliers

It is very important to establish a good relationship, built on trust, with your vendors/purveyors. Discrepancies such as short or over shipments of orders can be resolved in an amicable fashion.

Common Purchasing Methods

- **"Call or Market Sheet"** buying, as previously mentioned, refers to comparing quotations from no less than three potential suppliers.
- **"Blank cheque"** buying refers to purchasing at any cost.
- **"Cost plus"** buying refers to the Vendor's cost plus other charges. Be fully aware what other charges could be before entering a deal. Example: If it says that the goods are **F.O.B.** Vancouver, it means the "freight on board" is paid for up to Vancouver, but shipping from Vancouver to your city is your responsibility.
- **"Bidding—Open or Sealed"** a formal method of buying—the Buyer invites several purveyors or the open market to quote prices (written) on specific products. Bids are often placed on certain quantities, qualities, packaging, service and frequency; however, it is not uncommon to receive bids based solely on Cost.
- **"Tender"** or tendering is the process of making an offer on a bid. Offers may be conditional.
- **"Contract buying"** often follows the bidding or tendering process and is formalized by a written agreement with very specific terms and payment conditions (up-front, throughout, and at the end of the contract).

Receiving Procedures

- Step one—compare Invoice with Purchase Order
- Step two—count number of boxes and part-boxes and/or weigh product
- Step three—open boxes with knife and check content for: appropriate quantity, quality, freshness, signs of defrosting, dampness
- Step four—if everything is OK sign invoice
- Step five—if there are discrepancies, tape or tie open boxes for return and request a "Credit note" from driver clearly identifying the returned product type, quantity, and cost; otherwise, if extra product was shipped that you wish to keep, issue a "Debit note" to the driver clearly identifying the retained product type, quantity and cost.
- Step six—record delivery on the "Receiving summary sheet" as well as any Credit or Debit note.
- Step seven—load products on a platform truck or similar device and distribute to the requisitioner or the appropriate storage area/facility (dry, refrigerated store or freezer)
- **Step eight—update bin cards**

A recommended practice at the point of receiving is to have a scale which can print the weight of received goods directly on the invoice to confirm the received weight. Remember to remove ice or other cooling or packaging material prior to weighing.

All products should be labelled with the receiving and expiry date for proper stock rotation and inventory control.

Bin Card					
Product Name: Tomato paste					
A.P. Information: Catelli			Product #: 00001		
Unit Information: 1 cs = 12 × 2 ltr cans					
Date:	Quantity IN:	Cost:	Date:	Quantity OUT:	Balance:
01/01/XXXX	24	60.00			24
			02/01/XXXX	3	21
			03/01/XXXX	9	12
04/01/XXXX	12	30.00			24
			05/01/XXXX	15	9
Totals:	36	90.00	31/01/XXXX	27	9

Inventory

Perpetual Inventory

A functional option in addition to the Perpetual Inventory is a "Par-stock — Purchasing — Re-order add-on" with an estimated cost calculator built-in.

Perpetual Inventory from Bin-Card:

Product Name:	Product Code/SKU	Period ending: DD/MM/YY	Quantity IN # #:	A.P. Cost $	Quantity OUT: DD/MM/YY # #:		Perpetual Inventory	Actual Inventory	(Act-Perp) Variance	Actual Inventory Cost
Tomato Paste Catelli (12 x 2)	0001	xx/xx/xxxx	36	90.00	xx/xx/xxxx	27	9	8	-1	20.00
Next item										
Next item										
TOTALS	xxxxxxxx	xxxxxxxx	36	90.00	xxxxxxxx	27	9	8	-1	20.00

Purchasing Information:

Par Stock #:	Re-Order Quantity:	Cost of Re-Order:
20	12	30.00
20	12	30.00

Four illustrations of blank and completed *Perpetual Food* and *Beverage Inventory* sheets are appended at the end of this chapter.

Par-Stock Definition

Quantity on-hand to operate for a specific period of time. Although there are no specific guidelines, it is the author's opinion to have a minimum of two days of perishable goods on hand prior to the next delivery. Dry goods are usually less fragile and subsequently often bought in larger quantities and should be on a separate par-stock list than perishable items.

Physical Inventory

Inventory Sheet	Inventory area:						
Taken by:	Date:		Extended by:			Date:	
						Order up to Par-stock	
ITEM-BRAND DESCRIPTION	Item Weight/Size Count/Vol.	Unit Size Count	Unit #'s in Stock	Cost per Unit	Inventory Extended Cost $	Par Stock	Re-order #'s Units
Tomato Paste	Case/ 12/ 2L	1 x 2L	8	2.50	20.00	20	12
					0.00		0
					0.00		0
					0.00		0
					0.00		0
					0.00		0
					0.00		0
					0.00		0
					0.00		0

Number of items in Inventory: 8

Value of Inventory $: 20.00

Don't Just Count Your Inventory, Control It

FIFO (First In First Out) rules—Label food products with the receiving date, expiration date, and proper (usage) description. Inventory, simply put, is the quantity of goods on hand. In the food service business, we purchase raw foods, products, and materials, convert them into menu-able products for our guests and, hopefully, produce profits for our operation in the process. To be a successful Chef, Food and Beverage manager or Kitchen manager you need to positively impact profitability by controlling Product and Labour Cost.

Inventory for Profit

Basic inventory management procedures center around having just enough of what is needed (given period of time) and limiting waste, thereby maximizing profits.

Taking Inventory

For maximum control, inventory should be taken daily—alternatively, weekly, monthly or quarterly. By law, in order to produce an Income Statement, inventory needs to be taken once a year. Although daily inventory is labour intensive, if it is narrowed down to costly items it will provide important data. Apparent theft, inappropriate handling, spoilage, and breakage can be addressed in a timely fashion. Once a week, or month, has gone by, it is almost impossible to find out what caused shortages. Inventory items need to be assessed for validity with the item removed from menu, yet still in inventory.

A commonly used inventory method is the A, B, C method.

A Daily/Weekly High value, easily transportable, as well as perishable. Re-order on an as-needed basis only.	B Weekly/Monthly Lesser value than A, expiration date (aroma, freshness, temperature, humidity) sensitive.	C Monthly/Quarterly Least costly, not perishable, common ingredient, large quantity-discount purchasing.

Managing your business utilizing inventory information by preparing a simple internal income statement

Revenue minus C.O.G.S. (O.I. + P. − C.I.) = G.P. or C.M.

Revenue minus C.O.G.S. (Cost of Goods Sold) equals Gross Profit or CM Contribution Margin.

In this case, Actual Food or Beverage Cost %, compared to Projected Cost %, will allow you to detect differences (variances) and subsequently provide you with maximum control.

Many businesses utilize computer software P.O.S. (Point of Sales Systems) connected to an Inventory System providing a great variety of reports at will. In order to calculate the C.O.G.S. one must know the Value of the O.I. (Opening Inventory) and the C.I. (Closing Inventory) and the Purchases.

Inventory Turnover

Usually it is the Chef's and/or Manager's responsibility to ensure that there is sufficient product on hand to operate for a determined period of time. Insufficient stock and stockpiling could lead to problems, such as: Increased food cost due to spoilage, expired/stale dated product, excessive amounts of money tied up in products for sale, labour cost in moving inventory around, increased opportunity for theft, and possibly accidents caused by tight spaces.

A common technique used in establishing and monitoring inventory adequacy is to calculate how often inventory items have been purchased within an accounting period (usually one month). This purchasing frequency will depend on many factors, such as inventory space, market price of products, and available cash to be tied-up in storage.

To measure how frequently inventory has been consumed (used-up) and re-stocked during an accounting period, management uses an Inventory turnover calculation method — also referred to as Rate of Inventory turnover.

Firstly it must be acknowledged that not all products purchased are intended to turn over within one accounting period. Perishables should be turned over considerably more often while products that improve with age, such as some wines, may be kept purposely for an extended period of time.

Inventory Rate Formulae

Average Inventory = $\dfrac{\text{Opening Inventory (O.I.) plus (+) Closing Inventory (C.I.)}}{\text{divided by 2}}$ = Average

Inventory turnover = $\dfrac{\text{Product Cost (Food or Beverage)}}{\text{divided by Average Inventory}}$

Food Cost = $18,500.00

Applied Example

Avg. Inv. = $\dfrac{\text{O.I. \$7,655.00 plus C.I. (\$7,775.00)}}{\text{divided by 2}}$ = ($7,715.00)

INV. TURNOVER CALC. = $\dfrac{\text{Food Cost} = \$18,500.00}{\text{divided by \$7,715.00 equals}}$ = 2.398 or 2.4

In the above example, provided the inventory rate is consistently 2.4, the inventory rate for the year will be 28.8 times, or once every 1.806 weeks. Most establishments consider inventory sufficient if it lasts for one to two weeks. Using two weeks as a guideline, the provided example is slightly less than the guideline.

Product Inventory Extended Cost Calculations

As previously mentioned, every company must report the value of their inventory at least once a year. Product inventory is a "Short-term asset" and is listed on a "Balance Sheet" in the group of Assets.

There are five methods of calculating the value of the inventory. You may select any one of them, but you may not select more than one method for one operating period (maximum one year).

ACTUAL Cost Approach: In this method the unit cost of each purchase during the inventory period is multiplied by the number of remaining units from each period. See the following example. This method works well if the product has been marked with cost price stickers (# of units times cost of unit as purchased).

L.P.P. (Last Purchase Price Cost Approach): In this method it is assumed that the "Last invoiced" price is the price you paid throughout the reporting period. This method is the easiest of the four methods and commonly used by small businesses since invoices don't need to be researched. This method is often mistaken with the LIFO approach.

L.I.F.O. (Last In First Out Cost Approach): In this method the purchase price from the Opening Inventory and subsequent purchases during the inventory period, up to the number of items in inventory, is used to calculate the value of the inventory. This method is used, if applicable, to utilize the lowest purchase cost to deflate the value of the inventory, increasing the Cost of Goods Sold and subsequently reducing net income.

F.I.F.O. (First In First Out—Average of Last Purchases): In this method the cost of the remaining units as purchased during the inventory period is divided by the number of units bought, and the resulting average unit cost is multiplied with the number of units in stock.

Chapter 8 Purchasing, Receiving, Storing, Inventory and Inventory Costing—Simplified

Weighted AVERAGE Cost Approach: In this method the cost of all purchases during the inventory period plus the cost of the Opening Inventory is divided by the number of units bought and the units from the opening inventory. The resulting average unit cost is multiplied with the number of units in stock. Because of its complexity and accuracy, this method is the basis of commonly used computer inventory programs.

I suggest you consult an accountant before implementing any of these methods.

"Konrads'" Dill Pickles Monthly Inventory

Calculate the $ Value of the Inventory based on the following info:
Purchased item: Dill Pickles (Jar = 2 L)
Purchase Dates and Quantities and Costs: | Par stock | 11 | 2 L Jars |

	Date:	Quantity	Jar/Cost	Ext.Cost	Perpetual	
O.I.	02/01/XX	13	1.95	25.35	13	13
Issued	03/01/XX	3			-3	10
Purch	04/01/XX	7	1.98	13.86	7	17
Issued	08/01/XX	7			-7	10
Purch	11/01/XX	8	2.07	16.56	8	18
Issued	16/01/XX	10			-10	8
Purch	18/01/XX	5	2.14	10.70	5	13
Issued	22/01/XX	5			-5	8
Purch	25/01/XX	8	2.20	17.60	8	16
Issued	28/01/XX	9			-9	7
Purch	31/01/XX	4	2.25	9.00	4	11
Total Purchases only:		32	10.64	67.72		
Total including O.I.:		45	12.59	93.07		

| Avg. Pail Cost As Purchased | 1 | 2.13 | 2.12 |

| Avg. Cost plus Opening Inv. | 1 | 2.10 | 2.07 |

On February 01 Inventory is taken ⇒ | 11 | jars are in stock
What is the Total $ Value of the Inventory using the....

ACTUAL Cost approach:

(Actual Cost of available stock as purchased)

| 24.40 |

L.I.F.O. Cost approach:
(Cost of O.I. and subsequent purchases up to corresponding # of units in inventory)

| 21.45 |

F.I.F.O. Cost approach:

(Average of available stock as purchased)

| 24.38 |

L.P.P. Cost approach:

(Last Cost as purchased is used for calculation)

| 24.75 |

Weighted AVERAGE Cost approach:

(Average of all purchases + O.I.)

| 22.75 |

Four illustrations of blank and completed Perpetual Food and Beverage inventory sheets follow on the next four pages.

Chapter 8 Purchasing, Receiving, Storing, Inventory and Inventory Costing—Simplified

Perpetual Inventory System: Dry Goods
by Klaus Theyer C.C.C.

O.I. or Purchasing Date: _____   Inventory date: _____

#	Product from Bin Card			Product description				Purchased Quantity IN:	Total Purchase Cost:	Inventory Information				Re-Order, Purchase Info		
	Product Name:	Brand Name:	Code #	A.P. Quantity in #	Unit size:	Unit Cost:	Number of Units O.I.			Requisitioned OUT:	Perpetual Inventory:	Actual Inventory:	Inventory Variance:	Inventory Extended Cost:	Par Stock:	Re-Order Quantity:	Cost of Re-Order:
1	Tomato, Paste	Primo	822914	24	369 Ml	1.15	2.00	24		8		17			24		
2	Tomato, Plum Peeled	Stanis	868566	6	100 Oz	3.87	6.00	18		6		18			24		
3	Dressing, Caesar Ultimate	Hellmans	207616	2	4 L	19.20	1.00	1		1		0.5			2		
4	Mayonnaise, Real	Hellmans L/S	621579	2	4 L	16.05	0.50	2		1		1.5			2		
5	Vinegar, Champagne	Vilux	292000	6	750 Ml	2.25	2.00	6		1		6			6		
6	Vinegar, White Pure Distilled	GFS	694134	4	5 L	3.06	1.00	3		1		3			4		
7	Vinegar, Red Wine	GFS	694169	2	5 L	8.45	0.50	2		1		1.5			2		
8	Vinegar, Balsamic	De Nigelo	761842	12	500 Ml	3.38	6.00	6		2		9			12		
9	Capers, small	Kouri	796344	2	4 L	25.30	0.25	2		1		1			2		
10	Pickle, Sour Gherkin	Whyte	208900	2	4 L	13.13	0.00	2		1		1			2		
11	Olive, Queen Stuffed	GFS	101240	2	4 L	17.25	0.50	2		1		0			2		
12	Oil, Olive Pure Kosher	Gallo	847003	6	3 L	20.13	2.00	4		1		5			8		
13	Oil, Olive Xtra Virgin	Horio	153095	1	3 L	164.95	0.25	1		1		0.5			3		
14	Oil, Veg w/antifoam	GFS	722723	1	16 L	20.65	0.50	2		1		1.5			2		
15	Pasta, Fettuccine	GFS	685992	1	9.07 Kg	21.65	0.25	1		1		0			2		
16	Pasta, Penne Rigatte	GFS	686093	1	9.07 Kg	21.65	0.50	1		1		0			1		
17	Pasta, Spaghetti 20"	GFS	685968	1	9.07 Kg	21.45	0.25	1		1		0			1		
18	Rice Arborio Ital	Aurora	809047	1	5 Kg	10.20	0.25	1		1		0.5			1		
19	Rice, Long Grain Converted	Uncle Bens	691801	1	20 Kg	38.60	0.25	0		0		1			1		
20	Spice, Salt Iodized	Sifto	699594	1	20 Kg	10.95	1.00	0		0		1			1		
21	Spice, Salt Sea	T/east	686972	1	1 Kg	7.87	1.00	2		1		2.5			3		
22	Spice, Pepper Blk Cracked	McCormick	809039	1	520 Gr	15.63	0.00	2		1		1			2		
23	Spice, Pepper Blk Fine	T/east	666727	1	540 Gr	13.92	0.25	2		1		1			2		
24	Spice, Pepper Wht Ground	T/east	696579	1	600 Gr	19.01	0.25	2		1		1			2		
25	Spice, Nutmeg Ground	T/east	696471	1	525 Gr	21.50	0.00	1		0		1			1		
26	Spice, Onion Powder	T/east	686875	1	600 Gr	11.55	0.50	1		0		1			1		
27	Spice, Paprika, Hot	T/east	867217	1	540 Gr	8.65	0.00	1		1		0.5			1		
28	Spice, Cinnamon Ground	T/east	686786	1	550 Gr	9.22	0.00	1		1		0.5			1		
29	Herb, Thyme Leaf	T/east	194960	1	175 Gr	6.81	0.50	1		0		0.5			1		
30	Herb, Rosemary Leaf	T/east	696625	1	275 Gr	9.85	0.50	1		0		0.5			1		
31	Herb, Basil Sweet Leaf	T/east	686735	1	190 Gr	5.27	1.00	3		2		1			3		
32	Herb, Bay Leaf Whole	T/east	686743	1	60 Gr	5.85	0.50	1		0		0.25			1		
	TOTALS:																

118 Chapter 8 Purchasing, Receiving, Storing, Inventory and Inventory Costing—Simplified

Perpetual Inventory System: Dry Goods
by Klaus Theyer C.C.C.

O.I. or Purchasing Date: _____   Inventory date: _____

#	Product Name	Brand Name	Code #	A.P. Quantity in #	Unit size	Unit Cost:	Number of Units O.I.	Purchased Quantity IN:	Total Purchase Cost:	Requisitioned OUT:	Perpetual Inventory:	Actual Inventory:	Inventory Variance:	Inventory Extended Cost:	Par Stock:	Re-Order Quantity:	Cost of Re-Order:
1	Tomato, Paste	Primo	822914	24	369 Ml	1.15	2.00	24	27.60	8	18.00	17	-1	19.55	24	7	8.05
2	Tomato, Plum Peeled	Stanis	868566	6	100 Oz	3.87	6.00	18	69.66	6	18.00	18	0	69.66	24	6	23.22
3	Dressing, Caesar Ultimate	Hellmans	207616	2	4 L	19.20	1.00	1	19.20	1	1.00	0.5	-0.5	9.60	2	2	38.40
4	Mayonnaise, Real	Hellmans L/S	621579	2	4 L	16.05	0.50	2	32.10	1	1.50	1.5	0	24.08	2	1	16.05
5	Vinegar, Champagne	Vilux	292000	6	750 Ml	2.25	2.00	6	13.50	1	7.00	6	-1	13.50	6	0	0.00
6	Vinegar, White Pure Distilled	GFS	694134	4	5 L	3.06	1.00	3	9.18	1	3.00	3	0	9.18	4	1	3.06
7	Vinegar, Red Wine	GFS	694169	2	5 L	8.45	0.50	2	16.90	1	1.50	1.5	0	12.68	2	1	8.45
8	Vinegar, Balsamic	De Nigelo	761842	12	500 Ml	3.38	6.00	6	20.28	2	10.00	9	-1	30.42	12	3	10.14
9	Capers, small	Kouri	796344	2	4 L	25.30	0.25	2	50.60	1	1.25	1	-0.25	25.30	2	1	25.30
10	Pickle, Sour Gherkin	Whyte	208900	2	4 L	13.13	0.00	2	26.26	1	1.00	1	0	13.13	2	1	13.13
11	Olive, Queen Stuffed	GFS	101240	2	4 L	17.25	0.50	1	17.25	1	0.50	0	-0.5	0.00	2	2	34.50
12	Oil, Olive Pure Kosher	Gallo	847003	6	3 L	20.13	2.00	4	80.52	1	5.00	5	0	100.65	8	3	60.39
13	Oil, Olive Xtra Virgin	Horio	153095	1	3 L	164.95	0.25	1	164.95	1	0.25	0.5	0.25	82.48	3	3	494.85
14	Oil, Veg w/antifoam	GFS	722723	1	16 L	20.65	0.50	2	41.30	1	1.50	1.5	0	30.98	2	1	20.65
15	Pasta, Fettucine	GFS	685992	1	9.07 Kg	21.65	0.25	1	21.65	1	0.25	0	-0.25	0.00	2	2	43.30
16	Pasta, Penne Rigatte	GFS	686093	1	9.07 Kg	21.65	0.50	1	21.65	1	0.50	0	-0.5	0.00	2	1	21.65
17	Pasta, Spaghetti 20"	GFS	685968	1	9.07 Kg	21.45	0.25	1	21.45	1	0.25	0	-0.25	0.00	1	1	21.45
18	Rice Arborio Ital	Aurora	809047	1	5 Kg	10.20	0.25	1	10.20	1	0.25	0.5	0.25	5.10	1	1	10.20
19	Rice, Long Grain Converted	Uncle Bens	691801	1	20 Kg	38.60	0.25	1	38.60	0	1.25	1	-0.25	38.60	1	0	0.00
20	Spice, Salt Iodized	Sifto	699594	1	20 Kg	10.95	1.00	0	0.00	0	1.00	1	0	10.95	1	0	0.00
21	Spice, Salt Sea	T'east	686972	1	1 Kg	7.87	1.00	2	15.74	1	2.00	2.5	0.5	19.68	3	1	7.87
22	Spice, Pepper Blk Cracked	McCormick	809039	1	520 Gr	15.63	0.00	2	31.26	1	1.00	1	0	15.63	2	1	15.63
23	Spice, Pepper Blk Fine	T'east	686727	1	540 Gr	13.92	0.00	2	27.84	1	1.00	1	0	13.92	2	1	13.92
24	Spice, Pepper Wht Ground	T'east	696579	1	600 Gr	19.01	0.25	2	38.02	1	1.25	1	-0.25	19.01	2	1	19.01
25	Spice, Nutmeg Ground	T'east	696471	1	525 Gr	21.50	0.00	1	21.50	0	1.00	1	0	21.50	1	0	0.00
26	Spice, Onion Powder	T'east	686875	1	600 Gr	11.55	0.50	1	11.55	0	1.50	1	-0.5	11.55	1	0	0.00
27	Spice, Paprika, Hot	T'east	867217	1	540 Gr	8.65	0.00	1	8.65	1	0.00	0.5	0.5	4.33	1	1	8.65
28	Spice, Cinnamon Ground	T'east	686786	1	550 Gr	9.22	0.00	1	9.22	1	0.00	0.5	0.5	4.61	1	1	9.22
29	Herb, Thyme Leaf	T'east	194960	1	175 Gr	6.81	0.50	1	6.81	0	1.50	0.5	-1	3.41	1	1	6.81
30	Herb, Rosemary Leaf	T'east	696625	1	275 Gr	9.85	0.50	1	9.85	0	1.50	0.5	-1	4.93	1	1	9.85
31	Herb, Basil Sweet Leaf	T'east	686735	1	190 Gr	5.27	1.00	3	15.81	0	2.00	1	-1	5.27	3	2	10.54
32	Herb, Bay Leaf Whole	T'east	686743	1	60 Gr	5.85	0.50	1	5.85	0	1.50	0.25	-1.25	1.46	1	1	5.85
	TOTALS:					$ 578.45	29.25	97	$ 904.95	39	87.25	78.75	-8.5	$ 621.12	121	48	$ 960.14

Note: For column R use =roundup(Q8-N8,0) and copy all the way to R39

Chapter 8 Purchasing, Receiving, Storing, Inventory and Inventory Costing—Simplified

Perpetual Inventory System: Bar INVENTORY
by Klaus Theyer C.C.C.

Product from Bin Card:

#	Product Name:	LCBO#	Bottle Content in Ml	O.I. or Purchase Date:	Quantity Purchased IN (btl's)	Unit Cost:	Purchase Cost:	Inventory Date:	Product Requisitioned OUT (btl's)	Perpetual Inventory:	Actual Inventory:	Variance: - or +	Inventory Extended Cost:	Par Stock:	Purchasing: Re-Order Quantity:	Cost of Re-Order:
1	Ballantine	3186	1140		6	36.95			4.5		2			3		
2	Chivas Regal 12Y old	68312	1750		4	95.30			3		1			2		
3	Hpnotiq Liquor	600981	750		6	39.95			5		1			5		
4	Canadian Club	34637	1750		5	52.95			3		2			4		
5	Seagreams Crown Royal	10108	1750		3	59.25			1.75		1			2		
6	J.D. Sour Mash	89177	1136		2	41.95			1		1			2		
7	Alberta Pure Vodka	53082	1750		6	51.20			4		2			3		
8	McGuinness Silk Tassel	39404	1750		4	51.20			2		2			3		
9	Sour Puss	38505	1750		6	48.50			5		1			6		
10	Gilbey's Gin	67166	1750		6	51.45			4		2			4		
11	Tanqueray Dry Gin	96263	1750		3	54.45			1		2			4		
12	Sapphire London Dry	582973	1750		2	54.95			2		1			2		
13	Bacardi Gold Rum	85811	1750		6	52.45			4		2			4		
14	Whalers Vanilla Rum	150102	1136		6	44.95			5		1			6		
15	Lamb's Palm Breeze (P.E.T.)	57893	1750		6	51.20			4		2			3		
16	St Remy Brandy	234203	1750		4	51.45			4		0			4		
17	D'Eaubonne VSOP Napoleon	6320	1140		2	34.15			1.75		0			1		
18	Courvoisier XO	158865	750		2	214.95			1		1			1		
19	Remy Martin XO Excellence	563468	750		2	214.95			1		1			1		
20	Hennessy VSOP	43703	750		2	84.75			1		1			4		
21	Dujardin VSOP Brandy	128413	1140		6	34.15			2		3			2		
22	Janneau Grand Armagnac*	473785	750		4	38.95			3		1			2		
23	Calvados Boulard	296228	750		2	47.45			0.75		1			2		
24	Sauza Silva Tequila	17384	1140		6	46.35			5		1			2		
25	Walkers Peppermint Schnapps	11262	750		3	20.95			2		1			2		
26	Stroh Rum	10101	750		4	54.50			3		1			2		
27	Grand Marnier	187633	1750		4	99.20			2		2			3		
28	Skyy Vodka	6502	750		4	42.95			1		3			3		
29	Kahlua Coffee Liqueur	577973	1750		6	52.95			5		1			3		
30	Tia Maria	630913	750		6	27.95			4		1			3		
31	Drambuie	1867	750		6	41.45			3		3			4		
32	Disaronno Amaretto	31864	375		3	15.95			2		1			2		
	TOTALS:															

120 Chapter 8 Purchasing, Receiving, Storing, Inventory and Inventory Costing—Simplified

Perpetual Inventory System: Bar INVENTORY
by Klaus Theyer C.C.C.

#	Product from Bin Card: Product Name:	LCBO#	Bottle Content in Ml	O.I. or Purchase Date:	Quantity Purchased IN (btl's)	Unit Cost:	Purchase Cost:	Inventory Date:	Product Requisitioned OUT (btl's)	Perpetual Inventory:	Actual Inventory:	Variance: - or +	Inventory Extended Cost:	Par Stock:	Re-Order Quantity:	Cost of Re-Order:
1	Ballantine	3186	1140		6	36.95	221.70		4.5	1.5	2	0.5	73.90	3	1	36.95
2	Chivas Regal 12Y old	68312	1750		4	95.30	381.20		3	1	1	0	95.30	2	1	95.30
3	Hpnotiq Liquor	600981	750		6	39.95	239.70		5	1	1	0	39.95	5	4	159.80
4	Canadian Club	34637	1750		5	52.95	264.75		3	2	2	0	105.90	4	2	105.90
5	Seagreams Crown Royal	10108	1750		3	59.25	177.75		1.75	1.25	1	-0.25	59.25	2	1	59.25
6	J.D. Sour Mash	89177	1136		2	41.95	83.90		1	1	1	0	41.95	2	1	41.95
7	Alberta Pure Vodka	53082	1750		6	51.20	307.20		4	2	2	0	102.40	3	1	51.20
8	McGuinness Silk Tassel	39404	1750		4	51.20	204.80		2	2	2	0	102.40	3	1	51.20
9	Sour Puss	38505	1750		6	48.50	291.00		5	1	1	0	48.50	6	5	242.50
10	Gilbey's Gin	67166	1750		6	51.45	308.70		4	2	2	0	102.90	4	2	102.90
11	Tanqueray Dry Gin	96263	1750		3	54.45	163.35		1	2	2	0	108.90	4	2	108.90
12	Sapphire London Dry	582973	1750		2	54.95	109.90		2	0	1	1	54.95	2	1	54.95
13	Bacardi Gold Rum	85811	1750		6	52.45	314.70		4	2	2	0	104.90	4	2	104.90
14	Whalers Vanilla Rum	150102	1136		6	44.95	269.70		5	1	1	0	44.95	6	5	224.75
15	Lamb's Palm Breeze (P.E.T.)	57893	1750		6	51.20	307.20		4	2	2	0	102.40	3	1	51.20
16	St Remy Brandy	234203	1750		4	51.45	205.80		4	0	0	0	0.00	4	4	205.80
17	D'Eaubonne VSOP Napoleon	6320	1140		2	34.15	68.30		1.75	0.25	0	-0.25	0.00	1	1	34.15
18	Courvoisier XO	158865	750		2	214.95	429.90		1	1	1	0	214.95	1	0	0.00
19	Remy Martin XO Excellence	583468	750		2	214.95	429.90		1	1	1	0	214.95	1	0	0.00
20	Hennessy VSOP	43703	750		2	84.75	169.50		1	1	1	0	84.75	1	0	0.00
21	Dujardin VSOP Brandy	128413	1140		6	34.15	204.90		2	4	3	-1	102.45	4	1	34.15
22	Janneau Grand Armagnac*	473785	750		4	38.95	155.80		3	1	1	0	38.95	2	1	38.95
23	Calvados Boulard	296228	750		2	47.45	94.90		0.75	1.25	1	-0.25	47.45	2	1	47.45
24	Sauza Silva Tequila	17384	1140		6	46.35	278.10		5	1	1	0	46.35	2	1	46.35
25	Walkers Peppermint Schnapps	11262	750		3	20.95	62.85		2	1	1	0	20.95	2	1	20.95
26	Stroh Rum	10101	750		4	54.50	218.00		3	1	1	0	54.50	2	1	54.50
27	Grand Marnier	187633	1750		4	99.20	396.80		2	2	2	0	198.40	2	0	0.00
28	Skyy Vodka	6502	750		4	42.95	171.80		1	3	3	0	128.85	3	0	0.00
29	Kahlua Coffee Liqueur	577973	1750		6	52.95	317.70		5	1	1	0	52.95	3	2	105.90
30	Tia Maria	630913	750		6	27.95	167.70		4	2	1	-1	27.95	3	2	55.90
31	Drambuie	1867	750		6	41.45	248.70		3	3	3	0	124.35	4	1	41.45
32	Disaronno Amaretto	31864	375		3	15.95	47.85		2	1	1	0	15.95	2	1	15.95
					137	1,909.75	7,314.05		90.75	46.25	45	-1.25	2,562.30	92	47	2,193.15

Note: For column Q use =roundup(P6-M6,0) and copy all the way to Q37

Chapter 9

Labour Cost, Scheduling Methods and Calculations

Labour cost is perhaps the most difficult-to-control cost in any commercial food service establishment. Though difficult to predict, since no one ever knows what is on the potential customers' "dining preference" mind, having the appropriate amount of staff on hand is perhaps the most important task for management. If the Staff-to-Customer ratio is too low, it may result in speed and level of service below customers' expectations and unhappy customers; if the ratio is too high it will lead to increased labour cost, which affects budgeted payroll negatively and may affect tip- and bonus-dependent staff adversely. This goes hand-in-hand with pre-preparation for goods to be sold and is one of the most common factors in Over – Under production.

Record keeping of customer count, customer preferences, daily sales, and conditions of sales (such as weather, day of the week, holiday, or other special days such as Mother's Day) will provide a good basis for estimation of production needs and staff scheduling. The result of this process is referred to as "Historical Record."

What Makes Up Labour/Staff Cost

Minimum wage is set by the various Provincial governments. In Ontario, the minimum wage rose on March 31, 2010 to $10.25 per hour and at the time of this writing, May 2013, has not changed. There are different levels of minimum wage based on status – student under 18, adults, and/or liquor servers.

Minimum Wage Increases for General and Specific Job Categories	
Minimum Wage Rate in Ontario	**March 31, 2010 wage rate**
General Minimum Wage	$10.25 per hour
Students under 18 and working not more than 28 hours per week or during a school holiday	$9.60 per hour
Liquor servers	$8.90 per hour
Hunting & Fishing Guides: for less than five consecutive hours in a day	$51.25 per day
Hunting & Fishing Guides: for five or more hours in a day whether or not the hours are consecutive	$102.50 per day
Home-workers (people doing paid work in their home for an employer)	110 percent of the general minimum wage

- ▶ **Direct Labour Cost:** Pay and mandatory benefits based on required skill level (**CPP**, Canada Pension Plan; **EI**, Employment Insurance; **WSIB** Workers Safety Insurance Board; **Vacation Pay**; **EHT**, Employers Health Tax). These mandatory deductions are subject to possible adjustments every January 1st and July 1st.
- ▶ **Indirect labour cost; Absenteeism,** staff turnover and training, under-performance to standards, workplace accidents, Occupational Health and Safety Act.
- ▶ **Additional Benefits:** Profit sharing, pension plans, health-related insurances, performance bonuses, commissions, share options, staff meals, company car.

Employer's Payroll Cost Example (Payroll July to December 2010): Employee "A" earns $10.50 per hour and works 40 hours a week: Gross pay = $420.00.

C.P.P. = 4.95%	20.79	
E.I. = 2.562%	10.76	
Vacation Pay = 4%	16.80	
E.H.T. = 0.98%	4.12	(0.98% if total payroll is $200,000 or less)
W.S.I.B. = 1.65%	6.93	(average food service/handling rate)
Cost of mandatory benefits	$59.40	or 14.142% of Gross Pay
Total Employer Cost	$479.40	(plus cost for payroll administration)

Actual employee cost per hour is **$11.99** without any of the above-mentioned possible additional benefits.

As previously mentioned, Labour Cost is most commonly calculated and budgeted against potential and actual sales. Like all other costs, it is calculated as a percentage fraction of sales; see example in Chapter 1 — Introduction to Elements of Cost.

Labour Cost Control is a process used by management to direct, regulate, and restrain employees' actions in order to obtain desired levels of performance at appropriate levels of cost.

Labour cost is identified as a Semi-Variable Cost (partially fixed–management, and partially variable–hourly paid staff based on projected sales). Most establishments where the payroll does not change in dollar value from pay-period to pay-period consider payroll a Fixed cost.

Labour cost may be calculated against total sales, department sales, produced quantity, item, unit (plate), and cost per customer.

Labour cost is directly influenced by the sophistication of menu items, as well as level and type of service provided. The cost of employees rises with required skills level.

Staff Cost Starts with the Hiring Process

- ▶ **Job-Description:** Job Description clearly identifies the skill level and experience needed based on established Quality and Quantity standards of expected performance and subsequently determines the compensation level.
- ▶ **Want-ad:** based on job description and requiring candidate to submit a resume.
- ▶ **Selection for interview:** offered to the most suitable candidates.
- ▶ **Hiring and training:** training cost occurs since both the trainer and trainee are not working to full capacity. A specific time frame needs to be identified; upon completion of training, the trainee is expected to be "up-to-speed" based on the established performance standards.
- ▶ **Performance standard evaluation:** based on Quality and Quantity standards of expected performance.

The illustrated Payroll calculation template on the following page is based on current prescribed benefits assuming that the Employer's health tax rate is 0.89% and the WSIB rate is 1.65%. The most common WSIB rate for Restaurants and Catering is 1.65% for 2012 whereas the rate for Hotels, Motels and Camping was 2.65%.

If the calculated average cost per hour based on the Base-pay-per-hour is $11.50 whereas the average cost per hour based on the Total payroll cost including benefits is $13.12. That is a $1.62 per hour difference. Not realizing this difference could lead to incorrect Budget calculations with Profit-infringing consequences.

The illustrated template and many others are available at www.menuforprofit.com. Please contact the author if you would like to have it modified for your specific needs.

Some Easy and Effective Ways of Controlling Labour Cost

- ▶ Master schedule and labour capacity chart—see Scheduling
- ▶ Job descriptions
- ▶ Selection and hiring process
- ▶ On-the-job training
- ▶ Skilled supervisor/manager
- ▶ Standard recipes with identified production time
- ▶ Production and cleaning schedules
- ▶ Supervised Sign in and Sign out sheets
- ▶ Careful scheduling based on Sales forecasts and historical records
- ▶ Appropriate production equipment and facility layout
- ▶ Time-Punch clocks—Electronic Finger or Hand readers (Biometrics)

Overhead and Payroll has become one the largest expense/cost in most food-service establishments. This adds considerable pressure to Managers and Chef's responsibility of scheduling and maintaining a highly efficient workforce, often leaving insufficient time to train new staff and/or provide upgrading to existing staff.

A Final Word or Two about Labour Cost

A topic where very little is written in textbooks dealing with cost, yet it is an instrumental part of cost control, is dishonest staff and customers. This is a great concern of every employer. Many articles have been written about this topic, and many seminars have been held trying to identify what makes a **cheat** and a **thief** and how one can protect themselves.

There are many things that can be done to deter a thief:

- ▶ Screen potential employees during the hiring process.
- ▶ Provide clear directions (a written company policy dealing with theft) during the hiring process.
- ▶ Explain what is acceptable and unacceptable, how management practises prevention, and how unacceptable behaviour will be handled.
- ▶ Enforce methods such as approved purchase orders, frequent inventories, receiving records, limited access, cash control, locks and keys.

Canadian Payroll Calculations for 2013 (Simplified example)

compiled by Klaus Theyer CCC (New Rates are set at the beginning of the year and mid-year)

Employees who are paid a certain wage per hour, or any other time period, are subject to mandatory deductions which are withheld by the employer, as well as, the employer must make additional contributions on behalf of the employee. **See example:**

NOTE: Federal and Provincial Income Tax are not part of this calculation since they are solely withheld from the employee.

Explanation of Acronyms:

C.P.P.	Canada Pension Plan	http://www.servicecanada.gc.ca/eng/isp/cpp/cpptoc.shtml
E.I.	Employment Insurance	http://www.servicecanada.gc.ca/eng/ei/menu/eihome.shtml
Vac. Pay	Vacation Pay, currently 4% of regular pay, with increments depending on length of employment	
E.H.T.	Employers Health Tax (Ontario)	http://www.rev.gov.on.ca/en/tax/eht/
W.S.I.B.	Workplace Safety & Insurance Board	http://www.wsib.on.ca/wsib/wsibsite.nsf/public/homepage

E.H.T. Up 200K = 0.98% over 200K is 1.101%, over 230,000 is 1.223%, over 260,000 is 1.344%, over 400,000 is 1.95%

2012 C.P.P. Annual MAX contribution:	$ 2,306.70	Self-employed C.P.P. maximum contribution	$ 4,613.40
2012 E.I. Annual MAX contribution:	$ 839.97		

Employees

Mandatory Deductions		Annual	
Type	Amount	Maximum	
C.P.P.	4.95%	$ 2,306.70	< same % >
E.I.	1.83%	$ 839.97	< % x 1.4 >
E.H.T.	n/a		
W.S.I.B.	Group# 919		
Vac. Pay	n/a		

Employers

Mandatory Contributions		Annual	
Type	Amount	Maximum	
C.P.P.	4.95%	$ 2,306.70	
E.I.	2.562%	$ 1,175.96	incr. from 2011 by $53.21 or $74.49
E.H.T.	.98% to 1.95%		< of total payroll >
W.S.I.B.	1.65%		< of total payroll >
Vac. Pay	4.00%		< of total payroll >

Calculation Example:

Ensure to use the info from cells E34 to I 34 in formulas for E35 to I 39

For Vac.Pay regular hours only are considered, no overtime is calculated

	Employees I.D.	Base-pay per hour	Weekly hrs worked	Total pay	Vac.Pay 4.00%	C.P.P. 4.95%	Mandatory Benefits E.I. 2.562%	E.H.T. 0.98%	W.S.I.B. 1.65%	Cost of Weekly Benefits $	Employee Pay per Week including Benefits	Cost of Benefits of each Employee %
35	Min. Wage	$ 10.25	40	$ 410.00	$ 16.40	$ 20.30	$ 10.50	$ 4.02	$ 6.77	$ 57.98	$ 467.98	14.142%
36	A	$ 11.00	40	$ 440.00	$ 17.60	$ 21.78	$ 11.27	$ 4.31	$ 7.26	$ 62.22	$ 502.22	14.142%
37	B	$ 11.50	40	$ 460.00	$ 18.40	$ 22.77	$ 11.79	$ 4.51	$ 7.59	$ 65.05	$ 525.05	14.142%
38	C	$ 12.00	40	$ 480.00	$ 19.20	$ 23.76	$ 12.30	$ 4.70	$ 7.92	$ 67.88	$ 547.88	14.142%
39	D	$ 12.50	40	$ 500.00	$ 20.00	$ 24.75	$ 12.81	$ 4.90	$ 8.25	$ 70.71	$ 570.71	14.142%
40	XXXXXX	XXXXXX	Totals:	$ 2,290.00	$ 91.60	$ 113.36	$ 58.67	$ 22.44	$ 37.79	$ 323.85	$ 2,613.85	14.142%
41	Averages:	$ 11.45	40	$ 458.00	$ 18.32	$ 22.67	$ 11.73	$ 4.49	$ 7.56	$ 64.77	$ 522.77	14.142%

Your Answers based on Row E 41 to I 41 from calculations below:

	Employer	Employees
	$ 113.36	$ 113.36
	$ 58.67	$ 41.91
	$ 22.44	
	$ 37.79	
	$ 91.60	

There are things that can be done to deter a cheat, which indirectly is a thief as well.

- Get informed about the various methods that can be used to steal. Understand all aspects of your point of sales system and read it frequently.
- Try to visualise how each employee is directly or indirectly exposed to the opportunity to steal — remove opportunities as much as you can without infringing on productivity.

The following statistic is from the Rick Green eSeminars on Loss prevention website at www.ebridge.tv/LPG. Mr. Green, General Manager of Loss Prevention Group, has been in the Security/Loss Prevention field since 1977 and is an acknowledged and respected specialist in this field. The perfect situation for theft requires all of the following conditions: Opportunity, Need, and Attitude. The approximate percentage of the population that will or have stolen if the conditions were right: is 70%.

The percentage of the population who will always steal if given the opportunity is 25%. It is definitely something to seriously think about.

Scheduling Methods and Costing

Scheduling Methods and Costing is defined as a decision-making function that plays an important role in most manufacturing and service industries, enabling organizations to operate with a minimum of human resources.

Ever since labour cost has become one of the highest cost in foodservice it has become even more important than ever to schedule your employees for the required level of customer service, production efficiency and overall function of the department and establishment.

Although the method of scheduling varies in relation with the requirements of the particular type of establishment, the principles of scheduling remain uniformly the same.

Scheduling not only assists in planning labour and production cost for the establishment, it also allows employees to plan their own time. Scheduling has to accommodate the needs of the employer as well as the needs of the employee.

Schedules should be prepared well in advance of their effective date allowing employees to plan their own time. Scheduling is commonly based on projected daily sales and production needs, for a set period of time, usually one week, as well as for vacation entitlements, respecting applicable labour laws.

Sounds simple enough but it is a challenge which is not easily tackled since it depends on many variables;

- Type of establishment and complexity of menu offerings
- Layout of production and service areas
- Opening hours and seating capacity
- Job positions and descriptions, and availability of qualified and reliable staff
- Budget for Sales/Labour Cost (Annual, monthly, weekly and departmental) based on anticipated customer/sales volume
- Average Salary/Wages of employees by department and positions
- Absenteeism, mandatory and negotiated benefits
- Legal implications of scheduling — Employment Standards Act

Type of Establishment and Complexity of Menu Offerings

The level of expected service is in direct relation with the type of establishment. Customers at a fast food establishment are expecting to serve themselves whereas customers of a fine dining establishment and/or a five star hotel have an expectation to be catered to their accustomed and promised level of service. Also, fast food establishments often utilise pre-prepared products which require minimum handling and preparation whereas fine dining establishments utilise market fresh products which involves handling and skilled labour to cook and serve.

Layout of Production and Service Areas

As fewer steps a cook or server has to make, as more efficiently customer satisfaction can be achieved. If the layout of the establishment is designed with an effective production flow in mind, and if the distance from the counter/pass to the customer is not too far, food and beverage will be served at an appropriate temperature.

Opening Hours and Seating Capacity

Will determine the number of shift(s) and seating capacity the number of employees based on a guest and employee ratio for the front and the back of the house.

Job Positions and Descriptions, and Availability of Qualified and Reliable Staff

Based on the type of establishment needed positions have to be identified and job descriptions prepared for each position. This will clearly identify the level of expertise required for each position.

Budget for Sales/Labour Cost (Annual, monthly, weekly and departmental based on anticipated customer/sales volume)

In the budgetary process the two most often used methods to establish sales are the "Top down" or the "Bottom up" method. (See chapter for budgets)

As previously mentioned the sales budget is strongly influenced based on reservations and walk-ins, strongly influenced by the forecasted weather, seasons, vacation month, statuary holidays, celebrated days and the festive season.

In all scenarios sales will have to be forecasted for a period of time and multiplied with the desired labour cost percentage to establish the anticipated labour cost budget. (Sales × DLC % = Labour Budget)

The calculated labour cost budget divided by the average cost per labour hour will establish the available number of hours. (LCB$ ÷ AVG LC p/hr = # of hrs)

Average Salary/Wages of Employees by Department and Positions

From my experience it is advisable to split the departmental schedule into several parts. For the Kitchen there should be one schedule for *Management* or *Fixed Salaried* labour like Chefs and Sous chefs, one for *Hourly Labour* like line and prep-cooks, and optionally one for *Hourly Labour* such as dish/pot washers and custodians. Some establishments allocate labour cost for dish/pot washers and custodians to *Overhead Cost* since they not only work for the kitchen but also for the restaurant.

For the front of the house; one schedule for managers, one for hosts, servers, and bus-persons, as well as one for bartenders and cocktail servers.

The above would have to be duplicated for additional banquet facilities or catering venues.

Absenteeism, Mandatory and Negotiated Benefits

In Canada, mandatory benefits add approximately 14% to the base salary for hourly and full time employees. Other costs of company benefits like group insurances for life and/or health, and/or retirement plans need to be known in order to calculate the actual payroll cost. Other factors which may be overlooked are rather unpredictable costs to payroll are absenteeism, accidents, severance pay, cost of training or upgrading and contracts or legal costs.

Legal and Other Implications of Scheduling—Employment Standards Acts

Federal and provincial laws provide strict guidelines for maximum working hours per day or week before overtime has to be paid, paid and unpaid times for breaks, vacation entitlement, shift-work as well as regulations for different age groups and persons who serve alcohol.

In addition to legal requirements, if the establishment is unionized, negotiated contracts must be adhered to.

Now that we have reviewed the most common factors influencing payroll cost, the actual payroll cost can be calculated.

Recognising the fact that in Ontario mandatory benefits (Canada Pension Plan, Employment Insurance, Workers Safety Insurance Board, Employers Health Tax and Vacation Pay) add approximately 14% to the hourly/weekly or monthly base pay; if an employee earns $15.00 per hour the actual cost is $ 17.10. ($15.00 x 14% = $2.10) ($2.10 + $15.00 = $17.10). Forgetting the mandatory benefits could cause an excess payroll cost which in turn reduces the budgeted profit.

If forecasted sales are $10,000.00 and payroll is budgeted at 18% allocated payroll cost is $1,800.00 and if $10,000.00 sales are achieved it is a perfect scenario. However, if sales don't reach the targeted $10,000.00 the scheduled labour cost will be higher than budgeted, and subsequently reduce profit. On the contrary, if sales exceed the budgeted $10,000.00 the scheduled labour cost will be lower than budgeted, and subsequently increase profit.

Therefore, payroll cost should be monitored on a daily basis with Labour Cost Worksheets and schedules for salaried and hourly employees in conjunction with Sales projection to make adjustments as quickly as necessary. It is an ongoing balancing act, equal in importance to Break-even-point calculations.

It is advisable that prior to creating a work schedule, create a Labour Capacity Chart to determine how many customers per hour can be handled by each position considering complexity of menu offerings and service style and methods.

Labour Capacity Chart example
by Klaus Theyer CCC

Title of Job-position **# per each individual**	\multicolumn{5}{c}{Number (#) of Customers per hour}
	10	25	50	75	100
Food Production Area					
Manager/Chef	1	1	1	1	1
Sous Chef(s)	1	1	1	1	1
Line/Prep Cooks	1	2	3	3	4
Expediters	0	0	0	1	1
Dish/Pot washers	1	1	1	1	2
Front of the house					
Manager	1	1	1	1	1
Host/ess	0	0	1	1	2
Server	1	2	4	5	7
Bus-person	0	1	1	2	3
Bartender	1	1	1	2	2

Monthly Labour Cost Worksheet example
For Management and Fixed Salaried Labour (omit cents)

by Klaus Theyer CCC

Week # Day	Date dd/mm/yy	Sales $	Labour Budget %	Labour Budget $	Actual Labour Cost $	Over or Under $	Over or Under %	Actual Labour Cost %

Monthly Totals:

NOTES:

There are many options available for the actual creation of a schedule. From paper and pencil to using a spreadsheet program, to computer software designed for various situations of scheduling, to programs which integrate with POS's and track labour cost by signing in and signing out.

Smaller establishments may not invest in costly POS and their various add-ons, but prefer to have the option of designing a schedule set-up to suit their needs. The design of a schedule does not have to be limited to communicate with staff; it can easily be enhanced to monitor and quickly control labour cost situations.

My colleague Konrad Weinbuch CMC used to create schedules with Microsoft Excel. The following scenario is fictional and not knowingly associated with any actual occurrence.

In the following illustration Konrad started the MS Excel workbook by identifying the positions available in this establishment and their current Salaries or wages for the Full-time (Fixed Cost employees) and Hourly or (Variable Cost employees). To be used in further calculations he noted the desired labour cost percentage in relation to actual sales.

The "Lazy Duck" Restaurant (Cost of Labour)

by Konrad Weinbuch CMC

The Executive Chef at the "Lazy Duck" has to prepare the weekly Schedule for the week of dd/mm/yy (Monday to Sunday, Sunday being Mother's Day)

The Restaurant is open for Breakfast, Lunch and Dinner, as well as for Special Events/Caterings.

As an essential Guideline in preparing the Schedule, the Chef uses a weekly Forecast.

Kitchen Management Annual Salaries:

		per week
Executive Chef	$71,000.00	$1,365.38
1st Sous Chef	$53,000.00	$1,019.23
Sous chef	$43,000.00	$826.92
		$3,211.54

List of hourly wage Staff: (starting with the highest on the Seniority List)

Name of Employee	Position	Hourly Wage $	Fixed Days Off
	Chef de Partie Breakfast and Lunch	$20.90	Saturday - Sunday
	Demi Chef de Partie Breakfast and Lunch	$18.90	Monday-Tuesday
	Chef de Partie Dinner and Events	$20.90	Sunday-Monday
	Commis Pantry Breakfast and Lunch	$16.90	Saturday-Sunday
	Chef de Partie Tournant	$20.90	none
	Demi chef de Partie Dinner Events	$18.90	Tuesday-Wednesday
	Demi chef de Partie Dinner Events	$18.90	Thursday-Friday
	Commis Pantry Dinner	$16.90	Monday-Tuesday
	Demi Chef de Partie Tournant	$18.90	none
	Commis	$16.90	none
	Commis	$16.90	none
	Commis	$16.90	none
	Commis	$16.90	none

Note: Hourly Wages do not include standard mandatory benefits.

Labour Cost Percentage Allowance for total Payroll : 15.70%

Chapter 9 Labour Cost, Scheduling Methods and Calculations

Once this page was completed the names of the individuals needed for that week, based on forecasted sales revenue were entered.

	A	B	C	D
1	The "Lazy Duck" Restaurant (Cost of Labour)		by Konrad Weinbuch CMC	1A
2				
3	The Executive Chef at the "Lazy Duck" has to prepare the weekly Schedule for			
4	the week of dd/mm/yy (Monday to Sunday, Sunday being Mother's Day)			
5	The Restaurant is open for Breakfast, Lunch and Dinner, as well as for Special Events/Caterings.			
6				
7	As an essential Guideline in preparing the Schedule, the Chef uses a weekly Forecast.			
8	Kitchen Mangagement Annual Salaries:		per week	
9	Executive Chef	$71,000.00	$1,365.38	
10	1st Sous Chef	$53,000.00	$1,019.23	
11	Sous chef	$43,000.00	$826.92	$3,211.54
12	List of hourly wage Staff: (starting with the highest on the Seniority List)			
13	Name of Employee	Position	Hourly Wage $	Fixed Days Off
14	Paul	Chef de Partie Breakfast and Lunch	$20.90	Saturday - Sunday
15	Adam	Demi Chef de Partie Breakfast and lunch	$18.90	Monday-Tuesday
16	Christina	Chef de Partie Dinner and Events	$20.90	Sunday-Monday
17	Eva	Commis Pantry Breakfast and Lunch	$16.90	Saturday-Sunday
18	Thomas	Chef de Partie Tournant	$20.90	none
19	Stephanie	Demi chef de Partie Dinner Events	$18.90	Tuesday-Wednesday
20	Joseph	Demi chef de Partie Dinner Events	$18.90	Thursday-Friday
21	Kim	Commis Pantry Dinner	$16.90	Monday-Tuesday
22	Ben	Demi Chef de Partie Tournant	$18.90	none
23	Edna	Commis	$16.90	none
24	Billy	Commis	$16.90	none
25	Kyle	Commis	$16.90	none
26	Alex	Commis	$16.90	none
27	Note: Wages/Salaries do not include standard mandatory benefits.			
28	Labour Cost Percentage Allowance for total Payroll :		15.70%	
29				

132 Chapter 9 Labour Cost, Scheduling Methods and Calculations

A *Sales forecast* could be derived from different sources but Chef Konrad preferred to open a new sheet in Excel, appended to the Position allocation sheet so that the information can interactively flow from one page to the next. The sales forecast calculation was made by estimating the number of customers and the average cheque for each meal period, as well as considering special functions or holidays. This particular example was prepared for the week ending with a special Mother's Day buffet and Konrad also listed the cook's positions needed in the dining room.

	A	B	C	D	E	F	G	H
1	The "Lazy Duck" Restaurant (Sales Forecast)							by Konrad Weinbuch CMC
2								
3	Sales Forecast for the week of dd/mm/yy (Sunday being Mother's Day)							
4							Brunch	10.00 - 2.00
5	Average Cheque for Breakfast:		$11.50				Breakfast	7.00 - 11.00
6	Average Cheque for Lunch:		$18.60				Lunch	11.30 - 2.00
7	Average Cheque for Dinner:		$32.90				Dinner	6.00 - 10.00
8								
9	Staff required for Mother's Day Brunch Service:				1 Carver			
10					1 Chef for Omelette Station			
11					3 Runners			
12								
13		Monday	Tuesday	Wednesday	Thursday	Friday	Saturday	Sunday
14	Breakfast	155	170	195	210	210	145	120
15	**Brunch**	0	0	0	0	0	0	450 @ **$36.50**
16	Lunch	98	120	125	140	140	65	0
17	Lunch Events	0	80 @ $22.00	45 @ $21.50	0	150 @ $23.50	0	0
18	Dinner	90	115	110	120	175	180	65
19	Dinner Events	0	0	60 @ $38.00	30 @ $42.00	80 @ $41.50	0	0
20	Total Revenue	$6,566.30	$9,730.50	$11,434.00	$10,227.00	$17,621.50	$8,798.50	$19,943.50
21	**Total Weekly Revenue**		$84,321.30					
22								
23	Total Labor Cost Allowance	15.70%	equals $	$13,238.44				
24								

Once the weekly sales forecast (weekly sales budget) was completed, it was easy to calculate the available funds for labour cost based on the desired labour cost percentage, and create an actual staffing schedule with labour cost projection calculation. A new interactive Sheet was added to the Excel Workbook.

One of the many options available is to hide information so that they may not be readily seen by everyone. The next Excel sheet displays the normally hidden—for office use only—cells from J7 to L25.

	A	B	C	D	E	F	G	H	I	J	K	L
1	The "Lazy Duck" Restaurant (Weekly Schedule)							by Konrad Weinbuch CMC				
2	Schedule for the week of dd/mm/yy (Sunday being Mother's Day)											
3												
4	Actual Sales/Revenue =		$84,321.30		SVC allowance =		$13,238.44		Mandatory benefits add 14.142% to Scheduled Cost			
5												
6												
7	Name	MONDAY	TUESDAY	WEDNESDAY	THURSDAY	FRIDAY	SATURDAY	SUNDAY	Total Hours	Total Weekly Scheduled Cost	MB % 14.142%	Total Weekly Actual Cost
8	PAUL	6.00 - 2.30	6.00 - 2.30	6.00 - 2.30	6.00 - 2.30	6.00 - 2.30	6.00 - 2.30	off	40			
9	ADAM	off	off	7.00 - 3.30	7.00 - 3.30	7.00 - 3.30	6.00 - 2.30	off	40			
10	CHRISTINA	off	7.00 - 3.30	2.30 - 11.00	2.30 - 11.00	2.30 - 11.00	off	6.00 - 2.30	40			
11	EVA	7.00 - 3.30	7.00 - 3.30	7.00 - 3.30	7.00 - 3.30	7.00 - 3.30	off	off	40			
12	THOMAS	off	8.00 - 4.30	8.00 - 4.30	8.00 - 4.30	8.00 - 4.30	8.00 - 4.30	off	40			
13	STEPHANIE	2.30 - 11.00	off	off	2.30 - 11.00	2.30 - 11.00	2.30 - 11.00	2.30 - 11.00	40			
14	JOSEPH	2.30 - 11.00	2.30 - 11.00	2.30 - 11.00	off	2.30 - 11.00	2.30 - 11.00	2.30 - 11.00	40			
15	KIM	off	off	2.30 - 11.00	2.30 - 11.00	2.30 - 11.00	2.30 - 11.00	2.30 - 11.00	40			
16	BEN	7.00 - 3.30 B	7.00 - 3.30 B	off	off	8.00 - 4.30 B	8.00 - 4.30 B	8.00 - 4.30 B	40			
17	EDNA	2.30 - 1.00 P	2.30 - 1.00 P	off	off	7.00 - 3.30 B	7.00 - 3.30 B	7.00 - 3.30 B	40			
18	BILLY					2.30 - 9.00	8.00 - 4.30	8.00 - 4.30	20			
19	KYLE					2.30 - 9.00	9.00 - 3.30	8.00 - 4.30	20			
20	ALEX					10.00 - 4.30	10.00 - 5.30		6			
21	Hourly Wages:											
22	Chef de Partie:					Total Weekly Pay Variable (Hourly wage)						
23	Demi Chef de Partie:					Total Weekly Pay Fixed (Managers)						
24	Commis:					Total Weekly Payroll Semi Variable Cost						
25						OVER(-) or UNDER(+)						

134 Chapter 9 Labour Cost, Scheduling Methods and Calculations

The "Lazy Duck" Restaurant (Weekly Schedule)
Schedule for the week of dd/mm/yy (Sunday being Mother's Day)

by Konrad Weinbuch CMC

Actual Sales/Revenue = $84,321.30   **SVC allowance =** $13,238.44   Mandatory benefits add 14.142% to Scheduled Cost

Name	MONDAY	TUESDAY	WEDNESDAY	THURSDAY	FRIDAY	SATURDAY	SUNDAY	Total Hours	Total Weekly Scheduled Cost	MB % 14.142%	Total Weekly Actual Cost
PAUL	6.00 - 2.30	6.00 - 2.30	6.00 - 2.30	6.00 - 2.30	off	6.00 - 2.30	off	40	$836.00	$118.23	$954.23
ADAM	off	off	7.00 - 3.30	7.00 - 3.30	7.00 - 3.30	6.00 - 2.30	6.00 - 2.30	40	$756.00	$106.91	$862.91
CHRISTINA	2.30 - 11.00	2.30 - 11.00	2.30 - 11.00	2.30 - 11.00	2.30 - 11.00	off	off	40	$836.00	$118.23	$954.23
EVA	7.00 - 3.30	7.00 - 3.30	7.00 - 3.30	7.00 - 3.30	7.00 - 3.30	off	off	40	$836.00	$118.23	$954.23
THOMAS	off	8.00 - 4.30	8.00 - 4.30	8.00 - 4.30	8.00 - 4.30	8.00 - 4.30	off	40	$676.00	$95.60	$771.60
STEPHANIE	2.30 - 11.00	off	2.30 - 11.00	2.30 - 11.00	2.30 - 11.00	2.30 - 11.00	off	40	$756.00	$106.91	$862.91
JOSEPH	2.30 - 11.00	2.30 - 11.00	off	2.30 - 11.00	2.30 - 11.00	2.30 - 11.00	off	40	$756.00	$106.91	$862.91
KIM	off	off	2.30 - 11.00	2.30 - 11.00	2.30 - 11.00	2.30 - 11.00	2.30 - 11.00	40	$676.00	$95.60	$771.60
BEN	7.00 - 3.30 B	7.00 - 3.30 B	off	off	8.00 - 4.30 B	8.00 - 4.30 B	8.00 - 4.30 B	40	$756.00	$106.91	$862.91
EDNA	2.30 - 1.00 P	2.30 - 1.00 P	off	off	8.00 - 4.30 B	7.00 - 3.30 B	7.00 - 3.30 B	40	$676.00	$95.60	$771.60
BILLY					2.30 - 9.00	9.00 - 3.30	8.00 - 4.30	20	$338.00	$47.80	$385.80
KYLE					2.30 - 9.00	8.00 - 4.30	20	$338.00	$47.80	$385.80
ALEX					10.00 - 4.30	10.00 - 5.30	6	$101.40	$14.34	$115.74

Hourly Wages:		Total Weekly Pay Variable (Hourly wage)	$8,337.40	$1,179.08	$9,516.48
Chef de Partie:	$20.90	Total Weekly Pay Fixed (Managers)	$3,211.54	Actual =>	$3,665.71
Demi Chef de Partie:	$18.90	Total Weekly Payroll Semi Variable Cost	$11,548.94	Actual =>	$13,182.19
Commis:	$16.90	OVER(-) or UNDER(+)	$1,689.51	Actual =>	$56.25

Chapter 9 Labour Cost, Scheduling Methods and Calculations 135

The following Excel sheet, for which another interactive Excel Sheet was opened, is a Canadian and Provincial (Ontario) Mandatory Benefit calculation sheet, to establish the actual cost of the payroll including mandatory benefits.

This sheet has been created based on the principals of the Canadian Payroll Calculations for 2013 Excel sheet as displayed in the Labour Cost part of this chapter.

The "Lazy Duck" Restaurant (Cost of Labour mandatory benefits calculation) by Konrad Weinbuch CMC
Schedule for the week of dd/mm/yy (Sunday being Mother's Day)

Mandatory Benefits Canadian Payroll Calculations

Name	Total weekly Pay	Vacation Pay	C.P.P.	E.I.	E.H.T.	W.S.I.B.	Cost of weekly Benefits	Weekly Pay incl. Benefits
		4.00%	4.95%	2.562%	0.98%	1.65%		
PAUL	$836.00							
ADAM	$756.00							
CHRISTINA	$836.00							
EVA	$676.00							
THOMAS	$836.00							
STEPHANIE	$756.00							
JOSEPH	$756.00							
KIM	$676.00							
BEN	$756.00							
EDNA	$676.00							
BILLY	$338.00							
KYLE	$338.00							
ALEX	$101.40							
Total VLC								
Managers								
Total SVC	$3,211.54	$128.46	$158.97	$82.28	$31.47	$52.99	$454.18	$3,665.71

The "Lazy Duck" Restaurant
(Cost of Labour mandatory benefits calculation)

Schedule for the week of dd/mm/yy (Sunday being Mother's Day)

by Konrad Weinbuch CMC

Mandatory Benefits Canadian Payroll Calculations

Name	Total weekly Pay	Vacation Pay	C.P.P.	E.I.	E.H.T.	W.S.I.B.	Cost of weekly Benefits	Weekly Pay incl. Benefits
		4.00%	4.95%	2.562%	0.98%	1.65%		
PAUL	$836.00	$33.44	$41.38	$21.42	$8.19	$13.79	$118.23	$954.23
ADAM	$756.00	$30.24	$37.42	$19.37	$7.41	$12.47	$106.91	$862.91
CHRISTINA	$836.00	$33.44	$41.38	$21.42	$8.19	$13.79	$118.23	$954.23
EVA	$676.00	$27.04	$33.46	$17.32	$6.62	$11.15	$95.60	$771.60
THOMAS	$836.00	$33.44	$41.38	$21.42	$8.19	$13.79	$118.23	$954.23
STEPHANIE	$756.00	$30.24	$37.42	$19.37	$7.41	$12.47	$106.91	$862.91
JOSEPH	$756.00	$30.24	$37.42	$19.37	$7.41	$12.47	$106.91	$862.91
KIM	$676.00	$27.04	$33.46	$17.32	$6.62	$11.15	$95.60	$771.60
BEN	$756.00	$30.24	$37.42	$19.37	$7.41	$12.47	$106.91	$862.91
EDNA	$676.00	$27.04	$33.46	$17.32	$6.62	$11.15	$95.60	$771.60
BILLY	$338.00	$13.52	$16.73	$8.66	$3.31	$5.58	$47.80	$385.80
KYLE	$338.00	$13.52	$16.73	$8.66	$3.31	$5.58	$47.80	$385.80
ALEX	$101.40	$4.06	$5.02	$2.60	$0.99	$1.67	$14.34	$115.74
Total VLC	$8,337.40	$333.50	$412.70	$213.60	$81.71	$137.57	$1,179.08	$9,516.48
Managers	$3,211.54	$128.46	$158.97	$82.28	$31.47	$52.99	$454.18	$3,665.71
Total SVC	$11,548.94	$461.96	$571.67	$295.88	$113.18	$190.56	$1,633.25	$13,182.19

Up to this point Chef Konrad has done a great job, his projection came in just below budgeted cost, which helps to increase the profit. However, the true facts will only be known at the end of the day and the actual revenue has been calculated. If the actual revenue exceeds the forecast, the owner(s) and the chef will be happy, if, however actual revenue does not meet the forecast, the owner(s) and the chef will try to balance the payroll for the following weeks.

A Few Summary Pointers about Scheduling

- ▶ Create a "Master Schedule" encompassing all areas of the operation with break-outs for all "Profit and Cost/Loss Centres" including the cost of one shift for each position. This will be an essential part of creating an annual or periodical budget.
- ▶ Refer to "Historical records" of revenue and menu items sales mix – it will reveal not only customers' preferences for offered food and beverage items, it subsequently will also show what items are not popular, assisting in the purchasing and inventory process. Understanding the complexity of the offered menu items will determine the needed skill level from your employees.
- ▶ Another benefit of historical records, in conjunction with current reservations, is that it should assist with prevention of "over or under staffing" which can affect profit and customer satisfaction, as well as staff burn-out or unproductive idleness.
- ▶ Know the strengths and abilities of the employees.
- ▶ Consider your employee needs, but the business must come first.
- ▶ Post schedules for a two-week duration. It creates stability and allows staff to manage their own time.
- ▶ Establish a policy of process for schedule changes. For example; if an employee needs time off from scheduled work hours, it is the employee's responsibility to find a suitable substitute from the existing employee pool, however, changes need to be authorized by a supervisor or manager.
- ▶ It is advisable to have a list of potential part-time and/or temporary employees to fill in for emergencies and vacation scheduling.

Chapter 10

Menu Analysis and Sales Mix

Menu Analysis and Menu Engineering

The basis of the menu analysis technique that follows was developed some years ago by Michael L. Kasavana and Donald I. Smith and was described in a book they published in 1982.[*] Known as menu engineering, the technique is now widely known and respected and has been the subject of numerous papers and articles. (The following is modified to conform to the attached sample worksheet for the benefit of studious Culinarians.)

Although some may not agree with all the conclusions drawn by Kasavana and Smith, their approach to menu analysis is both interesting and revealing. This publication does not fully expose their method, which can best be obtained from their book.

Since this method was published, others have surfaced. It would be good practice to investigate the various methods of menu analysis available today and select a method best suited to individual needs.

The principal reason for performing a Menu Analysis has not changed: To determine which menu item performs satisfactorily by being popular with the customers and subsequently is a "Good Seller," yet producing the expected amount of "Contribution — Gross Profit" in comparison to all other offered "comparable" menu items.

When performing a menu analysis it is very important to categorize menu items to be evaluated by meal periods as offered; Breakfast, Lunch, Afternoon Tea, Dinner, as well as by types of offerings such as Main Courses (with possible subcategories such as Pasta and Pizza dishes, Fish, Shellfish, Meats, Poultry, Game, Specials, House speciality or ethnic origin items, Health food and/or dietary choices and Vegetarian/Vegan offerings), Appetizers, Soups, Salads, Sandwiches, and Desserts. This list can be expanded or reduced to suit any establishment.

This method of analysis can be applied to any type of menu, such as beverage, hot – cold, alcoholic and non-alcoholic, take-out, catering, banquet and special occasions, cycle (cyclical) menus, a la carte, table d'hôte, du jour, market and California-type menu.

In order to perform a menu analysis, it is essential to work with accurate data. Although a full menu analysis is quite labour intensive, it does provide a means for monitoring the effectiveness of offerings to maximize profits. Additionally, it provides some general insights that are useful for potentially increasing the profitability of a menu.

---

[*]Michael L. Kasavana and Donald I. Smith, *Menu Engineering – A Practical Guide to Menu Analysis*. Lansing, MI: Hospitality Publications, 1982.

Column C: Menu Mix Percent

The menu mix percent for each item is calculated by dividing the number of units sold by the total number of units sold for all items. For example, Lobster bisque accounted for 20 portions out of the total portion sales for all items: 264.

The menu mix percent for this item is calculated as follows:

$$\frac{20}{264} = .1768 \text{ or } 7.58\%$$

The menu mix percent for each of the other items is calculated in the same way.

Column F: Item CM

The Item Contribution Margin is the amount available from each sale to contribute toward meeting all other costs of operation and, when those costs have been met, to provide profit. (CM) is defined as **sales price minus variable cost per unit.** For simplicity reasons and for purposes of this analysis, product cost is treated as the *only* variable cost. **Therefore, the CM for Lobster bisque is determined by subtracting the portion cost for the item from its sales price, as follows:**

Sales Price	$7.50
– Food Cost	$3.35
= CM	$4.15

Column I: Menu CM

The menu contribution margin is calculated by multiplying the number of units sold for each menu item by its contribution margin. Thus, for Lobster bisque,

20 Units Sold × $4.15 CM = **$83.00 Menu CM**

Editor's Note: Alternatively, CM may be calculated by subtracting Menu Cost *(Column G)* from Menu Sales *(Column H)*. This calculation indicates the total of contribution margins provided by the particular menu item.

The sum of all the individual totals is **found in Box P.**

Box R (In column H)

The figure in *Box R* is the average contribution margin, determined by dividing the total in *Box P* by the total number of units sold, found in *Box M*. For the illustrated worksheet the calculation is:

$$\frac{\$1,529.31 \text{ Total CM (Box P)}}{264 \text{ Units Sold (Box N)}} = \$5.79$$

Box S (in columns F to J)

The figure in **Box S** requires careful consideration. This is the percentage of an entire menu represented by each item on that menu, multiplied by 70 percent.*

There are ten items on the menu, each is one-tenth, or 10 percent, of the menu. Similarly, if there were five items on the menu, each would be one-fifth, or 20 percent, of the total. The figure in **Box T** is calculated by dividing one menu item by the total number of items and then **multiplying the result by .7 (7 percent)**.

Thus, $\frac{1 \times .7}{10} = .07$, or 7%

This figure will be used when making entries in **Column K,** as discussed.

Column J: CM Category

The entries in this column, **L for "Low"** and **H for "High,** are made after comparing the contribution margin for each menu item **(Column F)** with the average contribution margin for the menu **(Box T)**. If the contribution margin for a given menu item is lower than the average contribution margin, the entry for that item in **Column J is "L" for low.** If the contribution margin is higher than average, the entry is **"H" for high.**

For example, the contribution margin for Lobster bisque is $4.15, which is somewhat lower than the average contribution margin for the menu, $5.79. Thus, the entry for that item in **Column J** is an **"L" for low.**

Column K: MM Category

The entries in **Column K** (L and H for "Low" and "High") are determined by comparing the menu mix percentage for each item in **Column C** with the figure in **Box S**. For example, the menu mix percentage for Lobster bisque is 7.58%. Compared to **the 7.0% figure in Box S, this is high,** so the entry for Lobster bisque is the letter **H**.

The menu mix percentage for Lady Curzon is 4.55% and, because this is **lower than the 7.0% in Box T**, the letter L has been entered.

Because all entries in **Columns J and K** must be one of two letters (either H or L), there are four possible combination of letters: **H / H, L / L, H / L, & L / H**. These four possible combinations are used to identify menu items and, in the unique language of menu engineering, each has been given a name:

- **H | H is a Star.** A Star is a menu item that produces both high contribution margin and high volume. These are the items that food service operators would prefer to sell.
- **L | L is a Dog.** A Dog is a menu item that produces a comparatively low contribution margin and accounts for relatively low volume. These are probably the least desirable items to have on a menu.

  Editor's note: This scenario often applies to private Clubs and Ethnic establishments that cater to a specific audience who directly or indirectly demand the menu offering.
- **L | H is a Plowhorse.** A Plowhorse is a menu item that produces a low contribution margin but accounts for relatively high volume. These are items that are popular with customers but contribute comparatively little profit per unit sold.

---

*This is a figure established by Kasavana and Smith and based wholly on their own experience. They state that 70 percent produces the most useful analysis.

▶ **H | L is a Puzzle.** A Puzzle is a menu item that produces a high contribution margin but accounts for comparatively low sales volume.

Editor's note: This scenario can be found in private Clubs and Ethnic establishments that cater to a specific audience who directly or indirectly demand the menu offering.

Once the worksheet is completed and results are analyzed, the establishment may use different approaches, described as follows, and then determine the changes, if any, that would improve the menu. An illustrated example is appended.

Dogs

Because dogs are both unprofitable and unpopular, they should be removed from the menu and replaced with more profitable items unless (a) there is a valid reason for continuing to sell a dog (as with an item that promotes other sales) or (b) its profitability can somehow be increased to an acceptable level. This will require changes to the item in some way. One way of changing an item from a dog to a puzzle is to increase contribution margin per unit, which might be done by increasing the sales price.

Plowhorse

Plowhorses are popular but relatively unprofitable. This/these item(s) should be kept on the menu, but attempts should be made to increase their contribution margins without decreasing volume. One possibility would be to decrease standard portion size slightly and at the same time improve the appearance of the product.

Puzzles

Puzzles are comparatively profitable but relatively unpopular. They should be kept on the menu, but attempts should be made to increase their popularity without substantially decreasing their profitability. There are any number of ways to do this; including repositioning items to more favourable locations on the menu, featuring items as specials suggested to diners by servers, and/or changing appearances or menu descriptions of these items to increase their appeal.

Stars

Stars are both profitable and popular and should normally be left alone, unless there is some valid reason for change. Because of the popularity of Stars, it is sometimes possible to increase their menu prices without affecting volume, thus increasing their profitability.

Scenarios of possible changes:

▶ **Lady Curzon,** was replaced with Minestra, an item with a higher contribution margin ($1.00 lower Cost). While sales volume did not change, the higher contribution margin changed the classification of the item from Dog to Puzzle. In addition, total revenues, total contribution margin, and average contribution margin were all increased.

▲ **Tomato Shrimp,** a Plowhorse, **the Selling Price was increased in price by $1.50.** Volume was not affected because of the popularity of the item, its relatively low sales price, and the minimal price increase. While the item remains a Plowhorse, total revenues, total contribution margin, and average contribution margin were all increased.

▲ **Puzzle's** often just need to be repositioned on the menu and suggested to customers by servers. **This may result in increased sales volume,** reclassifying the item from Puzzle to Star.

Following this exercise, Management decided to abandon their policy of **One-Price-Selling-Price** for this category of menu items and to gradually adjust Cost and Selling Prices to obtain a satisfactory Cost Percentage and Gross Profit Margin, while closely monitoring Customers' reaction.

A frequent review of the analysed results is highly recommended.

The following columns/cells contain the necessary information, as used in the appended menu engineering worksheet:

In the Excel worksheet on www.menuforprofit.com as numbers are entered in the "B column/rows" the total "of the number of items used" will be summarized in A27. In the appended example the number of items used is 10.

A. Menu items described and categorized (from menu)

B. Number of menu items sold (from sales record – POS)

C. Calculation of Menu item sales mix percentage also referred to as Menu mix or Popularity Index (Individual item sold divided by total items sold × 100)

D. Individual item Food/Beverage cost (from Standard recipe)

E. Menu item Selling price (from menu)

F. Individual item Contribution Margin/Gross profit (F – E)

G. Total item cost based on number of items sold (C × E)

H. Menu item Sales/Revenue (F × C)

I. Sold menu item Contribution margin or Gross profit (I – H)

J. Result of classification based on calculation from Line 24

K. Result of classification based on calculation from Line 25

L. Result of classification based on calculation from Line 28 to 31

For an effective visual display of results as entered, the "Menu items information" cells and the "Menu classification cells" will change colour to simulate a traffic light.

RED = Dog = Stop

YELLOW = Plowhorse = Caution

GREEN = Go = Star

For the Puzzle we selected ORANGE

The Spreadsheet has been field-tested and works as intended.

144 Chapter 10 Menu Analysis and Sales Mix

Menu Analysis Worksheet (Input information into White/Blanc cells ONLY)

Name of Property: **Any Place Hotel**
Name of Outlet: **Prestige Fine Dining**

For the period from: September 01 2013 To: September 31 2013 File Name: SoupsJan2013DinnerPrestige

A	B	C	D	E	F	G	H	I	J	K	L
Menu Items Information	Number of Menu Items # Sold	(M M) Menu Mix in percentage	Item Ingredient Cost	Item Sales Price	Item Contribution Margin	Menu Cost (C.O.G.S.)	Menu Items Sales Revenue	Menu C M M.C.M.	I C M Category	M M Category	Menu Item Classification
		M M %	I.P.C.	S.P.	(E – D)	(B × D)	(B × E)	(H – G)	L or H	L or H	S, D, PH, or PZ
Soups - Hot & Cold											
Tomato basil puree	27	10.23%	$ 1.28	$ 7.50	6.22	34.56	202.50	167.94	H	H	Star
Tomato shrimp bisque	19	7.20%	$ 2.85	$ 7.50	4.65	54.15	142.50	88.35	L	H	Plowhorse
Curried red lentil	32	12.12%	$ 0.98	$ 7.50	6.52	31.36	240.00	208.64	H	H	Star
Consommé w/ wild mushrooms	25	9.47%	$ 2.09	$ 7.50	5.41	52.25	187.50	135.25	L	H	Plowhorse
Navy bean	19	7.20%	$ 1.01	$ 7.50	6.49	19.19	142.50	123.31	H	H	Star
Chicken dumpling bouillon	52	19.70%	$ 1.25	$ 7.50	6.25	65.00	390.00	325.00	H	H	Star
Lobster bisque	20	7.58%	$ 3.35	$ 7.50	4.15	67.00	150.00	83.00	L	H	Plowhorse
Consommé w/ liver dumpling	28	10.61%	$ 1.90	$ 7.50	5.60	53.20	210.00	156.80	L	H	Plowhorse
Consommé Celestine	30	11.36%	$ 1.05	$ 7.50	6.45	31.50	225.00	193.50	H	H	Star
Lady Curzon	12	4.55%	$ 3.50	$ 7.50	4.00	42.00	90.00	48.00	L	L	Dog
Type item name here											
Type item name here											
Totals ==>	264	100%				450.21	1,980.00	1,529.79			

"A25" equals the numbers of listed menu items in column "B" **10**

M	N	O	P	Q	R	S
Total of B21	Tot. of G	Tot. of H	= H − G	= N / O (%)	= P / M	(1 ÷ A25 x .7) formatted to a percent
264	450.21	1,980.00	1,529.79	22.74%	5.79	7.00%
	$ 19.26	$ 75.00	55.74	450.21		

For Column J: (H : L) Compare F of each item with R. If F is lower than R then L, if higher than R then H
For Column K: (H : L) Compare M M% of each item with S, if lower than S then L, if higher than S then H.

The Sales-Mix percentage in K23 is pre-set to 70% out of 100% as per M. L. Kasavana & D. I. Smith. To change this pre-set value, enter a new value here: **70%**

For more detailed information please see "The Financial Menu" A Chef's Companion to Cost Control by Klaus Theyer CCC, ISBN 978-7575-8723-8

Column J:K:L: Scenario

J = ICM	K = MM	L = Class
H	H	equals => Star	S = STAR = Best performer in Popularity and Contribution Margin
H	L	equals => Dog	D = DOG = Worst performer in Popularity and Contribution Margin
L	H	equals => Plowhorse	PH = PLOWHORSE = Quite Popular but offers Lower Contribution Margin
L	L	equals => Puzzle	PZ = PUZZLE = Not very Popular but offers Higher Contribution Margin

Menu Analysis ~ This illustrated Menu engineering method was developed by Michael L. Kasavana & Donald I. Smith, published in 1982. Transcribed, modified and presented for teaching purposes by Klaus Theyer CCC and Karen M. Nair IT/Learning Professional, Humber College 1992/2013

Menu Analysis

Menu Analysis Worksheet (Input information into White/Blanc cells ONLY)

Name of Property: _____ Name of Outlet: _____

For the period from: _____ To: _____ File Name: _____

Menu Items Information

A	B	C	D	E	F	G	H	I	J	K	L
Menu items	Number of Menu items # Sold	(M M) Menu Mix in percentage	Item Ingredient Cost	Item Sales Price	Item Contribution Margin	Menu Cost M.C. or (C.O.G.S.)	Menu items Sales Revenue	Menu C M M.C.M.	I C M Category	M M Category	Menu Item Classification
Soups - Hot & Cold	M M	M M %	I.P.C.	S.P.	(E − D)	(B × D)	(B × E)	(H − G)	L or H	L or H	S, D, PH, or PZ
Type item name here											
Type item name here											
Type item name here											
Type item name here											
Type item name here											
Type item name here											
Type item name here											
Type item name here											
Type item name here											
Type item name here											
Type item name here											
Totals ==>	0	0%	$ -	$ -	0.00	0.00	0.00				

	M	N	O	P	Q	R	S
"A25" equals the numbers of listed menu items in column "B"	Total of B21	Tot. of G	Tot. of H	= H − G	= N / O (%)	= P / M	
0	0	0.00	0.00	0.00	0.00%	0.00	

The Sales-Mix percentage in K23 is pre-set to 70% out of 100% as per M. L. Kasavana & D. I. Smith. To change this pre-set value, enter a new value here: **70%**

(1 + A25 × .7) formatted to a percenta... 0.00%

(100 ÷ # of items × .7) or (100% ÷ # of items × 70%)

For more detailed information please see "The Financial Menu" A Chef's Companion to Cost Control by Klaus Theyer CCC, ISBN 978-7575-8723-...

Column J:K:L: Scenario

	J = ICM	K = MM	L = Class
The combination of	H	H	S = STAR = Best performer in Popularity and Contribution Margin
The combination of	L	L	Dog	D = DOG = Worst performer in Popularity and Contribution Margin
The combination of	H	L	Plowhorse	PH = PLOWHORSE = Quite Popular but offers Lower Contribution Margin
The combination of	L	H	Puzzle	PZ = PUZZLE = Not very Popular but offers Higher Contribution Margin

For Column J: (H : L) Compare F of each item with R, if F is lower than R then L, if higher than R then H

For Column K: (H : L) Compare M M% of each item with S, if lower than S then L, if higher than S then H.

Menu Analysis ~ This illustrated Menu engineering method was developed by Michael L. Kasavana & Donald I. Smith, published in 1982. Transcribed, modified and presented for teaching purposes by Klaus Theyer CCC and Karen M. Nair IT/Learning Professional, Humber College 1992/2013

Sales Mix Calculations

A full Menu Analysis as previously described and illustrated is an excellent method of evaluating Menu items, by group, periodically. However, for a daily quick analysis, attention must be given to Popularity of items and to the Sales Mix (Menu Mix). Recipe and Selling prices have been calculated to satisfy the "Desired and/or Ideal cost" yet, in order to offer items on a menu in a group such as Appetizers, Soups, Main courses, Desserts and Beverages with a uniform Selling price (i.e., all soups are sold for $7.50), it is unavoidable to have a fluctuation in Cost percentages. The ideal situation is to sell the items with the lowest cost more often than items with a higher cost and subsequently achieve a higher Gross profit margin compared to each item selling in equal number of units.

See the two examples that follow.

Simple Menu Analysis for Book
by Klaus Theyer C.C.C.

	A	B	Menu Item:	# Sold	Sales Menu Mix Popularity Index %	COGS Item Cost	COGS Total Cost	Menu Selling Price	Revenue Total Sales	Project. Product Cost %	Item GP or CM	Actual Product Cost %	Total Sold Item GP or CM	Contrib. Margin %	Contrib. Margin to Rev. %
5		1	Minute steak	73		4.83		14.95							
6		2	Shrimp (Tiger)	121		6.59		18.95							
7		3	Swordfish	105		5.18		14.95							
8		4	Chicken	140		2.14		7.25							
9		5	Lobster	51		8.64		21.00							
10		6	Scallops	85		3.39		9.95							
11		7	Beef medallions	125		4.04		10.95							
12		8	Pasta Primavera	155		2.25		5.95							
13		9	Meatloaf	97		2.75		6.95							
14		10	Cabbage Rolls	55		2.05		6.95							
15		11	Potato Skin	82		1.22		4.95							
16		Total:					xxxxxx		xxxxxx						
17		Averages:									xxxxxx		xxxxxx		
18															
19	Projected Cost Percentage:			minus											
20	Actual Cost Percentage:			equals	Variance:										
21															
22	Highest Seller by # Sold:					Highest Rev. in $:				AVG Item GP~CM $:					
23	Lowest Seller by # Sold:					Lowest Rev. in $:				Highest Item GP~CM $:					
24						Highest GP in $:				Lowest Item GP~CM $:					
25	Best Cost %:					Lowest GP in $:									
26	Worst Cost %:														

148 Chapter 10 Menu Analysis and Sales Mix

Simple Menu Analysis for Book
by Klaus Theyer C.C.C.

	A B C	D	E	F	G	H	I	J	K	L	M	N	O
	Menu Item:	# Sold	Sales Menu Mix Popularity Index %	Item Cost	COGS Total Cost	Menu Price Selling Price	Revenue Total Sales	Project. Product Cost %	Item GP or CM	Actual Product Cost %	Total Sold Item GP or CM	Contrib. Margin %	Contrib. Margin to Rev. %
1	Minute steak	73	6.70%	4.83	352.59	14.95	1,091.35	32.31%	10.12	32.31%	738.76	9.74%	6.35%
2	Shrimp (Tiger)	121	11.11%	6.59	797.39	18.95	2,292.95	34.78%	12.36	34.78%	1,495.56	19.72%	12.85%
3	Swordfish	105	9.64%	5.18	543.90	14.95	1,569.75	34.65%	9.77	34.65%	1,025.85	13.53%	8.81%
4	Chicken	140	12.86%	2.14	299.60	7.25	1,015.00	29.52%	5.11	29.52%	715.40	9.43%	6.15%
5	Lobster	51	4.68%	8.64	440.64	21.00	1,071.00	41.14%	12.36	41.14%	630.36	8.31%	5.42%
6	Scallops	85	7.81%	3.39	288.15	9.95	845.75	34.07%	6.56	34.07%	557.60	7.35%	4.79%
7	Beef medallions	125	11.48%	4.04	505.00	10.95	1,368.75	36.89%	6.91	36.89%	863.75	11.39%	7.42%
8	Pasta Primavera	155	14.23%	2.25	348.75	5.95	922.25	37.82%	3.70	37.82%	573.50	7.56%	4.93%
9	Meatloaf	97	8.91%	2.75	266.75	6.95	674.15	39.57%	4.20	39.57%	407.40	5.37%	3.50%
10	Cabbage Rolls	55	5.05%	2.05	112.75	6.95	382.25	29.50%	4.90	29.50%	269.50	3.55%	2.32%
11	Potato Skin	82	7.53%	1.22	100.04	4.95	405.90	24.65%	3.73	24.65%	305.86	4.03%	2.63%
Total:		1089	100.00%	43.08	4,055.56	122.80	11,639.10	XXXXXX	79.72	XXXXXXX	7,583.54	100.00%	65.16%
Averages:		99.0	9.09%	3.92	XXXXXX	11.16	XXXXXX	35.08%	7.25	34.84%	XXXXXXX	9.09%	5.92%
Projected Cost Percentage:								35.08%					
Actual Cost Percentage:								34.84%					
				equals	Variance:	minus		0.24%					
Highest Seller by # Sold:				155		Highest Rev. in $:		2,292.95		AVG Item GP–CM $:		7.25	
Lowest Seller by # Sold:				51		Lowest Rev. in $:		382.25		Highest Item GP–CM $:		12.36	
				Best Cost %:	24.65%	Highest GP in $:		1,495.56					
				Worst Cost %:	41.14%	Lowest GP in $:		269.50		Lowest Item GP–CM $:		3.70	

In the above illustration the best seller by numbers sold is: (155) the Pasta Primavera with a below average CM% and an above average Cost %.

Best Seller by Revenue is: Tiger Shrimp ($2,292.85); the Cost % is below average and it has the highest CM%.

Chapter 11

Breakeven Point Calculations for Value and Units

The Breakeven Point—Value

In order to calculate a breakeven point (where sales cover all costs, but no profit is made), you should be familiar with the following commonly used abbreviations and terminology:

- ▶ **S = SALES and/or REVENUE**
  Revenue refers to all Sales earned in exchange for Goods and Services (not including Taxes, as Taxes are NOT Revenue)

- ▶ **VC = VARIABLE COST**
  Refers to "All Costs that *are* changing with Sales volume"

- ▶ **VR = VARIABLE RATE – Equation VR = (VC ÷ S)**
  This Rate is calculated by dividing VARIABLE COSTS by SALES

- ▶ **CR = CONTRIBUTION RATE – Equation CR = (1 – VR)**
  Contribution Rate is a dividing factor and is established by either taking the whole number "1" and subtracting the Variable Rate expressed in a whole number (or fraction thereof) or replacing the number "1" with 100% and subtracting the Variable Rate in a percentage number. Either way is correct; however, *DO NOT* mix the two methods.

- ▶ **FXC = FIXED COST**
  Refers to "All Costs that *do not* change with Sales volume." (For the purpose of BEP calculations, Labour cost is usually considered a Fixed Cost.)

- ▶ **CM = CONTRIBUTION MARGIN – Equation CM = (S – VC)**
  Is the Dollar Amount remaining after subtracting the Variable Cost of an item from its sales price.

- ▶ **P = PROFIT – Equation P = (S – VC – SVC – FXC)**
  Profit refers to "Revenue minus Variable, Semi-Variable, and Fixed Costs"

Chapter 11 Breakeven Point Calculations for Value and Units

▶ **BEP = THE BREAKEVEN POINT** is calculated by dividing the Fixed Cost with the Contribution Rate:

▶ BEP = $\dfrac{\text{FXC (Fixed Cost)}}{\text{CR (Contribution Rate)}}$

To establish what **Sales are needed** to earn a desired amount of Profit, the formula should read:

Formula # 1   S = $\dfrac{\text{FXC (Fixed Costs)} + \text{P (Profit Expectations)}}{\text{CR (Contribution Rate)}}$

More useful formulas:

Formula # 1	Formula # 2	Formula # 3
CR = $\dfrac{\text{FXC} + \text{P}}{\text{S}}$	P = (S x CR) − FXC	FXC = (S x CR) − P

The Breakeven Point—Units

▶ **U = UNIT**
Singular or smallest (dividable) part of re-sellable (production) items.
Individual unit sales data is needed in order to calculate the breakeven point.

▶ **PSTS = PROPORTIONAL SHARE OF TOTAL SALES**
Ratio of Unit sales in comparison to Total Unit Sales within a given time period or the Ratio of Dollar sales in comparison to Total Dollar Sales within a given time period.

▶ **AVERAGE SALES OR COVER**
The result of dividing total dollar sales for a period by the number of customers served in that period; an average dollar figure representing the average amount spent by customers.

▶ **AVERAGE VARIABLE COST**
The result of dividing total variable cost for a period by the number of customers served in that period.

▶ **AVERAGE CONTRIBUTION MARGIN**
The dollar difference between average sales and average variable cost; the dollar amount remaining after average variable cost is subtracted from the average sale.

▶ **AVERAGE VARIABLE RATE**
The ratio of average variable cost to average sale, normally expressed in decimal form.

▶ **UNIT SALES REQUIRED TO BREAKEVEN**
The number of average sales required to achieve breakeven volume.

Review the Excel example on the next pages.

Chapter 11 Breakeven Point Calculations for Value and Units

Breakeven Point Calculations (Items Sold, Two Methods)

by Konrad Weinbuch CMC

	A	B	C	D	E	F	G	H	I	J	K
1	**Breakeven Point Calculations (Items Sold, Two Methods)**										
2											
3	Breakeven is the point at which total income equals total costs										
4	Breakeven may be expressed in Number of units (covers), or in a **Dollar $ amount** (Value), that must be sold in order to produce a profit of zero.										
5											
6	The Average Cheque of a restaurant reveals an average sale per customer (Cover) of										
7	for the dinner service period (Appetizer, Main Course and Dessert)						$45.00				
8	How many covers (customers served) have to be sold in order to break even?										
9	What should the total sales be to break even?										
10											
11	Item	Selling Price $	Food Cost $	Other VC $	Items total VC $	Contribution Margin $	FXC $ for the Period	Items BEP in #	Sales required to break even $	Variable Rate	Contribution Rate	Sales required to break even
12		xxxxxx	xxxxxx	xxxxxx	= C + D	= B - E	xxxxxx	= G / F	= H * B	= E / B	= 1 - J	= G / K
13	Appetizer	$9.00	$2.97	$1.97								
14	Main Course	$27.00	$9.31	$3.39		$1,795.00						
15	Dessert	$9.00	$2.55	$2.11		$1,795.00						
16	**Cost of Cover $**											
17												
18	How many Covers have to be sold to break even?				BEP Formula: FXC / ($P - Total VC) (From H16)							

4 decimal places please

152 Chapter 11 Breakeven Point Calculations for Value and Units

Breakeven Point Calculations (Items Sold, Two Methods)

by Konrad Weinbuch CMC

Breakeven is the point at which total income equals total costs

Breakeven may be expressed in Number of units (covers), or in a **Dollar $ amount** (Value), that must be sold in order to produce a profit of zero.

The Average Cheque of a restaurant reveals an average sale per customer (Cover) of $45.00

How many covers (customers served) have to be sold in the dinner service period (Appetizer, Main Course and Dessert)?

What should the total sales be to break even?

	A	B	C	D	E	F	G	H	I	J	K	L
10											4 decimal places please	
11	Item	Selling Price $	Food Cost $	Other VC $	Items total VC $	Contribution Margin $	FXC $ for the Period	Items BEP in #	Sales required to break even $	Variable Rate	Con-tri-bution Rate	Sales required to break even
12		xxxxxx	xxxxxx	xxxxxx	= C+D	= B − E	xxxxxx	= G/F	= H*B	= E/B	= 1 − J	= G/K
13	Appetizer	$9.00	$2.97	$1.97	$4.94	$4.06	$1,795.00	442.12	$3,979.06	0.5489	0.4511	$3,979.06
14	Main Course	$27.00	$9.31	$3.39	$12.70	$14.30	$1,795.00	125.52	$3,389.16	0.4704	0.5296	$3,389.16
15	Dessert	$9.00	$2.55	$2.11	$4.66	$4.34	$1,795.00	413.59	$3,722.35	0.5178	0.4822	$3,722.35
16	Cost of Cover $	$45.00	$14.83	$7.47	$22.30	$22.70		79.07	$3,558.37	0.4956	0.5044	$3,558.37
17												
18	How many Covers have to be sold to break even?				BEP Formula: FXC / (SP − Total VC) (From H16)				79.07			

Chapter 12

Essential Basic Math Templates, References, Exercises and Workshops

Index

1. Conversion Sheet Page One
2. Conversion Sheet Page Two
3. Conversion Sheet Page Three
4. Percentage Pie Charts
5. Baking Sheets Samples
6. Formula Page for Cost, Cost % & Selling Price as well as Yield Calculation Methods
7. Easy Workshop Example (blank)
8. Easy Workshop Example (completed)
9. Yield calculation example for a Suckling Pig (blank)
10. Yield calculation example for a Suckling Pig (completed)
11. Simple Menu Analysis for food items example (blank)
12. Simple Menu Analysis example (completed)
13. Yield calculation example for a Turkey (blank)
14. Yield calculation example for a Turkey (completed)
15. Yield Test comparison sheet (blank)
16. Yield Test comparison sheet (completed)
17. Simple Menu Analysis for Beverage items example (blank)
18. Simple Menu Analysis for Beverage items example (completed)
19. From One Dollar to a Googolplex chart (The difference a few zeros can make)

154 Chapter 12 Essential Basic Math Templates, References, Exercises and Workshops

Quick Conversion Factors for Kitchen and Bar
by Klaus Theyer CCC   January 2013   Page 1

NOTE: Significance of conversions should be limited to 4 decimal places.

FLUID Units abbreviations:

Tsp	Teaspoon
Tbsp	Tablespoon
Ml	Milliliter
Dl	Deciliter
M cup	Metric cup
Ltr	Liter
US fl Oz	US fl ounce
US Cup	Cup
US Gal	US Gallon
US Qrt	US Quart
US Pnt	US Pint
Imp fl Oz	Imperial fl ounce
Imp Cup	Imp cup
Imp Gal	Imperial Gallon
Imp Qrt	Imperial Quart
Imp Pnt	Imperial Pint
Btl	Bottle

SOLID Weight abbreviations:

Gr	Gram
Dk	Decagram
Kg	Kilogram
Oz	Ounce
Lbs	Pound

LENGTH Units Abbreviations:

Mm	Millimeter
Cm	Centimeter
Mtr	Meter
Km	Kilometer
Inch "	Inch
Ft '	Foot
Yd	Yard
Mi	Mile

NM is a Nautical Mile

Temperature definition & conversion:
C = Celsius   F = Fahrenheit
To Convert From F to C: (F - 32) ÷ 9 x 5 or (F - 32) ÷ 1.8
To Convert From C to F: (C x 9 ÷ 5) + 32 or (C x 1.8) + 32

Common C to F conversions:

C	F	
0	32	
-40	-40	
100	212	
121	250	
149	300	
177	350	
191	375	
204	400	
232	450	
260	500	
288	550	
315.5	600	
21.11	70.0	Room temperature
36.8	98.2	Body temperature
-273.15	-459.7	Absolute zero (0)
100	212.0	Boiling
0	32.0	Freezing

VOLUME (US Liquid Fluid)
1 US fl Oz = 29.57 Ml. 1 US Gal = 4 Qrt or 8 Pnt or 128 Fl Oz. 1 US Gal = 3.785 Ltr
1 US fl Oz x 0.960764769 = 1 Imp fl Oz or 1 US fl Oz x 0.961 = 1 Imp fl Oz
1 Ltr = 10 Dl = 1000 Ml = 33.818 US fl Oz

1 US fl Oz = 2 Tbls of liquid. 4 US fl Oz = 1/2 Cup. 8 US fl Oz = 1 Cup.
3 Tsp = 1 Tbls, 1 Tbls = 1/16 of a US Cup, 4 Tbls = 1/4 US Cup,
8 Tbls = 1/2 US Cup, 1/2 Lb (8 oz) of Butter = 1 Cup, 1 Lbs of Butter = 2 Cups,
2 US Cups = 1 Pnt, 2 Pnt = 1 Qrt, 4 Qrt = 1 US Gal or 3.785 Ltr

QUICK BAR measurement conversions:

	Imp Oz Shot	US Oz Shot	Ml
1	28.5		Ml
1		29.57	Ml
1 1/2		42.6	Ml

U.S. VOLUME Units - for accurate conversion
Multiply units times factor for Metric
one (1) unit x factor equals = Metric

			For simple Recipe conversion use:
1	Tsp	4.928365563	Ml	5
1	Tbsp	14.78509669	Ml	15
1	Fl Oz	29.5701934	Ml	29.6
1	Cup	0.236515470	Ltr	0.24
1	½ pint	0.23656155	Ltr	0.24
1	Pint	0.473123094	Ltr	0.47
1	Quarts	0.9462461880	Ltr	0.95
1	Gallons	3.784984752	Ltr	3.8

MIXED Volume Units - for accurate conversion
Multiply units times factor for Results
one (1) unit x factor equals = results

			For simple Recipe conversion use:
1 US	Tsp	0.166666667	US fl Oz	0.17
1 US	Tbsp	0.500000000	US fl Oz	0.5
1	Ml	0.033817837	US fl Oz	0.034
1	250 Ml	8.454459425	US fl Oz	8.500
1	Ltr	33.8178376894	US fl Oz	33.82
1	Ltr	2.1136148556	US Pnt	2.11
1	Ltr	1.056807428	US Qrt	1.06
1	Ltr	0.2642018569	US Gal	0.264

Metric Ml / US fl Oz / Imp fl Oz

	Metric Ml	US fl Oz	Imp fl Oz
1 Glass	148	5	5.2
1 Glass	177	6	6.25
1 Btl	187	6.3	6.6
1 Btl	341	11.5	12
1 Btl	500	16.91	17.6
1 Btl	750	25.4	26.4
1 Btl	1,000	33.81	35.2
1 Btl	1,500	50.72	52.8
1 Keg	20,000	676.28	703.9

Quick Conversion Factors for Kitchen and Bar

by Klaus Theyer CCC   January 2013

NOTE: Significance of conversions should be limited to **4 decimal** places.

VOLUME (Imperial Liquid Fluid)

1 Imp fl Oz = 28.413 Ml,   1 Imp Gal = 4 Qrt = 8 Pnt = 160 Fl Oz, 1 Gal = 4.546 Ltr
1 Imp fl Oz ÷ 1.0408375 = 1 US fl Oz or 1 Imp fl Oz ÷ 1.041 = 1 US fl Oz
1 Ltr = 10 Dl = 1000 Ml = 35.195 Imp fl Oz
1 US fl Oz = 29.574 Ml minus 1 Imp fl Oz (28.413 ml) = 1.161 Ml, hence the US fl Oz is 1.161 Ml, or (4.088%) larger than the Imp fl Oz

LENGTH Conversion Summary

Mm = Millimeter, Cm = Centimetre, Mtr = Meter, Km = Kilometer
1 Cm = 10 Mm, 1 Mtr = 100 Cm = 1000 Mm, 25.4 Mm = 1 Inch "
Inch " = Inch, Ft ' = Foot (feet), Yd = Yard, Mi = Mile, NM = Nautical Mile
12 Inch " = 1 Ft, 3 Ft = 1 Yd, 5280 Ft = 1 Mi, 1 Mi = 1760 Yd

IMP Volume Units - for accurate conversion
Multiply units times factor for Metric

	one (1) unit x factor equals = Metric		For simple Recipe conversion use:
1	Tsp	3.625116000	Ml	5
1	Tbsp	14.500464000	Ml	15
1	Fl Oz	28.410000000	Ml	28.4
1	Cup	0.227280000	Ltr	0.23
1	½ pint	0.284100000	Ltr	0.284
1	Pint	0.568200000	Ltr	0.57
1	Quarts	1.136400000	Ltr	1.14
1	Gallons	4.546000000	Ltr	4.55

MIXED Volume Units - for accurate conversion
Multiply units times factor for Results

	one (1) unit x factor equals = results		For simple Recipe conversion use:
1	Tsp	0.127600000	Imp fl Oz	0.13
1	Tbsp	0.510400000	Imp fl Oz	0.5
1	Ml	0.035198736	Imp fl Oz	0.04
1	250 Ml	8.80 Imp fl Oz		8.80
1	Ltr	35.198736360	Imp fl Oz	35.20
1	Ltr	1.759436818	Imp Pnt	1.76
1	Ltr	0.879718409	Imp Qrt	0.88
1	Ltr	0.219929602	Imp Gal	0.22

WEIGHT Units - for accurate conversion
Multiply units times factor for Result

	one (1) unit x factor equals = results		For simple Recipe conversion use:
1	Oz	28.34952312	Gr	28.35
1	Gr	0.035273962	Oz	0.035
1	Lb	0.453592370	Kg	0.454
1	Lb	453.592370400	Gr	454
1	Kg	2.204626199	Lb	2.205
1	Kg	35.273961955	Oz	35.3
1	Metric Ton	1.102311311	Ton	1.1
1	Ton	0.907184739	Metric T.	0.91

LENGTH Units - for accurate conversion
Multiply units times factor for Result

	one (1) unit x factor equals = results		For simple Recipe conversion use:
1	Mm	0.04	Inch "	0.04
1	Cm	0.39	Inch "	0.39
1	Mtr	39.4	Inch "	39.4
1	Mtr	3.28	Ft '	3.28
1	Mtr	1.09	Yd	1.09
1	Km	0.06	Mi	0.06
1	Km	0.54	Nautical NM	0.54
1	inch "	25.4	Mm	25.4
1	inch "	2.54	Cm	2.54
1	inch "	0.03	Mtr	0.03
1	foot '	0.3	Mtr	0.3
1	Yd	0.91	Mtr	0.91
1	Mi (land)	1.61	Km	1.61
1	Nautical NM	1.85	Km	1.85

156 Chapter 12 Essential Basic Math Templates, References, Exercises and Workshops

Quick Conversion Factors for Kitchen or Bar

http://www.esbconsult.com/esbcalc

#REF!   #REF!   #REF!

Page 2

Quick Bar measurements conversion

1 Imp oz Shot	= 28.41 ml			
1 ¼ Imp oz Shot	= 35.513 ml			
1 ½ Imp oz Shot	= 42.615 ml			
1 btl (26 imp fl oz) =	738.66 ml	.73866 L		
1 btl (40 Imp oz) =	1136.40 ml	1.14 L		
1 btl (250 ml) =	8.799 Imp oz	8.454 US oz		
1 btl (500 ml) =	17.599 Imp oz	16.909 US oz		
1 btl (750 ml) =	26.399 Imp oz	25.363 US oz		
1 btl (1 L) =	35.199 Imp oz	33.818 US oz		
1 btl (1750 ml) =	61.598 Imp oz	59.181 US oz		
1 btl (2 L) =	70.398 Imp oz	67.636 US oz		

LENGTH

#'s of Units	Unit	times	=	to
1	inches	25.40		millimeters
1	inches	2.54		centimeters
1	inches	0.0254		meters
1	foot	0.305		meters
1	yard	0.91		meters
1	mile (land)	1.61		kilometers
1	nautical miles	1.85		kilometers

in = inches, ft = foot (feet), yd = yard, mi = mile
12 inches = 1 foot, 3 feet = 1 yard, 5280 feet = 1 mile, 1 mile = 1760 yards

TEMPERATURE

F to C (F - 32) ÷ 9 × 5
C to F (C × 9 ÷ 5) + 32
F to C (F - 32) ÷ 1.8
C to F (C × 1.8) + 32

Fahrenheit	to Celcius	Fahrenheit	to Celcius
500	260	350	176.66
450	232.22	300	148.88
400	204.44	250	121.11
375	190.55	212	100

WEIGHT conversions

#'s of Units	Unit	times	=	to	For simple Recipe conversion
1	Ounces (oz)	28.34952312		Grams (gr)	28.4
1	Grams	0.035273962		Ounces	0.035
1	Pounds (lbs)	0.453592370040		Kilograms	0.454
1	Pounds (lbs)	453.5923704		Grams (gr)	454
1	Kilograms	2.204622619199		Pounds	2.205
1	Kilograms	35.273961955800		Ounces	35.3
1	Metric Tons	1.102311311		Tons	1.1
1	Tons	0.9071847399		Metric Tons	0.91

1 Kg = 100 Decagrams = 1000 Grams = 2.205 Lbs
1 Pound = 16 Ounces = 454 Grams = .454 Kilograms

#'s of Units	Unit	times	=	to
1	millimeters	0.04		inches
1	centimeters	0.394		inches
1	meters	39.37		inches
1	meters	3.281		feet
1	meters	1.094		yards
1	kilometers	0.6214		miles
1	kilometers	0.540		nautical miles

mm = millimeter, cm = centemeter, m = meter, km = kilometer
1 cm = 10 mm, 1 m = 100 cm = 1000 mm

Fahrenheit	to Celcius	Fahrenheit	to Celcius
32	0	Body 98.3	36.8
-40	-40	Room 70	21.11
-28	-33.33	Absolute 0	-273.15
-18	-27.78	-459.67	Absolute 0

The Percentage Pie   by Klaus Theyer C.C.C.

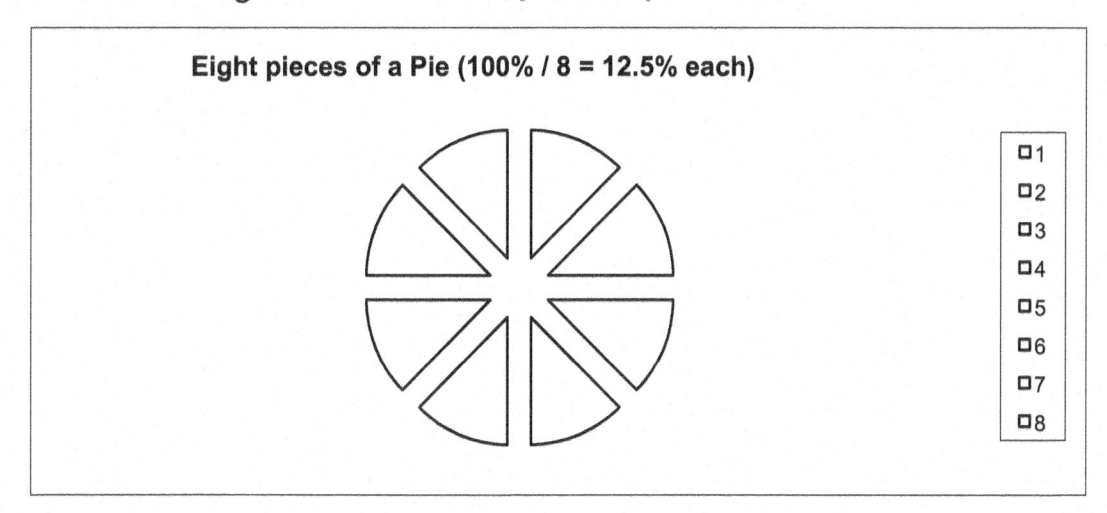

Eight pieces of a Pie (100% / 8 = 12.5% each)

☐1
☐2
☐3
☐4
☐5
☐6
☐7
☐8

If one eight of a pie is 12.5%, what percentage is one twelfth?

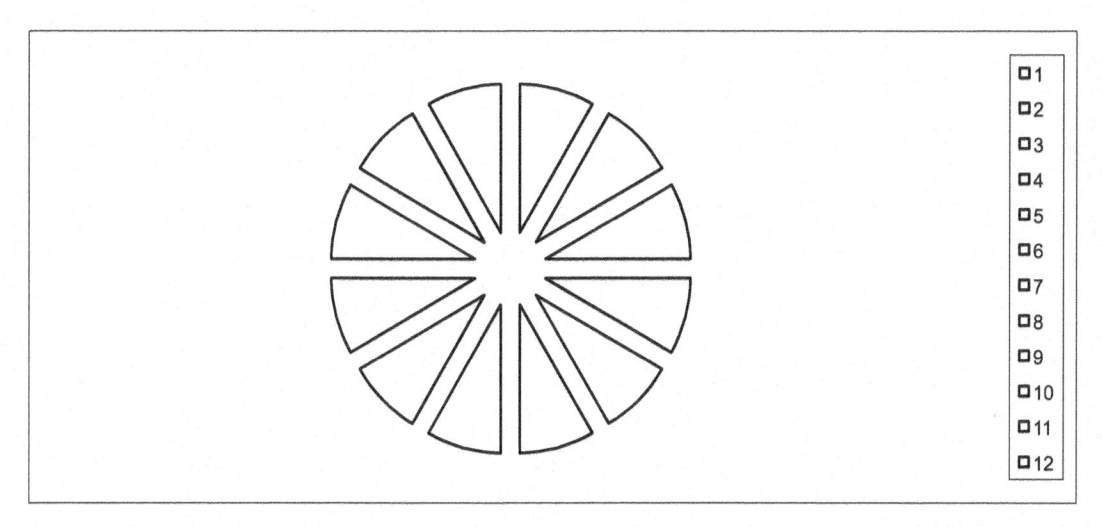

☐1
☐2
☐3
☐4
☐5
☐6
☐7
☐8
☐9
☐10
☐11
☐12

If one twelfth of a pie is 8.333%, what percentage is one sixteenth? (100 ÷ 16)

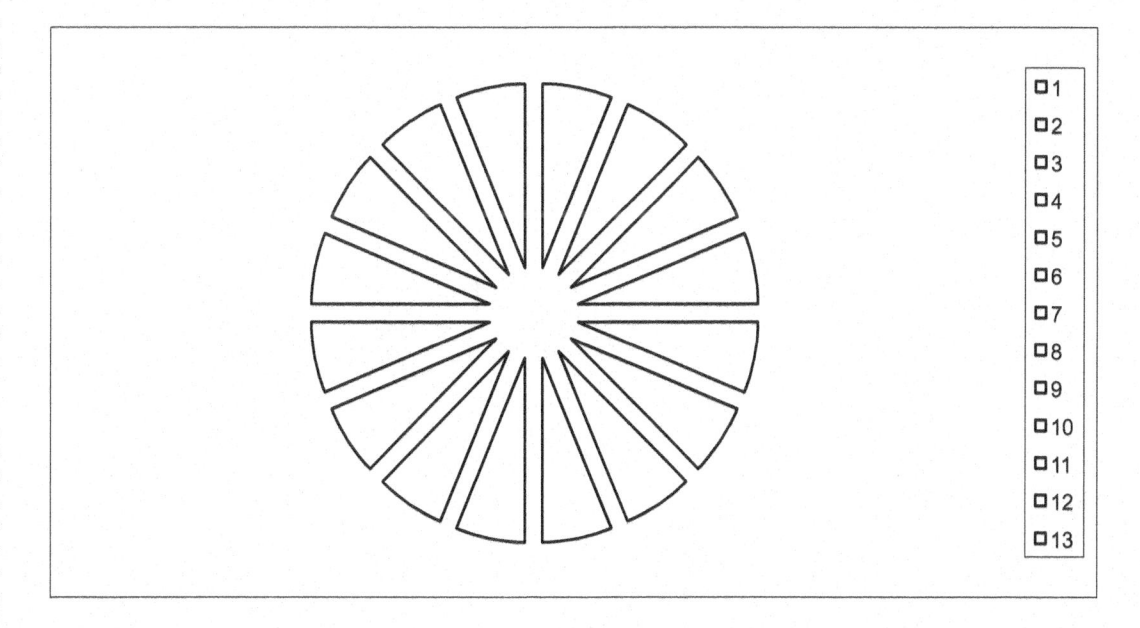

☐1
☐2
☐3
☐4
☐5
☐6
☐7
☐8
☐9
☐10
☐11
☐12
☐13

Standard Baking Sheet(s)

18" X 26" X 1" high   (45.72 cm X 66.04 cm X 2.54 cm)

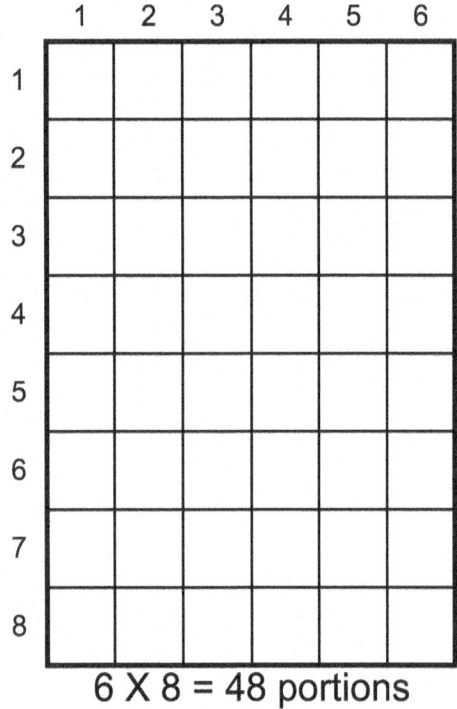

6 X 8 = 48 portions
(3" x 3.25" x 1") or
(7.6 x 8.23 x 2.5 cm rounded)

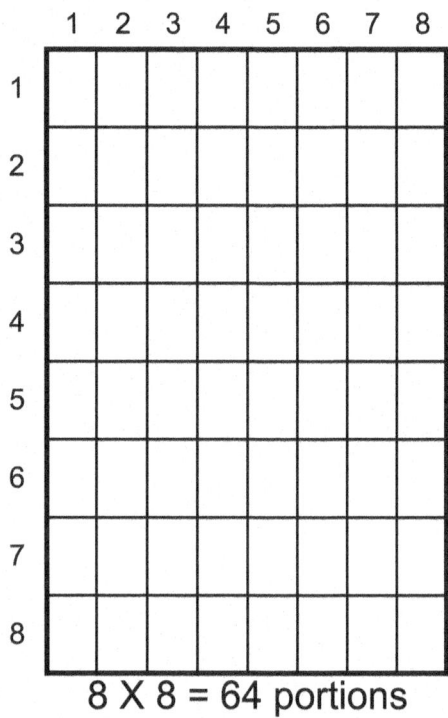

8 X 8 = 64 portions
(2.25" x 3.25" x 1") or
(5.7 x 8.23 x 2.5 cm rounded)

Recommendation:

Since the edges/rims/borders of the trays are slightly slanted, for cost calculations consider a yield percentage between 95 and 98%.

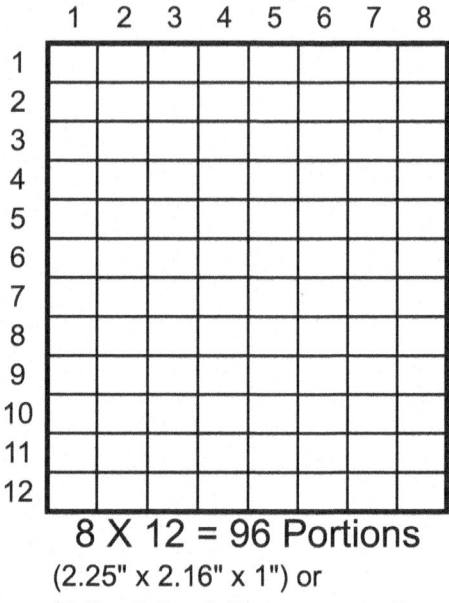

8 X 12 = 96 Portions
(2.25" x 2.16" x 1") or
(5.7 x 5.5 x 2.5 cm rounded)

Chapter 12 Essential Basic Math Templates, References, Exercises and Workshops 159

Sales, Cost, Cost %, formulae, by Klaus Theyer CCC

Explanation of abbreviations:
S.P. = Selling Price,   **C** = Cost,
C % = Cost percentage,
COGS = Cost Of Goods Sold,
R or Rev = Revenue,

Cost → Cost % → S.P. → Cost

The "3" basic formulas to calculate either Cost, Selling Price or Cost percentage:

(If your calculator has a % key and if you use it you may omit the x 100)

COST ÷ COST % = S.P.   S.P. × COST % = COST

COST ÷ S.P. x 100 = COST %   COST × Factor = S.P.

Common Yield, A.P., U.P., L, E.P., Y, %, $, formulae:

Explanation of abbreviations:
Yield = Edible remains of As Purchased   **A.P.** = As Purchased
U.P. = Usable remains of As Purchased   **E.P.** = Edible Portion
L = Loss, difference between A.P. And Edible Portion or Yield
Y = Yield, Consumable or Edible Portion   **%** = Percentage
$ = Value   The $ or % could apply to any descriptor above

E.P. or U.P. ÷ A.P. x 100 = Yield %   A.P. × Yield % = E.P.

E.P. or U.P. ÷ Yield % = A.P.   A.P. $ ÷ Yield % = E.P. $

E.P. $ × Yield % = A.P. $ A.P. $ ÷ E.P. Weight = E.P. $

L or U.P. ÷ A.P. = L or U.P. %   A.P. $ ÷ E.P. Count = E.P. Item $

A.P. Weight × Yield % = E.P. Weight

160 Chapter 12 Essential Basic Math Templates, References, Exercises and Workshops

Easy Workshop by Klaus Theyer C.C.C.

1. A Pie is divided into [8] portions.

2. One portion of this Apple Pie costs [5] portions are sold. What percentage % of the Pie is remaining?

3. What percentage % of the cost of a whole Pie is represented by one slice? [$ 0.60] Dollars to prepare. How much does it cost to make [12] Pies?

4. If you were to sell one slice for [$ 2.75] what is the Food Cost percentage %?

5. If the desired Food Cost percentage is [32.00%] what would the Selling Price have to be?

6. If the Food Cost is [25] percent % and the Selling Price is [2.50] what is the Product Cost in ¢?

7. To make one Pie, [1] Kg of Apples is needed, after peeling and trimming there is only [75%] left of the purchase weight. What is the actual weight, of the peeled and cored Apples in grams?

8. How many pounds (lbs) of A.P. Apples are needed if the recipe calls for [5] lbs of U.P. Apples?

9. If Apples average [8] oz each, how many Apples would you have to buy in the previous question? [ ] in ounces?

10. If the Apples cost [$ 1.21] per Kg, what is the total cost of the bought Apples [ ]

Sales mix - Menu mix - Popularity Index

Item Name	Sold	% of Sale
11 Cheeseburger	14	
12 Hamburger	18	
13 Hot Dog	12	
14 Poutine	6	
15 French Fries	36	
16 Chef Salad	10	
17 Apple Pie portion	22	
18 Ice Cream	11	
Total		

Item Name	Sold	% of Sale
19 Coffee Columbia	42	
20 Coffee Dark Roast	23	
21 Coffee Decaffeinated	12	
22 Coffee Arabica	18	
23 Coke/Pepsi	26	
24 Diet Coke/Pepsi	43	
25 Milk 2% (1/2 pint)	14	
26 Red Wine 5 oz glass	28	
Total		

Easy Workshop by Klaus Theyer C.C.C.

1. A Pie is divided into [8] portions. What percentage % of the Pie is remaining? [37.50%]

2. One portion of this Apple Pie costs [$ 0.60] Dollars to prepare. How much does it cost to make [12] Pies? [$ 57.60]

3. What percentage % of the cost of a whole Pie is represented by one slice? [12.50%]

4. If you were to sell one slice for [$ 2.75] what is the Food Cost percentage %? [21.82%]

5. If the desired Food Cost percentage is [32.00%] what would the Selling Price have to be? [$ 1.88]

6. If the Food Cost is [25] percent % and the Selling Price is [2.50] what is the Product Cost in ¢? [62.5]

7. To make one Pie, [1] Kg of Apples is needed, after peeling and trimming there is only [75%] left of the purchase weight. What is the actual weight, of the peeled and cored Apples in grams? [26.46] in ounces? [26.46]

8. How many pounds (lbs) of A.P. Apples are needed if the recipe calls for [5] lbs of U.P. Apples? [6.67]

9. If Apples average [8] oz each, how many Apples would you have to buy in the previous question? [13.33]

10. If the Apples cost [$ 1.21] per Kg, what is the total cost of the bought Apples [$ 3.66]

Sales mix - Menu mix - Popularity Index

Item Name	Sold	% of Sale		Item Name	Sold	% of Sale
11 Cheeseburger	14	10.85%		19 Coffee Columbia	42	20.39%
12 Hamburger	18	13.95%		20 Coffee Dark Roast	23	11.17%
13 Hot Dog	12	9.30%		21 Coffee Decaffeinated	12	5.83%
14 Poutine	6	4.65%		22 Coffee Arabica	18	8.74%
15 French Fries	36	27.91%		23 Coke/Pepsi	26	12.62%
16 Chef Salad	10	7.75%		24 Diet Coke/Pepsi	43	20.87%
17 Apple Pie portion	22	17.05%		25 Milk 2% (1/2 pint)	14	6.80%
18 Ice Cream	11	8.53%		26 Red Wine 5 oz glass	28	13.59%
Total	129	100.00%		Total	206	100.00%

162 Chapter 12 Essential Basic Math Templates, References, Exercises and Workshops

Cooking Yield Formulae and Scenarios by Klaus Theyer CCC

A.P. As Purchased	U.P. Usable Portion # 1	U.P. Usable Portion # 2	E.P. Edible Portion
represents 100% in Kg and $	Fraction of A.P. U.P. "1"	Fraction of A.P. U.P. "2"	Fraction of A.P. Yield
As Purchased	*Before Cooking*	*After Cooking*	*After portioning*
A.P. weight 25 Kg	U.P. weight 24 Kg Shrinkage/**Loss** Kg	U.P. weight 20 Kg Tot. Shrinkage Kg	E.P. weight 15 Kg Tot. Shrinkage Kg
A.P. $ Cost per Kg $5.50		E.P. Portion Size = 175 Gr	

Total (extended) Cost A.P. Is ($ per Kg x A.P. Kg) = ☐

Loss between A.P. and "before cooking U.P. "1"
(A.P. weight - U.P. one weight) = ☐ Kg   Loss % = (Loss "1" weight ÷ A.P. weight)   ☐

    Yield between A.P. and "before cooking U.P. "1" =   (U.P. "1" Kg ÷ A.P. Kg) =   U.P. Yield "1"

Loss between A.P. and "after cooking U.P. "2"
(A.P. weight - U.P. two weight) = ☐ Kg   Loss % = (Loss "2" weight ÷ A.P. weight)   ☐

    Yield between A.P. and "after cooking U.P. "2" =   (U.P. "2" Kg ÷ A.P. Kg) =   U.P. Yield "2"

Loss between A.P. and "after carving E.P. Yield"
(A.P. weight - E.P. Yield weight) = ☐ Kg   Loss % = (Total Loss weight ÷ A.P. weight)   ☐

    Yield between A.P. and "after carving E.P. Yield" =   (E.P. Kg ÷ A.P. Kg) =   E.P. Yield

As mentioned before, the purpose of calculating yield weight is to acknowledge the weight loss and to ensure compensation. **Example:** purchased 1 Kg of Pork leg at a cost of $5.50. Between preparation and cooking the loss is 40% of its weight, or 400 Gr, therefore you only have 60%, or 600 Gr left for sale, but you paid for 1 Kg (1000 Gr).

The formula for compensation is straight forward: (Divide A.P. $ with Y %) to calculate compensation for the
Cost of the weight Loss.   A.P. $ p. Kg is: ☐

    Yield % is: ☐   Yield adjusted Cost is: ☐   per K.g

Based on the above example, we can now calculate the cost of one 175 Gr portion.
The Cost of one Yield adjusted Kg (which equals 1000 Gr) is ☐
Cost of one Gram is: ($ ÷ 1000) ☐
Cost of a 175 Gr portion is: ☐

Another very useful application of Yield % is to calculate the Raw or A.P. weight
to be purchased in order to serve a certain number of portions. **Example:**
You prepare for a function for 60 people, each one is to get a 200 Gr (E.P.) portion
You know from experience that the Average Yield % is 60% of A.P.

Equation: # of Customers x portion size, divided by Yield % equals weight in Gr.
☐ Gr
divide Gr by 1000 equals Kg   ☐ Kg are needed to serve 60, 200 Gr portions.

Cooking Yield Formulae and Scenarios by Klaus Theyer CCC

A.P. As Purchased	U.P. Usable Portion # 1	U.P. Usable Portion # 2	E.P. Edible Portion
represents 100% in Kg and $ *As Purchased*	Fraction of A.P. U.P. "1" *Before Cooking*	Fraction of A.P. U.P. "2" *After Cooking*	Fraction of A.P. Yield *After portioning*
A.P. weight 25 Kg	U.P. weight 24 Kg Shrinkage/Loss 1 Kg	U.P. weight 20 Kg Tot. Shrinkage 5 Kg	E.P. weight 15 Kg Tot. Shrinkage 10 Kg
A.P. $ Cost per Kg $5.50		E.P. Portion Size = 175 Gr	

Total (extended) Cost A.P. Is ($ per Kg x A.P. Kg) = $ 137.50

Loss between A.P. and "before cooking U.P. "1"
(A.P. weight - U.P. one weight) =   1 Kg   Loss % = (Loss "1" weight ÷ A.P. weight)   4%

  Yield between A.P. and "before cooking U.P. "1" =   (U.P. "1" Kg ÷ A.P. Kg) =   U.P. Yield "1"   96%

Loss between A.P. and "after cooking U.P. "2"
(A.P. weight - U.P. two weight) =   5 Kg   Loss % = (Loss "2" weight ÷ A.P. weight)   20%

  Yield between A.P. and "after cooking U.P. "2" =   (U.P. "2" Kg ÷ A.P. Kg) =   U.P. Yield "2"   80%

Loss between A.P. and "after carving E.P. Yield"
(A.P. weight - E.P. Yield weight) =   10 Kg   Loss % = (Total Loss weight ÷ A.P. weight)   40%

Yield between A.P. and "after carving E.P. Yield" =   (E.P. Kg ÷ A.P. Kg) =   E.P. Yield   60%

As mentioned before, the purpose of calculating yield weight is to acknowledge the weight loss and to ensure compensation. **Example:** purchased 1 Kg of Pork leg at a cost of $5.50. Between preparation and cooking the loss is 40% of its weight, or 400 Gr, therefore you only have 60%, or 600 Gr left for sale, but you paid for 1 Kg (1000 Gr).

The formula for compensation is straight forward: (Divide A.P. $ with Y %) to calculate compensation for the
Cost of the weight Loss.   A.P. $ p. Kg is: $5.50

   Yield % is: 60%   Yield adjusted Cost is: $9.17   per K.g   (5.50 ÷ 60 x 100 = 9.17)

Based on the above example, we can now calculate the cost of one 175 Gr portion.
The Cost of one Yield adjusted Kg (which equals 1000 Gr) is $9.17
Cost of one Gram is: ($ ÷ 1000)   (9.17 ÷ 1000) $0.0092
Cost of a 175 Gr portion is: (9.17 ÷ 1000 x 175) $1.60

Another very useful application of Yield % is to calculate the Raw or A.P. weight
to be purchased in order to serve a certain number of portions. **Example:**
You prepare for a function for   60   people, each one is to get a   200 Gr (E.P.) portion
You know from experience that the Average Yield % is   60%   of A.P.

Equation: # of Customers x portion size, divided by Yield % equals weight in Gr.
((60 x 200) ÷ 60%) =   20000 Gr
divide Gr by 1000 equals Kg   20 Kg are needed to serve 60, 200 Gr portions.

164 Chapter 12 Essential Basic Math Templates, References, Exercises and Workshops

Simple Menu Analysis for Book
by Klaus Theyer C.C.C.

	A	B	C D E	F	G	H	I	J	K	L	M	N	O
5			Menu Item:	# Sold	Sales Menu Mix Popularity Index %	COGS Item Cost	Total Cost	Menu Selling Price	Revenue Total Sales	Project. Product Cost %	Item GP or CM	Actual Product Cost %	Total Sold Item GP or CM	Contrib. Margin %	Contrib. to Rev. Margin %
					(D6/D17) %		(D6xF6)		(D6 × H6)	(F6/H6) %	(H6-F6)	(G6/I6) %	(I6-G6)	(M6/M17) %	(M6/I17) %
6	1	Minute steak		73		4.83		14.95							
7	2	Shrimp (Tiger)		121		6.59		18.95							
8	3	Swordfish		105		5.18		14.95							
9	4	Chicken		140		2.14		7.25							
10	5	Lobster		51		8.64		21.00							
11	6	Scallops		85		3.39		9.95							
12	7	Beef medallions		125		4.04		10.95							
13	8	Pasta Primavera		155		2.25		5.95							
14	9	Meatloaf		97		2.75		6.95							
15	10	Cabbage Rolls		55		2.05		6.95							
16	11	Potato Skin		82		1.22		4.95							
17	Total:						xxxxxx		xxxxxx		xxxxxx		xxxxxx		
18	Averages:									=F17/H17		=G17/I17			
19	Projected Cost Percentage:														
20	Actual Cost Percentage:														
21			equals	Variance:	minus	=F19-F20									
22	Highest Seller by # Sold:					=max(range)		Highest Rev. in $:			Highest GP in $:		AVG Item GP~CM $:		
23	Lowest Seller by # Sold:					=min(range)		Lowest Rev. in $:			Lowest GP in $:		Highest Item GP~CM $:		
24				Best Cost %:				Highest GP in $:					Lowest Item GP~CM $:		
25															
26				Worst Cost %:				Lowest GP in $:							

Chapter 12 Essential Basic Math Templates, References, Exercises and Workshops 165

Simple Menu Analysis for Book
by Klaus Theyer C.C.C.

	Menu Item:	# Sold	Sales Menu Mix Popularity Index %	Item Cost	COGS Total Cost	Menu Selling Price	Revenue Total Sales	Project. Product Cost %	Item GP or CM	Actual Product Cost %	Total Sold Item GP or CM	Contrib. Margin %	Contrib. Margin to Rev. %
1	Minute steak	73	6.70%	4.83	352.59	14.95	1091.35	32.31%	10.12	32.31%	738.76	9.74%	6.35%
2	Shrimp (Tiger)	121	11.11%	6.59	797.39	18.95	2292.95	34.78%	12.36	34.78%	1495.56	19.72%	12.85%
3	Swordfish	105	9.64%	5.18	543.90	14.95	1569.75	34.65%	9.77	34.65%	1025.85	13.53%	8.81%
4	Chicken	140	12.86%	2.14	299.60	7.25	1015.00	29.52%	5.11	29.52%	715.40	9.43%	6.15%
5	Lobster	51	4.68%	8.64	440.64	21.00	1071.00	41.14%	12.36	41.14%	630.36	8.31%	5.42%
6	Scallops	85	7.81%	3.39	288.15	9.95	845.75	34.07%	6.56	34.07%	557.60	7.35%	4.79%
7	Beef medallions	125	11.48%	4.04	505.00	10.95	1368.75	36.89%	6.91	36.89%	863.75	11.39%	7.42%
8	Pasta Primavera	155	14.23%	2.25	348.75	5.95	922.25	37.82%	3.70	37.82%	573.50	7.56%	4.93%
9	Meatloaf	97	8.91%	2.75	266.75	6.95	674.15	39.57%	4.20	39.57%	407.40	5.37%	3.50%
10	Cabbage Rolls	55	5.05%	2.05	112.75	6.95	382.25	29.50%	4.90	29.50%	269.50	3.55%	2.32%
11	Potato Skin	82	7.53%	1.22	100.04	4.95	405.90	24.65%	3.73	24.65%	305.86	4.03%	2.63%
Total:		1089	100.00%	43.08	4,055.56	122.80	11,639.10	XXXXXX	79.72	XXXXXX	7,583.54	100.00%	65.16%
Averages:		99.0	9.09%	3.92	XXXXXX	11.16	XXXXXX	35.08%	7.25	34.84%	XXXXXX	9.09%	5.92%

Projected Cost Percentage:	35.08%
Actual Cost Percentage:	34.84%
equals Variance: minus	0.24%

Highest Seller by # Sold:	155	Highest Rev. in $:	2,292.95	AVG item GP–CM $:	7.25
Lowest Seller by # Sold:	51	Lowest Rev. in $:	382.25	Highest Item GP–CM $:	12.36
Best Cost %:	24.65%	Highest GP in $:	1,495.56	Lowest Item GP–CM $:	3.70
Worst Cost %:	41.14%	Lowest GP in $:	269.50		

166 Chapter 12   Essential Basic Math Templates, References, Exercises and Workshops

Turkey Yield by Klaus Theyer C.C.C.

Keep all calculations at THREE decimal places

Part one

Based on the following information, answer the accompanying questions:

Turkey A.P. Info

Cost	$	5.83	per Kg
Weight		7.26	Kg

U.P.	Weight	6.7	Kg

The percentage Yield for the cooked (**U.P.**) Turkey is ? ☐

After carving there are 2.6 Kg Bones left.

What is the edible (**E.P.**) weight in Kg ? ☐

The percentage Yield for the cooked (**E.P.**) Turkey is ? ☐

The cost of one E.P. cooked Kg is ? ☐

What is the cost of a 150 Gr portion is ? ☐

Side dishes (Line Cost) is $ 1.75

Total cost of one Turkey meal ? ☐

Part two

You are contemplating different Selling Price scenarios by using the most common method; Cost divided by Cost % = **S.P.**

Potential Selling Price based on listed Cost Percentages:

24.00%	26.00%	28.00%	30.00%	32.00%	34.00%

Now, the Menu Price is: $ 12.50   Actual Cost % is ? ☐

Part three

Based on the result of **Part one**, how many raw (**A.P.**) Turkeys would you have to buy to serve 410 Customers ?

Step one: # of Customers x portion size in Grams: ☐

Step two: Divide result by 1000 to convert to Kg: ☐

Step three: Divide Kg by Yield %: ☐

Step four: Divide A.P. Kg by A.P. weight of 1 Turkey: ☐

A.P. Cost $ to serve the 410 Customers ? ☐

Turkey Yield by Klaus Theyer C.C.C.

Keep all calculations at THREE decimal places

Part one

Based on the following information, answer the accompanying questions:

Turkey A.P. Info

Cost	$	5.83	per Kg
Weight		7.26	Kg

U.P.	Weight	6.7	Kg

The percentage Yield for the cooked (**U.P.**) Turkey is ? [92.29%]

After carving there are [2.6] Kg Bones left.

The percentage Yield for the cooked (**E.P.**) Turkey is ? [56.47%]

What is the edible (**E.P.**) weight in Kg ? [4.1]

The cost of one E.P. cooked Kg is? [$ 10.32]

What is the cost of a [150] Gr portion is ? [$ 1.549]

Side dishes (Line Cost) is [$ 1.75]

Total cost of one Turkey meal ? [$ 3.30]

Part two

You are contemplating different Selling Price scenarios by using the most common method; Cost divided by Cost % = **S.P.**

[$ 3.30]

Potential Selling Price based on listed Cost Percentages:

24.00%	26.00%	28.00%	30.00%	32.00%	34.00%
$ 13.74	$ 12.69	$ 11.78	$ 11.00	$ 10.31	$ 9.70

Now, the Menu Price is: [$ 12.50]   Actual Cost % is ? [26.39%]

Part three

Based on the result of **Part one**, how many raw (**A.P.**) Turkeys would you have to buy to serve [410] Customers ?

Step one: # of Customers x portion size in Grams: [61500]

Step two: Divide result by 1000 to convert to Kg: [61.5]

Step three: Divide Kg by Yield %: [108.90]

Step four: Divide A.P. Kg by A.P. weight of 1 Turkey: [15.00]

A.P. Cost $ to serve the 410 Customers ? [$ 634.89]

# Yield Test Comparison Sample
by Klaus Theyer CCC

Yield Tester's Name: _____

Calculate the "Yield % & Loss % and associated Cost" for each of the four items, to establish the most beneficial buy for your establishment.

Supplier Name	A.P. Cost per weight	Weight defined	A.P. Raw weight	U.P. Trim weight	U.P. weight	E.P. weight	Cooking Weight loss	E.P. Yield %	Total Loss weight	Total Loss %	Yield Cost per Kg
A	$9.20	Kg	9.250	0.830		8.000					
B	$9.75	Kg	9.150	0.820		7.850					
C	$9.15	Kg	9.050	0.815		7.850					
D	$9.46	Kg	9.000	0.840		7.800					

Totals:

Averages: [ ] [ ] Do not use =Average formula [ ] Do not use =Average formula [ ]

For the example "A,B,C,D," the average A.P. weight in Kg is: [ ]
The average yield in Kg is: [ ]
and the average yield percentage is: [ ]

Best Yield Weight: Supplier:
Best Yield Cost: Supplier:
Best Yield %: Supplier:
Least Trim Loss: Supplier:
Least Cooking Shrinkage: Supplier:

Based on these test results and comparing Actual with Averages it becomes quite clear which supplier provides the best product for your establishment. Regardless of the mathematical result, you will need to decide between quality, cost and yield.

Yield Test Comparison Sample
by Klaus Theyer CCC

Yield Tester's Name: _____

Calculate the "Yield % & Loss % and associated Cost" for each of the four items, to establish the most beneficial buy for your establishment.

	A	B	C	D	E	F	G	H	I	J	K	L	M
	Supplier Name	A.P. Cost per weight	Weight defined	A.P. Raw weight	U.P. Trim weight	U.P. weight	E.P. weight	Cooking Weight loss	E.P. Yield %	Total Loss weight	Total Loss %	Yield Cost per Kg
	A	$9.20	Kg	9.250	0.830	8.420	8.000	0.420	86.49%	1.250	13.514%	$10.64
	B	$9.75	Kg	9.150	0.820	8.330	7.850	0.480	85.79%	1.300	14.208%	$11.36
	C	$9.15	Kg	9.050	0.815	8.235	7.850	0.385	86.74%	1.200	13.260%	$10.55
	D	$9.46	Kg	9.000	0.840	8.160	7.800	0.360	86.67%	1.200	13.333%	$10.92
Totals:	$37.56		36.450	3.305	31.500		1.645	Do not use =Average formula	4.950	Do not use =Average formula	43.466
Averages:	$9.39		9.113	0.826	7.875		0.411	86.420%	1.238	13.580%	10.867

For the example "A,B,C,D," the average A.P. weight in Kg is: 9.113

The average yield in Kg is: 7.875

and the average yield percentage is: 86.42%

Best Yield Weight:	8.000	Supplier: A
Best Yield Cost:	$10.55	Supplier: C
Best Yield %:	86.74%	Supplier: C
Least Trim Loss:	0.815	Supplier: C
Least Cooking Shrinkage:	0.360	Supplier: D

Based on these test results and comparing Actual with Averages it becomes quite clear which supplier provides the best product for your establishment. Regardless of the mathematical result, you will need to decide between quality, cost and yield.

Informal Menu Analysis - Bar One
by Klaus Theyer C.C.C.

G = Gin based beverage
V = Vodka based beverages
T = Tequila based beverages
R = Rum based beverages

All Drink Names are from: www.mixed-drink.com

	A	B	C	D	E	F	G	H	I	J	K	L	M	N	O
				Sales		COGS	Menu	Revenue	Project.	Item	Actual	Total	Contrib.	Contrib.
			Menu Item:	# Sold	Menu Mix Popularity Index %	Item Cost	Total Cost	Price Selling Price	Total Sales	Product Cost %	GP or CM	Product Cost %	Sold Item GP or CM	Margin %	Margin to Rev. %
7		1	G-Red Cloud	73		1.95		7.95							
8		2	G-Typhoon	121		1.75		7.95							
9		3	G-Boomerang	105		1.85		7.95							
10		4	V-Sputnik	140		2.05		8.25							
11		5	V-Naked Pretzel	51		2.25		8.25							
12		6	V-Jungle Jane	85		2.15		8.25							
13		7	T-T-N-T	125		2.05		8.95							
14		8	T-Hot Pants	155		2.10		8.95							
15		9	T-Brave Bull	97		2.20		8.95							
16		10	R-Hop Frog	68		1.70		7.95							
17		11	R-Casa Blanca	77		1.90		7.95							
18		12	R-Dingo Salad	82		1.85		7.95							
19		Total:					XXXXXX		XXXXXX		XXXXXX		XXXXXX		
20		Averages:													

Projected Cost Percentage:
Actual Cost Percentage: ___ minus ___ equals Variance: ___

Highest Seller by # Sold: ___ Highest Rev. in $: ___ AVG Item GP~CM $: ___
Lowest Seller by # Sold: ___   Lowest Rev. in $: ___   Highest Item GP~CM $: ___
Best Cost %: ___   Highest GP in $: ___   Lowest Item GP~CM $: ___
Worst Cost %: ___   Lowest GP in $: ___

Chapter 12 Essential Basic Math Templates, References, Exercises and Workshops

Informal Menu Analysis - Bar One *by Klaus Theyer C.C.C.*

G = Gin based beverage V = Vodka based beverages T = Tequila based beverages
R = Rum based beverages

All Drink Names are from: www.mixed-drink.com

#	Menu Item:	# Sold	Sales Mix Popularity Index %	Item Cost	COGS Total Cost	Menu Price Selling Price	Revenue Total Sales	Project. Product Cost %	Item GP or CM	Actual Product Cost %	Total Sold Item GP or CM	Contrib. Margin %	Contrib. Margin to Rev. %
1	G-Red Cloud	73	6.19%	1.95	6.50	7.95	580.35	24.53%	6.00	1.12%	573.85	7.52%	5.84%
2	G-Typhoon	121	10.26%	1.75	211.75	7.95	961.95	22.01%	6.20	22.01%	750.20	9.84%	7.63%
3	G-Boomerang	105	8.91%	1.85	194.25	7.95	834.75	23.27%	6.10	23.27%	640.50	8.40%	6.51%
4	V-Sputnik	140	11.87%	2.05	287.00	8.25	1155.00	24.85%	6.20	24.85%	868.00	11.38%	8.83%
5	V-Naked Pretzel	51	4.33%	2.25	114.75	8.25	420.75	27.27%	6.00	27.27%	306.00	4.01%	3.11%
6	V-Jungle Jane	85	7.21%	2.15	182.75	8.25	701.25	26.06%	6.10	26.06%	518.50	6.80%	5.27%
7	T-T-N-T	125	10.60%	2.05	256.25	8.95	1118.75	22.91%	6.90	22.91%	862.50	11.31%	8.77%
8	T-Hot Pants	155	13.15%	2.10	325.50	8.95	1387.25	23.46%	6.85	23.46%	1061.75	13.92%	10.80%
9	T-Brave Bull	97	8.23%	2.20	213.40	8.95	868.15	24.58%	6.75	24.58%	654.75	8.58%	6.66%
10	R-Hop Frog	68	5.77%	1.70	115.60	7.95	540.60	21.38%	6.25	21.38%	425.00	5.57%	4.32%
11	R-Casa Blanca	77	6.53%	1.90	146.30	7.95	612.15	23.90%	6.05	23.90%	465.85	6.11%	4.74%
12	R-Dingo Salad	82	6.96%	1.85	151.70	7.95	651.90	23.27%	6.10	23.27%	500.20	6.56%	5.09%
	Total:	1179	100.00%	23.80	2,205.75	XXXXXXX	9,832.85	XXXXXX	75.50	XXXXXX	7,627.10	100.00%	77.57%
	Averages:	98.3	8.33%	1.98	XXXXXXX	8.28	99.30	23.97%	6.29	22.43%	XXXXXX	8.33%	6.46%

Projected Cost Percentage:	23.97%			
Actual Cost Percentage:	22.43%			
	equals Variance:	1.54% minus		

Highest Seller by # Sold:	155	Highest Rev. in $:	1,387.25	AVG item GP~CM $:	6.29
Lowest Seller by # Sold:	51	Lowest Rev. in $:	420.75	Highest Item GP~CM $:	6.90
Best Cost %:	21.38%	Highest GP in $:	1,061.75	Lowest Item GP~CM $:	6.00
Worst Cost %:	27.27%	Lowest GP in $:	306.00		

From ONE Dollar to a GOOGOLPLEX

In US. Dollars, as per Mr. Beakman, transcribed by Klaus Theyer CCC

One	1
Ten	10
Hundred	100
Thousand	1,000
Million	1,000,000
Billion	1,000,000,000
Trillion	1,000,000,000,000
Quadrillion	1,000,000,000,000,000
Quintillion	1,000,000,000,000,000,000
Sextillion	1,000,000,000,000,000,000,000
Septillion	1,000,000,000,000,000,000,000,000
Octillion	1,000,000,000,000,000,000,000,000,000
Nonillion	1,000,000,000,000,000,000,000,000,000,000
Decillion	1,000,000,000,000,000,000,000,000,000,000,000
Undecillion	1,000,000,000,000,000,000,000,000,000,000,000,000
Duodecillion	1,000,000,000,000,000,000,000,000,000,000,000,000,000
Tredecillion	1,000,000,000,000,000,000,000,000,000,000,000,000,000,000
Quattuordecillion	1,000,000,000,000,000,000,000,000,000,000,000,000,000,000,000
Quindecillion	1,000,000,000,000,000,000,000,000,000,000,000,000,000,000,000,000
Sexdecillion	1,000,000,000,000,000,000,000,000,000,000,000,000,000,000,000,000,000
Septendecillion	1,000,000,000,000,000,000,000,000,000,000,000,000,000,000,000,000,000,000
Octodecillion	1,000,000,000,000,000,000,000,000,000,000,000,000,000,000,000,000,000,000,000
Novemdecillion	1,000,000,000,000,000,000,000,000,000,000,000,000,000,000,000,000,000,000,000,000
Vigintillion	1,000,000,000,000,000,000,000,000,000,000,000,000,000,000,000,000,000,000,000,000,000

Usually, for numbers beyond a Trillion the Zeros are omitted - e.g. 1 Vigintillion = 10^{63}.

Googol   is a 1 with 100 Zeros behind
Googolplex   is a 1 with a googol of Zeros behind

There is no such "thing" as a Zillion, it is a figure of speech

If counted to a billion, counting one number per second, it would take you 31 years, 259 days, 1 hour, 46 minutes and 40 seconds...

As mentioned above, this scenario is based on US and/or Canadian Dollars, Europeans use a different system.

Index

2012 Preparing Your Income Tax Returns, 32

A

ABC inventory method, 113.
    see also Inventory
Absenteeism, 122, 126–127
Accounting terms, 17
Accrued means accumulated, 17
Actual cost pricing, 101
Actual costs, 9, 19, 114
Advertising cost, 86
Alternative cost, 8, 9, 86
Asset, 5–6
Asset to COGS conversion, 18
Atmosphere, 96
Average contribution margin, 150
Average sales, 150
Average variable rate, 150
Average yield percentage, 68

B

Baking sheets sample, 158
Balance sheet, 17, 22
Basic cost of goods sold, 20
Beer, 6
Benefits, as labour cost, 122
Beverage costs, 6
Bills of fare, 106
Breakeven point, 149–152
    calculations sheet, 151–152
    units, 150
    value, 149–150
Brewer's Retail, 6
Budget, 25–30
    annual, 29
    bottom-up approach, 29
    defined, 25
    financial goals and objectives of, 28
    and income statement, 29, 30
    top-down approach, 29
    types of, 26–27, 28
Budgeted cost, 8
Budget Plan, 8
Business, 15
Business report, 16
Butcher Yield test, 68, 69, 73, 74

C

Calculated selling price, 11
Canada Pension Plan (CPP), 122
Canada Revenue Agency, 31
Capital budget, 26
Capital cost, 86
Capital cost allowance, 31
Capital gain, 31
Capital loss, 31
Cash flow budget, 28
Celsius, 54
CFO (Chief Operating Officer), 28
Chicken yield, 70–72
Closed inventory, 19
Coffee, 6
Common yield, 67
Comparative analysis, 91
Competition, 85, 99–100
Competitive analysis, 91, 95
Competitive establishments, 92–94
Concept, 94, 96–97, 105
    atmosphere, 96
    checklist of characteristics, 97
    customer base, 96
    type of eatery, 96
    workforce, 96
Contribution margin, 149
Contribution rate, 149
Control cost, 84
Conversion, of quantities, 50
Conversion sheet, 154–156
Corporate budget, 28

Corporation, 15
Cost, 1–4
   in accounting terms, 1
   chef's areas of, 7
   classification of, 4–6
   controllable vs. non-controllable, 5
   defined, 1
   elements of, 1
   fixed costs, 5
   and inventory, 114–115
   labour, 5
   vs. price, 8
   projected, 9
   reduction of, 9
   terminology, 12
   variable costs, 4–5
Cost behaviour, 100
Cost centre, 2
Cost conscientious, 98
Cost control, 10
Cost control terms, 16, 17
Costing page, 77
Cost of Goods Sold (COGS), 6, 8, 17, 19–21
Cost of sale, 8
Cost plus pricing, 101
Credit note, 109
Customer base, 96
Customer profiling, 89

D

Daily food cost, 86
Debit note, 109
Decimal calculations, 35
Decimal place values, 36
Decimal to percent, 37
Demographics, 85, 89–91, 95
Demographic study, 89
Denominator, 39
Departmental budget, 26, 27
Depreciation, 31–33
   defined, 31
   example of, 31, 32, 33
   methods, 32, 33
Desired cost pricing, 10
Desired or ideal cost percentage, 10
Direct cost, 86
Direct labour cost, 122
Disposable income, 90

E

Easy workshop example, 160–161
Elements of cost, 1. *see also* Cost
   cost centre, 2
   profit centre, 2
   for sales, 2
Employers Health Tax (EHT), 122
Employment Insurance (EI), 122
Employment Standards Acts, 127
Establishments, list of competitive, 91
Expense, 1
Extended COGS calculation, 21
Extended cost, 84

F

Factor method, 99
Fahrenheit, 54
Fast-food restaurant, 94
Feasibility study, 89, 90
F.I.F.O. (first in-first out), 114
"First-Year-Rule," 32
Fixed asset, 5
Fixed budget, 26
Fixed cost (FXC), 5, 8, 9, 17, 149
Fixed selling price, 102
Flexible budget, 28
Food cost (FC), 5
Formula page for cost, 159
Four "W's" of purchasing, 105
Fraction of sales, 8
Fractions, 39–42
   adding, 39–40
   calculating, 39
   converting into decimals, 42
   dividing, 41
   multiplying, 40–41
   subtracting, 40

G

Goals, of budget, 28
Goods, depleted, 2
Green, Rick, 125
Gross profit, 10, 19
Gross profit pricing, 100–101

H

Head-on competition, 95
Hidden costs, 85
Hiring process, 122
Historical cost, 86
Hospitality, terms, 13–14
Hotel revenue and cost areas, 4
Hour, 55

I

Ideal cost, 86
Income statement, 16, 17
Indirect costs, 86
Indirect labour cost, 122
Inventory, 6, 19, 111–115
    ABC method, 113
    control, 112
    and costs, 114–115
    perpetual, 111
    physical, 112
    rate formula, 114
    taking, 112–113
    turnover, 113
Inventory sheets, 111, 117–120

K

Kasavana, Michael L., 139

L

Labour capacity chart, 127
Labour cost, 5, 8, 9, 121–125
    calculating, 127
    controlling, 123
    fixed salary, 126
    hourly, 126
    payroll, 121–123
    and scheduling, 125
    staff, 122
Labour cost percentage, 99
Length measurement, 55–56
L.I.F.O. (last in first out), 114
Limited (Ltd) company, 15
Line-plate cost, 86
Liquid asset, 5

Liquor, 6
Liquor Control Board of Ontario (LCBO), 6
L.L.P. (last purchase price), 114
Long-term budget, 26, 27
Loss, 65, 66
Loss leader principle, 100

M

Master budget, 26
Math, 35–64
    and conversions, 50–55
    decimal calculations, 35
    and length measurements, 55–56
    percent and percentages, 47–49
    recipe conversion, 57–64
    rounding, 36
    and weights and measures, 43–46
Menu analysis, 139–145
    calculating, 140–142
    example, 164, 165
    reason for, 139
Menu engineering, 139
Menu engineering worksheet, 140, 144–145
Menu item cost calculation, 85
Menu items, 24
Menu pricing, 19–21
    strategies, 24, 98
Methods and presentation page, 77, 78
Metric, 84
Mid-scale, or family restaurant, 95
Minimum wage, 121
Minutes, 55

N

Nadeau, Eric, 105
Numerator, 39

O

Occupancy cost, 5
Odd/even pricing, 102
One dollar to googolplex chart, 172
Opening inventory, 19
Operating budget, 26, 28
Overhead cost, 86, 126

P

P & L (profit and losses) statement, 17
Payroll, 121–123, 123
Payroll calculation template, 123
    payroll, 124
Percentage pie chart, 157
Percent/percentages, 47–49
Percent to decimal, 38
Perpetual inventory, 19, 111
Planned cost, 86
Plate cost, 86, 87, 88
Popularity, 85
Portion cost, 77
Practicality, 85
Prestige pricing, 102
Price, 1
    vs. cost, 8
Primary costs, 85
Prime cost, 8–11, 11
    and selling price calculation, 10
Product and labour budget, 28
Product cost, 9, 24
Product specification form, 107. *see also* Purchasing
Profit, 2, 15, 149
    defined, 2
    elements of, 2
Profitability, 16, 85
Profit centre, 2
Projected costs, 9
Projection forecast, 98
Proportional share of total sales, 150
Psychographics, 89
Psychological pricing, 102
Projected cost, 19
Purchase order (PO), 108
Purchase specification form, 106. *see also* Purchasing
Purchasing, 105–110
    methods, 110
    from multiple vendors, 108
    from one-stop vendors, 108
    process, 108–109
    product specification form, 107
    sample, 106
    "what," 105
    "when," 105, 107
    "where," 105, 108
    "why," 105, 106

R

Receiving, 110, 111
Receiving summary sheet, 109
Recipe, 77
Recipe conversion, 55, 57–58
Recipe input & costing page, 77, 78
Record keeping, 16
Records, 16
Reduction of cost, 9
Repair and maintenance budget, 28
Requisition, 108
Restaurant revenue and cost areas, 3
Restaurant styles, 94–95
Revenue, 17, 149
Rick Green eSeminars on Loss Prevention, 125
Rounding, 36

S

Sales, 2, 149
Sales forecast, 132, 133
Sales-related cost, 86
Sale-to-cost ratio, 24
Scheduling methods, 125, 137
Seasonal pricing, 102
Secondary costs, 85
Seconds, 55
Selling price, 10, 85
    strategies, 24
Selling price, setting, 94
Semi-variable cost, 86
Shareholder, 15
Short-term budget, 26
Simple menu analysis, 164, 165
    example, 170, 171
Smith, Donald I., 139
Soft drinks, 6
Staff meal cost, 86
Standard recipe, 77–78
Statement of income and expenses, 17, 22, 23, 25
Static budget, 28
Stock value, 19
System International (SI), 84

T

Tax return, 16, 17
Temperature measurements, 54

Terminology
  accounting, 16
  cost, 12
  cost control, 17
  menu or selling price strategies, 98
  units, 150
  value, 149–150
Theme, 94–96, 105
Theoretical cost, 86
Theyer, Klaus, 77, 78, 103
Today's Menu du jour, 6, 24
Toronto, 90, 91
Total cost, 86

U

Unit, 84, 150
Unit cost, 84
Unit of labour cost, 84
Upscale, or fine-dining restaurant, 95

V

Vacation pay, 122
Variable cost pricing, 101
Variable costs, 4–5, 8, 9, 17, 86, 149
Variable rate, 149
Vendor, 108, 109
Volume measurements, 50

W

Weighted average, 115
Weights and measures, 43–46
Weinbuch, Konrad, 35, 70, 71, 129
Wine, 6
Workers Safety Insurance Board (WSIB), 122
Workforce, 96

Y

Yield calculations, 65–75
  E.P., 65
  example, 162, 163, 166, 167
  exercise, 75
  A.P., 65
  in recipe, 66
  U.P., 65
Yield test comparison sheet, 168, 169

Z

ZBB (zero-based budgeting), 28